THE TOTAL TELEVISION SCRAPBOOK

by

Mark Arnold

and

Victoria Biggers

Books by Mark Arnold:

The Best of The Harveyville Fun Times!

Created and Produced by Total TeleVision productions

If You're Cracked, You're Happy, Part Won and Part Too

Mark Arnold Picks on The Beatles

Frozen in Ice: The Story of Walt Disney Productions 1966-1985

Think Pink: The DePatie-Freleng Story

Pocket Full of Dennis the Menace

The Harvey Comics Companion

Long Title: Looking for the Good Times; Examining the Monkees' Songs (with Michael A. Ventrella)

Aaaaalllviiinnn!: The Story of Ross Bagdasarian, Sr., Liberty Records, Format Films and The Alvin Show

The Comedy of Jack Davis

The Comedy of John Severin

Headquartered: A Timeline of The Monkees Solo Years (with Michael A. Ventrella)

Friendly Ghosts, Little Devils, Giants and Rich Kids: The Art and Creations of Warren Kremer

THE TOTAL TELEVISION SCRAPBOOK

by

Mark Arnold

and

Victoria Biggers

BearManor Media

2021

THE TOTAL TELEVISION SCRAPBOOK

First printing.

For information, contact:
Ben Ohmart - benohmart@gmail.com
BearManor Media
https://bearmanor-digital.myshopify.com

Cover illustration by Jim Engel.

Back cover by Matt Hansel

Typesetting and layout by Senthil Kumar.

Published in the USA by BearManor Media.

Library of Congress Cataloging-in-Publication Data
Arnold, Mark and Biggers, Victoria.
The Total TeleVision Scrapbook
by Mark Arnold and Victoria Biggers.
Includes index.

ISBN - 978-1-62933-777-7

DEDICATED TO

Buck Biggers – 6/2/27-2/10/13
Tread Covington – 7/9/25-7/9/14
Chet Stover – 4/19/25-1/12/16
Joe Harris – 1/5/28-3/26/17

ACKNOWLEDGEMENTS

Frank Andrina, Roman Arambula, Ralph Bakshi, Jerry Beck, Greg Beda, Bradley Bolke, Shaun Clancy, David R. Dunsford, Greg Ehrbar (sorry I misspelled your name in my Chipmunks book!), Hy Eisman, Jim Engel, Scot Ennis, Mark Evanier, Herbert Goldman, Stephen Grossfeld, Jim Halperin, Chip Hamlen, Matthew Hansel, Sophie Harris, Barry Haskell, Tom Heintjes, Heritage Auctions, Lee Hester, Reed Kaplan, Mike Kazaleh, Cliff MacMillan, Ben Ohmart, Patrick Owsley, Brian Pearce, Andrew Peterson, James Rash, Harvey Seigel, Scott Shaw!, Stu Shostak, Dan Slotnik, Bill Smith, Derek Tague, Darrell Van Citters, Mark A. Yurkiw. Apologies to anyone who I have forgotten. Your contributions are noted.

INTERVIEWS

Harvey Siegel Interview - March 15, 2014

CONTENTS

Foreword . . . xi

Introduction. . . . 1

1 Updated History of TTV . . . 2

2 An Interview with Harvey Siegel - March 15, 2014. . . . 11

3 King Leonardo and his Short Subjects . . . 30

4 Tennessee Tuxedo and his Tales . . . 49

5 The Underdog Show . . . 59

6 Comic Book Art and Other Stuff . . . 89

7 The Macy's Thanksgiving Day Parade Underdog Balloon . . . 154

8 The Beagles. . . . 168

9 Victoria's Scrapbook . . . 185

Bibliography . . . 249

Index . . . 250

About The Authors . . . 258

FOREWORD

by Phil Hall

When I was offered the opportunity to write the Foreword for this wonderful book, I approached the assignment with a dual sense of wonder and trepidation.

As a child growing up in New York City in the 1970s, many of the TTV characters were small-screen staples via syndicated reruns on WNEW-TV, a local station that was part of the now-defunct Metromedia broadcasting operation. I was a cartoon addict because my childhood dream was to become an animator. And while it didn't pan out – my artistic talent was utterly nonexistent – I particularly enjoyed the droll designs and memorable voice performances from this studio's output. The joy in writing this foreword was the recollection of a very happy childhood spent in front of the television, laughing along at Tennessee Tuxedo, Underdog and the other wonderfully warped creations.

But with the passage of time, I became detached from the simple joys of childhood and wound up pilloried by the responsibilities and supposedly sophisticated tastes of adulthood. Also, as television programming evolved over the years, those great cartoons from my early years seemed to vanish from view. While I could still recall many TTV episodes with great clarity, including their infectious theme songs and brilliant catch-phrases, they became increasingly distant items from a daily life that I could no longer claim.

My occasional forays into rediscovering the pleasures of my childhood have resulted in very mixed results. Some of the Bugs Bunny and Bullwinkle cartoons that included references that baffled the five- or ten-year-old version of me became remarkably vibrant when reconsidered in my guise as a college-educated adult. On the other hand, the jollity I experienced in decades past with the Hanna-Barbera television output failed to travel well into my grown-up years – characters and episodes that were too much fun back in the day were now highly resistible to my current tastes and humor levels.

Mercifully, I discovered via home entertainment formats and online videos that the TTV works were neither better nor worse than memory served up – they were just as perfectly entertaining to the grown-up version of me as they were to the childhood version of me. Watching Tennessee Tuxedo today as he flummoxes Stanley Livingstone or cheering as the politically-incorrect Go-Go Gophers disrupt the never-correct U.S. Cavalry is just as intoxicating now as it was too many decades ago.

The wonderful aspect of this new book – as well as Mark Arnold's earlier BearManor Media book *Created and Produced by Total Television Productions* – was the chance to enjoy the full scope of the TTV output. My childhood television viewing experience was absent of several TTV creations – including King Leonardo, Tooter Turtle, The Hunter and The Beagles – and it was through that book that I was able to track down and enjoy the full scope of this studio's imagination. The earlier book also brought back vaguely-recalled memories of TTV ephemera, such as *The Sing-a-Long Family* and *Gene Hattree* – neither of those works gained any traction in the wider pop culture, but in some strange way they lodged in my memory cells and could be called up when needed.

While individual TTV characters such as Underdog and Tennessee Tuxedo may have become household names, the TTV studio as a whole has not secured the popular admiration bestowed on the likes of Disney, Warner Bros., UPA or Hanna-Barbera, let alone the more contemporary animation funhouses. With this book, I hope that TTV can achieve the level of adulation that its characters and their creators deserve.

And while the too-self-confident Tennessee Tuxedo always insisted that he would not fail, TTV never failed to entertain and inspire – the grown-up me and the childhood me are united in that opinion.

Phil Hall is co-editor of Cinema Crazed and author of 10 books including *The History of Independent Cinema* and the recently released *Jesus Christ Movie Star*. His entertainment writing has been published in the *New York Times, New York Daily News* and *Wired*, and he is the host of the award-winning SoundCloud podcast *The Online Movie Show* and co-host of the award-winning radio talk show *Nutmeg Chatter*.

INTRODUCTION

by Mark Arnold

The cartoons created by Total TeleVision productions (yes, large V, small p, or TTV for short) from 1960-1970 were virtually a mystery for years. People knew the names of the voice over artists, but the other creators' names remained elusive except a quick and blurry scrawl of animators' names at the end of the original airings of *King Leonardo and his Short Subjects* from 1960-1963.

The only other clue was at the end of *The Beagles* (1966-1968) where the names Watts Biggers, Chet Stover, Joe Harris and Tread Covington appeared, listed as creators and producers and songwriters, but since hardly anybody watched that show and copies of it are still scarce today, these names meant virtually nothing.

For the most part, syndicated reruns that aired for years of *Tennessee Tuxedo and his Tales* (1963-1966) and *The Underdog Show* (1964-1967) offered no new revelations of who the creators of these shows were, so most assumed that they were made by Jay Ward of Rocky and Bullwinkle fame.

The first inkling of knowing anything about the TTV creators came with a lengthy article about Joe Harris in *Animato* #38, Summer 1997.

Next, Buck Biggers and Chet Stover wrote *How Underdog Was Born* in 2004 and I interviewed both of them for *Hogan's Alley* magazine in 2007, so two more pieces of the puzzle became clear.

When asked to write my first book for BearManor Media, I was asked if I could expand my interviews with Biggers and Stover into a book. I said I could, not knowing if I could get in contact with anyone further. Fortunately, I did and interviewed Joe Harris and the final missing puzzle piece. Tread Covington: a man with a name so strange, I had to ask Buck and Chet if he really existed, assuming that he was a fictional name like Ponsonby Britt was for Jay Ward Productions. He did and I interviewed him as well.

All four proved to be incredibly helpful and my book *Created and Produced by Total TeleVision productions* came out in 2009. While proud of my work, information, images and interviews that have occurred since that time has caused me to want to update that book for at least five years.

This is that update.

What this book includes is a revised original air date listing and some new interviews and MANY new images, plus first hand recollections and images by Buck Biggers daughter, Victoria, who reached out to me when she discovered a hidden scrapbook of her father's after he passed away.

What this book doesn't include is a retread of the history as told in those earlier books because those books are still relevant and accurate. Instead, the focus is on the images, to show the "art" of TTV.

Did I say images? YES, many. Enjoy!

—Mark Arnold.

1 Updated History of TTV

by Mark Arnold

Since 2009, TTV has been purchased by two companies! When we last met, TTV was owned by Classic Media. On July 23, 2012, DreamWorks Animation acquired Classic Media from Boomerang Media for $155 million. The company became a unit of DreamWorks Animation and was renamed DreamWorks Classics, LLC. On April 28, 2016, NBCUniversal announced it would be acquiring DreamWorks Animation for $3.8 billion. The acquisition was completed on August 22, 2016.

4/4/07

Mark —

Per your request.

Please return to:

W. Watts Biggers
Box 305
E. Sandwich, MA
02537

Thanks —

Watts

P.S. This picture is from about 1973.

Frank Andrina

MAY 29/08

HELLO MARK—.

I RECIEVED OUR INTERVIEW RECENTLY (A MONTH AGO)
I RETURNED FROM THE HOSPITAL
A SHORT TIME AGO. I HAD A MINOR
HEART ATTACK.
I HAVE MARKED OFF THE
ERRORS OF THE INTERVIEW AND
WILL CORRECT THEM AS SOON AS
POSSIBLE. —I'LL ALSO SEND
SOME DRAWINGS—.

THANKS FOR YOUR
PATIENCE

— FRANK

Hanna-Barbera

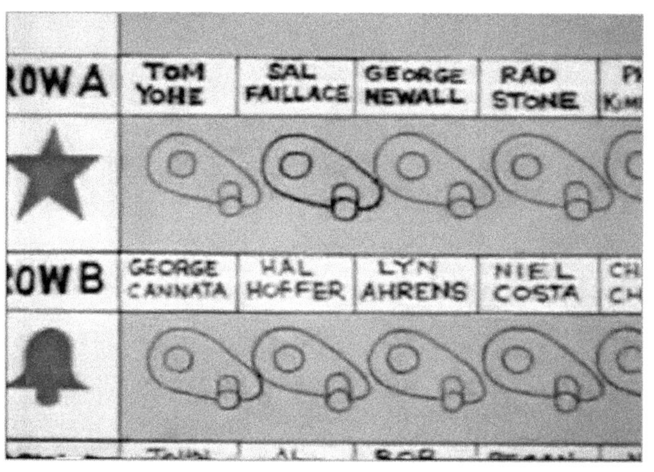

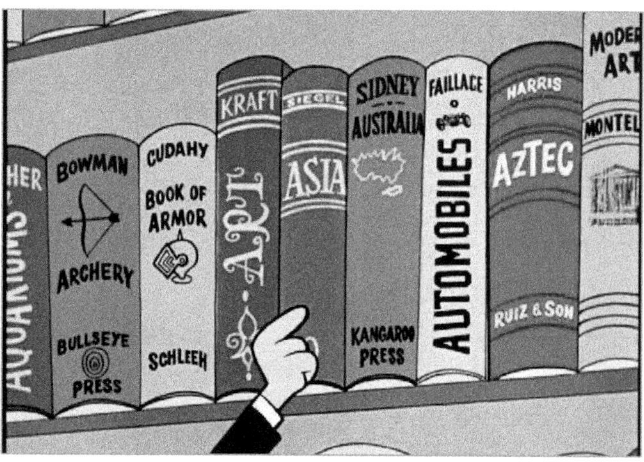

The TTV staff hid their names in *Tennessee Tuxedo* and the non-TTV *Schoolhouse Rock*.

Unpublished *Underdog* and *Tennessee Tuxedo* comic strips drawn by Hy Eisman.

UNDERDOG

UNDERDOG, WE MUST STOP SIMON BARSINISTER BEFORE HE RULES THE WORLD!
IT'S HIP HIP HIP AND AWAY WE GO!
NOW WE'RE IN FOR IT!
NO WE'RE NOT!
YOU FORGET I CONTROL GENERAL BALDYDASH AND HE CONTROLS THE ARMY!
GENERAL, UNDERDOG IS FLYING THIS WAY! SIMON SAYS... SHOOT HIM DOWN LIKE A **DOG!**
I WILL DO WHAT SIMON SAYS.

TENNESSEE TUXEDO

DUH, HEY TENNESSEE! I GOT A RIDDLE!
LET'S HEAR IT, CHUMLEY!
BUS STOP
OYSTE
WHAT IS THE...
OYSTER
...MOST FAMOUS **BUS** IN THE WORLD?
MOST FAMOUS BUS? WHY, WHAT ELSE...
OYSTE
...COLUMBUS OF COURSE!

animator
Harvey Siegel was the head of layouts (he hired me at Gamma)
Jaime Torres was 2nd operations manager under Jesus Martinez
Rodolfo Gonzara was layout man
Sergio de la Torre was layout man
Eduardo Olivares was layout man
Daniel Burgos was animator
Cesar Canton was animator
Angel Canton was animator
Julio Guerrero was animator
Tex Henson Was animator

7= yes

8= yes, a lot of incidental characters in all the shows

9= No

10= No

11= No

12= No

13= after Gamma I went to work in comics in Mexico City until I moved to the USA in August 1967 to work on animated commercials in Dallas Texas I did this until 1970 when I moved to Los Angeles California to work for Hanna & Barbera. On April 1975 I joined the Walt Disney studio and in October of that year my first Mickey Mouse comic strip daylies week was published.

In 1982 I began doing the sunday strip as well, I did this until November of 1989 when the strip was no longer published.

Since then I have kept myself busy working with different animation studios, like Marvel Productions, Warner Bros. and Hyperion productions.

Then I went on to teach animation in a local college until my retirement.

Román Arámbula.
march 2008
Burbank ca. USA

BEST AMIGO HARVEY SIEGEL (MICKEY MOUSE AND ROMAN ARNOLDO 1/17/79

JOE HARRIS
AP 45/100
JOE HARRIS
Golden Books
JOE HARRIS
JOE HARRIS
1963

30

MA: Did you create the sound effects?

TC: No, we had a certain stock library. The music we did was written by the four of us.

MA: That's pretty much all I have for now.

Mark –
Please forgive my delay and call (and I'll call you) to decipher my editing. At least it clears up a lot of points I was confusing about.
Best –
Fred

Oct 31 '08

Dear Mark -
You've been very
patient — however
what is sent
to you I'm afraid
isn't exactly
"stop the presses"
info — hope
it will be useful
in some way.

Best - Tread

JOE HARRIS
175 W 76TH ST. 4A
NYC NY 10023

NEW YOR
OS JUL 200

to MARK ARNOLD
15291 NORTON ROAD

Total TeleVision productions

inc., 366 Madison Avenue, New York 17, N.Y., OXford 7-4123

September 29, 1966

Mr. Al Kilgore
216-55 113th Drive
Queens Village, New York
11429

Dear Al:

I'd like to put down the schedule we discussed on the phone the other day so you'll have a record of what's coming up in the next few weeks. All dates are when due in my hands, so allow time for mailing.

	Underdog	109	9/30
	Underdog	110	10/7
*	Underdog	112	10/14
	Underdog	123	10/22
	Underdog	124	10/30
(Possibly)	Go Go Gophers	48	11/9

* As you know you'll be doing 111 or 112 as you decide, and sending drawings of backgrounds, props, costumes and incidental characters on to Gary Mooney:

Box 66
Millington, Maryland
21651

Best,

Joe

Joseph B. Harris

JH/gm

2 An Interview with Harvey Siegel - March 15, 2014

by Mark Arnold

GENERAL MILLS, INC. - GROCERY PRODUCTS DIVISION - 9200 WAYZATA BOULEVARD - MINNEAPOLIS, MINNESOTA 55440

CYRIL W. PLATTES

7 April 1964

Mr. Harvey Siegel
Producer-Director
Gamma Productions
Alvaro Obregon 284
Mexico 7, D.F.

Dear Harvey:

I want to thank you for the wonderful direction and execution you are giving our animated shows through Gamma Productions.

As with your direction on the Bullwinkle show, I am equally delighted with the Underdog and Hoppity Hooper films. You did so many extra little touches that helped make these shows great! Keep up the good work, and be assured that everything you do is most appreciated.

I expressed my feelings to Peter Piech, But I am sending a copy of this letter to confirm them.

Kindest Regards.

CWP/abc

cc: Peter Piech

P.S. Many thanks for the plaque. It's beautifully done, and I got quite a kick out of it.

Introduction: I hate to say that the biggest error in the original *Created and Produced by Total TeleVision productions* book was to say that Harvey Seigel was dead. Unfortunately, through my research, I had tracked down the wrong Harvey Seigel. I discovered the correct Harvey Seigel when I read *The Art of Jay Ward Productions* by Darrell Van Citters (2013), an excellent and highly recommended book for fans of TTV. Fortunately, I can make amends here with an interview I conducted since that original book came out...

MA: This is Mark Arnold for the revised Total Television book and today is March 15, 2014. Tell me a bit about yourself and how you got interested in animation.

HS: I worked for a very very important man in the animation field named Shamus Culhane. He's an ex-Disney animator. I got out of high school and went to work for Jimmy - Shamus we called him - almost immediately. In the meantime, during that period, I joined the Marine Corp reserve, and spent four years with the reserve being trained, getting ready for the Korean War which had come about early. So I started with Shamus Culhane. I mentioned the Marine Corp because it's one of my loves in life. Part of my two loves is I worked for the FBI up until about a year ago. So the two loves of my life are art and cartooning and judicial work with the government, actually, and having fun all the way.

MA: The two are vastly different.

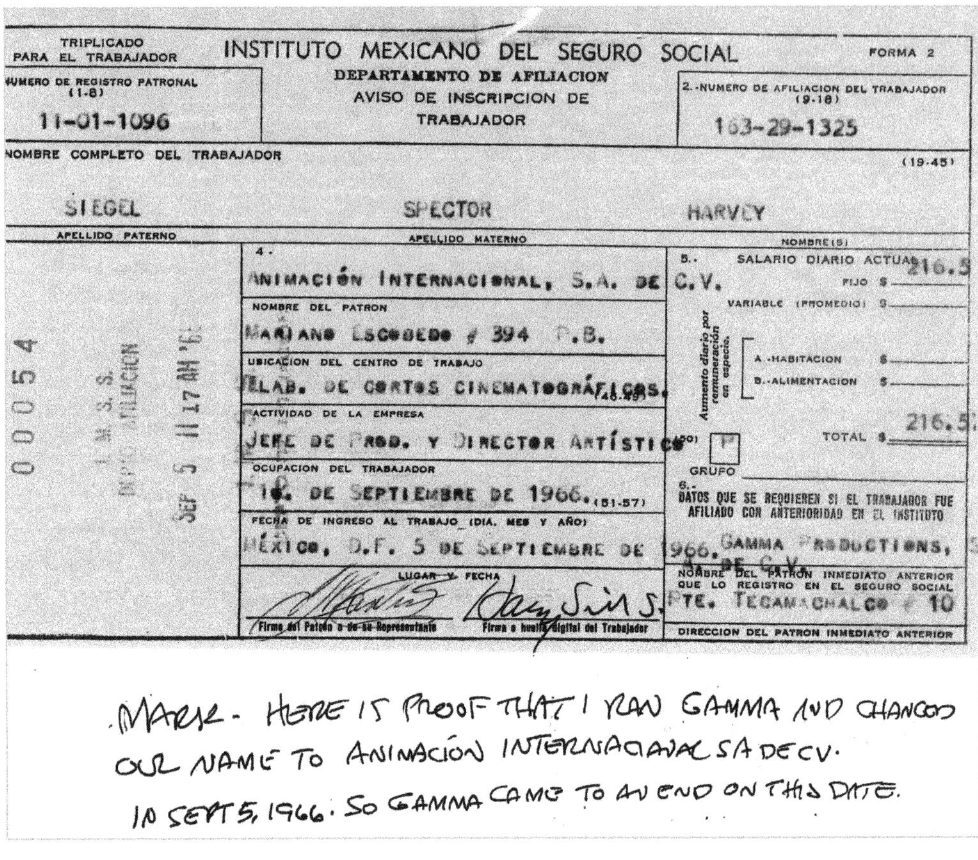

TRIPLICADO PARA EL TRABAJADOR

INSTITUTO MEXICANO DEL SEGURO SOCIAL

FORMA 2

DEPARTAMENTO DE AFILIACION
AVISO DE INSCRIPCION DE TRABAJADOR

NUMERO DE REGISTRO PATRONAL (1-8): 11-01-1096

2.-NUMERO DE AFILIACION DEL TRABAJADOR (9-18): 163-29-1325

NOMBRE COMPLETO DEL TRABAJADOR (19-45)

SIEGEL	SPECTOR	HARVEY
APELLIDO PATERNO	APELLIDO MATERNO	NOMBRE(S)

00054

I. M. S. S. DEPTO. AFILIACION SEP 5 11 17 AM '66

4.- ANIMACIÓN INTERNACIONAL, S.A. DE C.V.

NOMBRE DEL PATRON

MARIANO ESCOBEDO # 394 P.B.

UBICACION DEL CENTRO DE TRABAJO

ELAB. DE CORTOS CINEMATOGRÁFICOS. (46-49)

ACTIVIDAD DE LA EMPRESA

JEFE DE PROD. Y DIRECTOR ARTÍSTICO (50)

OCUPACION DEL TRABAJADOR

16 DE SEPTIEMBRE DE 1966. (51-57)

FECHA DE INGRESO AL TRABAJO (DIA, MES Y AÑO)

MÉXICO, D.F. 5 DE SEPTIEMBRE DE 1966.

LUGAR Y FECHA

Firma del Patrón o de su Representante — Firma o huella digital del Trabajador

5.- SALARIO DIARIO ACTUAL 216.5
FIJO $
VARIABLE (PROMEDIO) $
Aumento diario por remuneración en especie.
A.-HABITACION $
B.-ALIMENTACION $
TOTAL $ 216.5

P

GRUPO

6.- DATOS QUE SE REQUIEREN SI EL TRABAJADOR FUE AFILIADO CON ANTERIORIDAD EN EL INSTITUTO

GAMMA PRODUCTIONS, S.A. DE C.V.

NOMBRE DEL PATRON INMEDIATO ANTERIOR QUE LO REGISTRO EN EL SEGURO SOCIAL

PTE. TECAMACHALCO # 10

DIRECCION DEL PATRON INMEDIATO ANTERIOR

MARK - HERE IS PROOF THAT I RAN GAMMA AND CHANGED OUR NAME TO ANIMACIÓN INTERNACIONAL SA DE CV. IN SEPT 5, 1966. SO GAMMA CAME TO AN END ON THIS DATE.

HS: Yeah, yeah. I mentioned to you that I believe that I meet every Thursday with the department here with the assistant chief of police and the old SWAT team members. There's about six of us and we start to meet every Thursday at a Chinese restaurant. We discuss the latest things going on in armor and what's going on in the world and such. Wednesday afternoons I teach at St. Thomas Episcopal working with children. That's one of my loves also is working with kids. That's one of my joys in life right now, really. That's the present, but how I got started was Jimmy Culhane. I always liked cartooning and it's something that you're either born with or not born with. I always liked cartoons. I like humor and working with children. They've been my goals in life also. I'm just having a ball doing it even to this day. Right now I'm 85, and I feel like I'm mentally 12. How does that sound?

MA: Sounds good to me. Did you have any formal training or did you just learn on the job with Shamus?

HS: I had a scholarship to the Cooper Union School of Engineering and Architecture. Did you hear of that? Cooper Union?

MA: Ummmm, no. [I have since looked it up on Wikipedia.]

HS: Ok. It's a very fine university in New York City and it has scholarships. Abraham Lincoln gave speeches there and the elevator is a round elevator. It's full of engineering and architecture and fine art. I got a scholarship there. That's my basic fine art background, you might say. As far as a cartoon background, I basically worked with Culhane, who was a great, great teacher. He was a really hard taskmaster and worked with very very tough people. He knew what he wanted and if you worked with Shamus, you learned everything about animation from inking and painting and sipping coffee and the whole works. Right off the top.

MA: What projects did you work on with him?

HS: Trix rabbit, Lucky Charms, American Airlines, Gillette, Peter Paul Mounds and Almond Joy. This is all black and white television at that time.

MA: When you were working for Shamus, was that directly for General Mills?

HS: No. Mills came later. Shamus had his own shop. You lose accounts, you get accounts in our field. Eventually he had to close up. I worked for Shamus for about seven years. When he had to close his shop, I was approached by Peter Piech, who was involved with the Rocky and Bullwinkle show from the very beginning. I believe it was Cloyd and Gidney the moon men. That was our first on film - the moon men. And Peter, I knew Peter and he called me into his office one day to check out some new animation film that he was interested in. I was so interested. I guess you know Leonard Key and Ted Key?

MA: Yes.

HS: I bought Leonard's shares in that company. I spent $10,000 in that company. I sure wished I had kept it. I had no idea that it was going to be a hit; the way it was a hit. Leonard sold me his share and he stepped out and I worked with Peter Piech. George Carlson was their accountant at that time. He was also the VP of the company which was different from Jay Ward. Ward had his own company.

MA: Wasn't it called Producer's Associates of Television?

HS: Yeah, it was P.A.T.

MA: So, did you work for him directly?

HS: Yes. I worked with Peter Piech - Great name for a cartoon company, right? I'm trying to remember some of the names: Cynthia Carlin, Roger Carlin, were part of the P.A.T. group at the very beginning. George Carlson was the accountant at the very beginning. Peter went out and met with people and he was a good salesperson. He got involved somehow - I don't know how - but he got involved with Jay Ward. I was in service in Japan for about two years. My service was in psychological warfare. We called it psywar. I went all around Japan and loved it. Peter called and said, "Do you want to go back to Japan?" I said, "Definitely." The original intention was to produce the shows in Japan. I believe the name of the studio was called Tojo Studios that they had involved themselves with. I've heard rumors that there was not a studio, but there was a studio. The problem at that time was logistics. Nowadays, you have your cell phones and there are ways to get around. At that time, we just had local telephone lines and the logistics were terri-

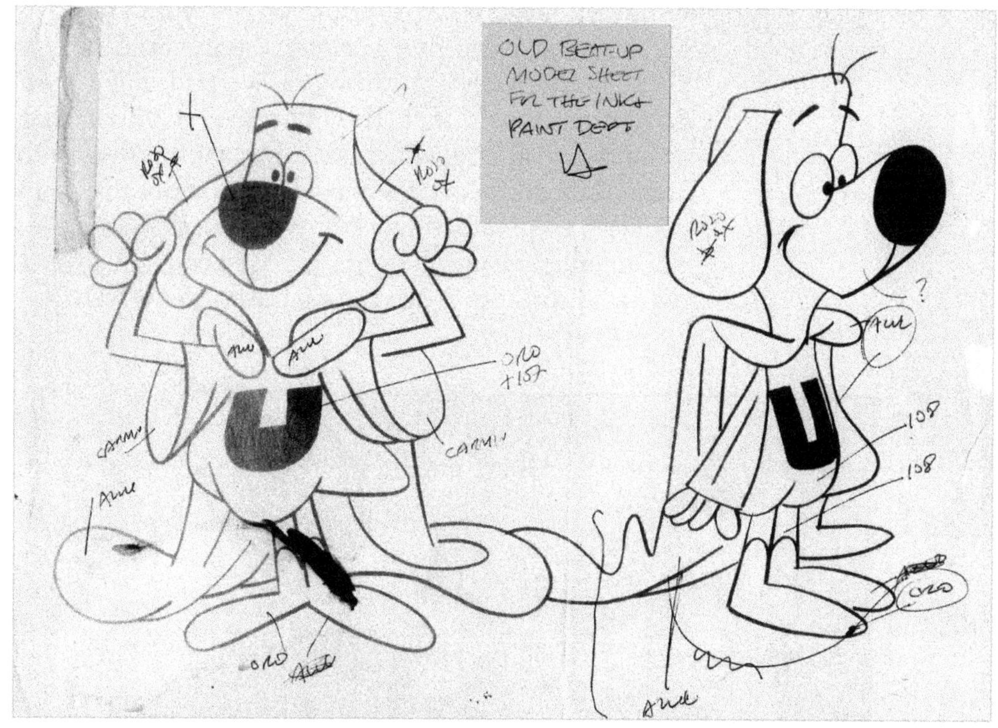

ble to make a phone call to get things moving. It was a really big problem. Between Peter and Jay, they decided on Mexico. I had no idea they were going to Mexico. I knew nothing about Mexico. That was the beginning of the Ward group and P.A.T. in Mexico. You know how that started, right? The book that Darrell Van Citters wrote. It's really fantastic. He really pinned everything down perfectly. I helped him along the way and my recollections of the beginnings of Mexico were really, really, really tough. We had nobody to work with, basically. We had about four or five Americans that came down, which is in Darrell's book. There was Ernie Terrazas. You don't need their names, do you? It's all in Darrell's book.

MA: Yeah. I know a couple of them, at least. Like Gerard Baldwin.

HS: Yeah, Gerard was working with Ward. He had a pretty big group. He had about four or five animators working with us. I would say that that show would not have succeeded. They really were going on a dream in Mexico. If not for one of our animators - I'm trying to think of the names - they are all listed in the book. Anyway, one of them was from Argentina, and he spoke perfect Spanish.

MA: Was it Sal Faillace?

HS: Sal died. He had a bad heart. Many years ago. Sal Faillace and George Singer. Well, at least four or five of them came down. We needed help, desperately. Peter did what he could on his end to not get in trouble for working in Mexico. For every five Mexicans, you could hire one American. In order to get so many Americans to work, we had to get permission from the Mexican government to do that. They had to give you a special form. You could work there as a visitante, which means you could work there six months, and then come back and work there again in six months as a visitante. I was one of the contacts, originally. I worked with the industry a lot. I was an FM2, and that document gave me all rights of a Mexican citizen except that I could not vote or own a liquor store or land along the border which they call the frontier. The FM2 gave me all those rights which is what we should do for the Mexican citizens here. We should give them every right that we have, but don't give them the privilege of voting. That's the problem. That's the way it worked in Mexico. We could not vote. We had every other right as a Mexican citizen. I just loved it down there. It was really fun and they're wonderful people.

MA: So you basically stayed because of that for a number of years then?

HS: Everything was 18 months, originally. I signed up for that and since I owned part of the company, I felt it would be very, very good for me and my family and with my wife at that time, Eileen, and my two children named Scott and Drew. I moved them all down to Mexico and became my home for 25 years. I did love it. It was really a wonderful experience. My kids all speak Spanish fluently. That's their mother tongue, really. They went to an American school there. There are many, many foreign schools in Mexico like the British Academy and so on. My kids went to the American school which taught them basically in English and Spanish. If you live in Mexico like we did - FM2 - you went to the University free of charge. My oldest son Drew - he was three years old then. Eventually he graduated high school and then went to University in Guadalajara - a medical school. He became a doctor and I didn't have to pay for anything. It was paid for by the government. Once you graduated, you were obligated to the government for a year or two, they assign you a job in a very small town or it could be in Guadalajara, but you had to give the government back in the form of payment of working for the government where they assign you a special place in the port to give back in other words. I didn't have to pay for Drew's medical school. He got out of the school and joined the US Navy and became a flight surgeon and he went to some school in North Carolina, which the Navy paid for. He became a Lt. Commander and a Commander and a flight surgeon. He loved flying and he did what he wanted to do, flying and doctoring. My other son, Scott, liked animation, liked live-action and that is what he's doing right now. He works freelance, both in the States and Mexico doing live-action commercials. My daughter, Laurie, she's down in Mexico. She's a dual citizen, Mexican-American right now. She has two passports, legally. Laurie lives near Carmen, it's called. It's close to Cancun, that area. It's a small town, but a very popular tourist place called Playa Del Carmen. Laurie still lives down there. We have a Chinese granddaughter now that speaks perfect Spanish. They'll be up here next month.

MA: You go back and forth still between Texas and Mexico?

HS: Yeah, yeah. It's a wonderful experience, really. I love the Mexican people. Never once did I have a problem down here. When you hear about Jay Ward's problems, there are many books written about Mexico. Earthquakes destroyed this building and these other things happened here. It was all BS. I told Darrell that we had earthquakes, but never once was a building destroyed. One of the books showed a building separated in half, you might say, and we jumped from one building to the next. It's stupid. That's ridiculous. The government would have shut us down so fast, you wouldn't know what hit you. So, that never happened.

MA: When I did my book, everyone generally said that everything ran pretty smoothly. It was a little rough at the very beginning. Of course, during TTV, this was quite a bit later, so all the really bad kinks were already worked out. They were talking about Tennessee Tuxedo and Underdog.

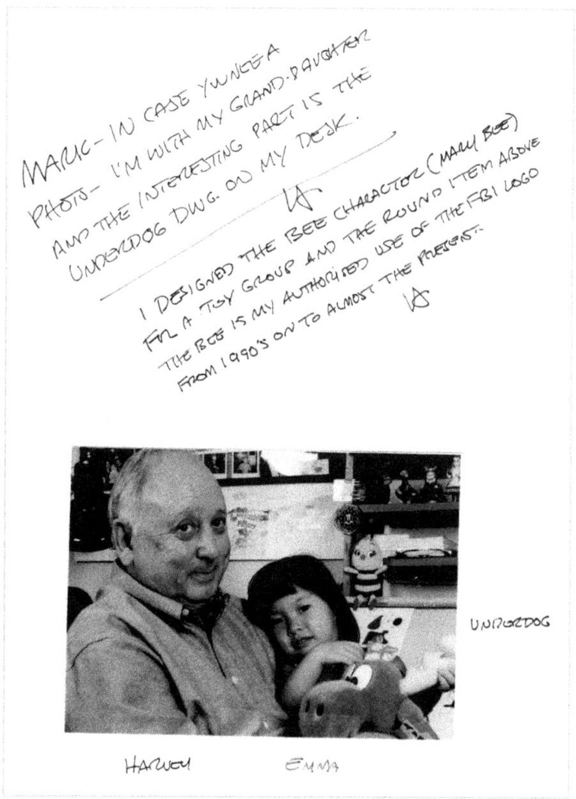

MARC - IN CASE YOU NEED A
PHOTO - I'M WITH MY GRAND-DAUGHTER
AND THE INTERESTING PART IS THE
UNDERDOG DWG. ON MY DESK.
I DESIGNED THE BEE CHARACTOR (MARY BEE)
FOR A TOY GROUP AND THE ROUND ITEM ABOVE
THE BEE IS MY AUTHORIZED USE OF THE FBI LOGO
FROM 1990'S ON TO ALMOST THE PRESENT.
UNDERDOG
HARVEY
EMMA

HS: Yeah, right. We finally had what was really capable, really. The problem we had was that we couldn't get animation cels into Mexico back then, and so we had to smuggle them in. Really truly. We couldn't get paint. They'd close the border on something like ink. It's called black magic ink. We couldn't get that so we had our ink made in Mexico, which was horrible. It was made with glycerin, so of course, during the rainy season, which we had, it would never dry. The cels would stick to each other in these big blobs. It was really terrible. The paint, of course, we had to use latex wall paint. We couldn't get cartoon colors, cel levels and cartoon colors. You're familiar with all that?

MA: To make them all the same shade and all that?

HS: Yeah. The company that was near LA, I guess it was in Culver City. It was the Cartoon Color company. Let's say you wanted red. In fact, I remember the numbers. It was 108 red. We couldn't get it in Mexico, because they made house paint in Mexico that was pretty similar. We had to get the closest thing we could to 108 red. With the cel levels, it would be on cel one and the buildings on cel four. Other characters would be cels three and two. The Cartoon Color company had those leveled out in cel levels, so that if you put one cel down, it changes the color of the cel underneath it. Let's say you use white on the bottom cel?

MA: Right.

HS: And then you put four levels on top of that, it would become grey, of course. We had to get the Cartoon Color company, they had all the cartoon levels for us, from grey to white. So we had to hire somebody and his job all day long was to get the colors as close as we could to the different colors of red, for instance. We had different jars of the paint to make them move from cel to cel. When you work with the Cartoon Color company, you can order 108 level one, 108 level two and so on, so it would never jump in color contrast. If you ever watch any of our old shows, you'll see. Even in old Bullwinkle, you'll see it jump from light brown to dark brown because they're not leveled. They're not cel leveled.

ANOTHER PHOTO WHICH MIGHT BE OF USE

MA: Did you ever run out of colors completely? Let's say you're doing red, did you run out of that?

HS: Well, no. Since we were using house paint, you'd never run out of colors because there were many houses, so then we had tons of paint. The problem we had was getting the right colors. Then there were people out there like RCA, which is a British company. They were very, very helpful and they were trying to help us in working with us to get cel levels for us. They were very, very cooperative on that. We did our best, but we did have the problem with ink. Black ink, you could get Higgins ink, but it wasn't for cels. And then during the rainy season, it would just blob right on top of that. The pressure of each cel on top of something would make it stick like glue. You'd get your cel back and you lost your image. These are the things we had to fight, and it made it really difficult. It was a lot of work. One of the major problems, really. Tape was no problem. Another major problem was that I had iodide and we had Oxford cameras. We used special lamps to get Kelvin ratings. We had a certain Kelvin rating and we had to use regular photo floods, which were not made for animation. We had to use that and we had to get a kelvinometer and get the right Kelvin rating. We had all these technical problems, and only if you worked in the field, you would appreciate the amount of problems that came up like just getting the right Kelvin rating. We were using Kodak film. Any wrong Kelvin rating, the film wouldn't give you the right saturation of color.

MA: Did you have all those problems all along or by the end it was all figured out?

HS: All along.

MA: Oh wow.

HS: Yes, we had problems all along, because of dealing with the Mexican government. You'd think they would try and help you, because you were working in Mexico, but we had 125 people working for us. You had certain laws and you had to work within the law of immigration. That was always one problem. Customs was another problem. There was a lot of smuggling. The animation cels you couldn't get, so the films we used for my shows were very, very thin. They weren't the normal thickness. We had a lot of problems with cel jumps. They would go all over the place sometimes. I spoke to Darrell about this. How familiar are you about animation?

MA: I've never worked in the field and am only familiar from what I have read.

HS: Darrell knew what we were talking about. The original optical cameras were set up for ACME pegs - the pegs that hold the bottom of the cel. Since we had to use the very, very thin cels, we had to use Oxberry pegs, which is a much sturdier peg. They call them pegs, actually. We had to use the Oxberry pegs, which is very rare. Most people use ACME. We had to use them because we couldn't get the cels that were normal size. I think normal cels are 005, I believe, and I believe we were using 003, which is what they would fit. That was really, really a major problem.

MA: It's amazing you got the cartoons done. When I interviewed Roman Arambula, he said that they never missed a deadline, as far as he knew.

HS: Yeah. Roman's a very good friend of mine. In fact, he gave me a drawing of Mickey Mouse and the rest of those characters. He loves me. He gave me a hat here somewhere if I can find it. My room here is a mess. I'll try to send you a copy of it.

MA: Let me ask you about a few people who worked there. Some I know have passed on. Some I don't know what happened to them. I think the one you were thinking of from Argentina was Bob Schleh?

HS: Ok, Bob, yeah. Without Bob Schleh, we wouldn't have gotten anything off the ground, really. Bob was a tremendous Disney talent and a fantastic animation artist. He was part of my family, you might say. The kids loved him and he was a very good friend. In one of the animation books, it said he commited suicide in Italy. It should have never been brought up because - I don't know if you want to know what happened or not?

MA: Sure.

HS: It was nothing illegal or anything like that. Bob retired in Italy and he gave all the money he earned and when it came time to retire, he had no money. He had spent it all. Bob was a very fine gentleman, really easy-going, and he just couldn't face it. I wished many times that he would have called us. We could have helped him out in a lot of ways, financially, and had just come to the house and stayed with us, or something, but he had lost everything. He was just a wonderful, wonderful person, really. Without Bob's help - he spoke perfect Spanish and none of us spoke Spanish. He just smoothed the way for everybody. He was just a gentleman. A really fine, fine person. That was Bob Schleh. George Carlson was also a wonderful man. We had a good crew. There was not one person that was bad, except one. I can tell you that George Singer - I had to fire him, and the fun part about it was that he was a terrific fine artist. He did fine painting in the hotel room at the Hotel Roosevelt - a very big hotel in Mexico City. They would show his work in the windows and so on. He started making more money than he ever made with us - thousands and thousands of dollars more. We were friends until the very end even with these things. He made a fortune selling paintings. It was like $50,000 a painting, so he thanked me for firing him so he could get back into fine art. I told Darrell the same story. It is true and it could happen and he was married to a Mexican national. Give me some other names now.

MA: Jesus Martinez.

HS: We called him "Chuy". Chuy owned part of Val-Mar - Valdez Martinez - the V-A-L is Valdez and M-A-R is Martinez. They owned a company called Val-Mar. The first name Valdez is Gustavo Valdez, who was in politics. I believe he was the governor of one of the states, I think Durango. I'm not too sure about that, but he was in politics. He was a really wonderful person and really wealthy. When I say wealthy, I mean millions of dollars under the mattress wealthy like that. The guy was Gustavo Valdez. Chuy was his brother-in-law. That's how he got involved. When we bought Val-Mar, and it became Gamma Productions, Chuy became in charge of production as far as the Mexican concern and any problems between the Mexicans and the Americans. We honestly never had a strike. A lot of books were written about how good it was, but it was a marvelous experience. Let's put it that way. The people were marvelous with no problems. They were nice people. If not for the government and their laws, it would have been much easier, let's put it that way. We had a place eventually getting things in Mexico. Brushes. Winsor-Newton brushes, for instance. We couldn't bring that to Mexico, because they made brushes down there for painting homes. A brush is a brush, but it's not a Winsor-Newton. A $5 brush for painting the house. These are the problems we faced, really.

MA: You'd think there would be some art supplies down there anyway.

HS: Oh yeah, you could get them, but where a brush might cost you $30 here in the States, a Winsor-Newton, it might be there at $110. Using house paint on the brush, where you weren't using regular art paint or acrylic paint, your brush would just be dead in a week. It was useless. We had to smuggle other stuff like brushes in our way. We had some good smuggling contacts at our company who took care of us.

(MARK - PLEASE LET ME KNOW YOU RECEIVED CHECK)

APRIL 2, 2014

HI MARK,

HERE IS A CHECK TO COVER THE BOOK FOR LORI PLUS POSTAGE. I FIGURE $40 SHOULD COVER ALL BUT IF NOT PLEASE LET ME KNOW.

HERE ARE SOME MORE NAMES THAT POPPED UP BEFORE I DRIFTED OFF TO SLEEP.

CHARLIE KIMBAL EDITOR

ALBERTO VALENZUELA ASST. EDITOR (BUT DID ALL THE WORK)

* EDITION, CHECK RUSHES FOR RE-TAKES AND MOVIEOLA (I HOPE I SPELLED THIS RIGHT) TOOK PLACE AT CHURUBUSCO STUDIOS IN MEXICO CITY. WE HAD NO MOVIEOLA AT GAMMA AND NEEDED ONE BUT NO FUNDS. WHEN I TOOK OVER GAMMA I PURCHASED ONE FROM HANS BEINLER, A LIVE ACTION PRODUCER.

CARLOS MANRIQUEZ WAS SUPPOSED TO DO THE CHECKING FOR CHIPPED INK AND PAINT BUT DID FAIL MANY TIMES LEAVING A MESS FOR ME TO O.K. THE WORK BEFORE BUD GOURLEY SENT THE FILM OFF TO WARD

SO AS YOU CAN SEE I WAS NOT JUST A LAYOUT MAN — I WAS FROM DAY 1 — CHARGE OF PRODUCTION, BUT CHIPPED IN ALL AREAS OF PRODUCTION INCLUDING INK & PAINT, BACKGROUNDS AND KEEPING ALL GOING. WITHOUT BOB SHEEH THIS WOULD HAVE BEEN A MONSTER TO HANDLE.

* AND SYNC UP SOUND TRACK TO IMAGE.

MA: Here's another person. Ernesto Terrazas.

HS: Ernie Terrazas, he was an animator. A Disney animator. He worked with Carlos Manriquez. Carlos was in charge of ink and paint. He was with us on the *Underdog* series, but Ernie was let go. Carlos Manriquez was in charge of ink and paint. We had like three people working in Ink and Paint at that time. Originally, Val-Mar was in a three or four story building, but Gustavo, being an architect also, decided to build a building of our own with the money. I didn't get involved with that situation. Somehow, along the way, we ended up with a building for ourselves all done for Gamma Productions in a place called Tecamachalco.

MA: Darrell does show photographs of both buildings.

HS: Yeah. I can't recognize it, really.

MA: It doesn't look the same at all?

BUD RAN THE MONEY AND SUPPLY PROBLEMS. CHUY MARTINEZ NICE GUY BUT DID NOTHING TO SPEAK OF.

$ GUSTAVO VALDEZ $, CHUY'S BROTHER IN LAW, WEALTHY BEYOND $ COMPREHENSION AND A GREAT FRIEND. HE THREW WONDERFUL PARTY'S AT HIS HACIENDA LOCATED IN THE "PEDRIGAL", A RICH MAN'S AREA IN THE CITY. HE SPARED NO EXPENSE MAKING THE FIESTA FOR THE KIDS AT GAMMA (AT LEAST TWICE A MONTH).

ERNESTO LOPEZ – ANIMATOR – GENTLEMAN

CARLOS SANDOVAL LOOKED EXACTLY LIKE MR. WHOOPEE. FUN LOVING GUY

TERESA REYES, MY AND BUDS SECRETARY.

AS FAR AS I CAN REMEMBER – WE NEVER, NEVER HAD A MAJOR PROBLEM WITH THE MEXICAN STAFF. NEVER!!

I LOOK BACK AT MY ORIGINAL PLAN FOR 18 MONTHS TO ALMOST 25 YEARS WITH FUN AND LEARNING ABOUT ANOTHERS COUNTRY.

WE COULD NOT IMPORT "KODAK" CELLS WHICH WERE CLEAR AND DID NOT AFFECT OF COLORS WHEN LAID DOWN ONE CELL ON TOP OF THE OTHER. WE USED 4 TO 5 CELL LEVELS AND WITH KODAK MY COLOR LEVELS WOULD HAVE BEEN EASIER.

WE HAD TO USE ANOTHER COMPANY CALLED "CELANESE" WHICH HAD A BLUE CAST AND DID AFFECT THE COLORS GREATLY.

HOPE THIS HELPS A BIT. IF I CAN THINK OF ANYTHING ELSE I WILL WRITE.

EXCUSE MY WRITING – AS I SAID I'M ON POWERFUL DRUGS WHICH REALLY HELPS MY SHRAPNEL PAIN IN MY BACK BUT MY BRAIN DOES GET SLIGHTLY WOOZY

BEST REGARDS

HARVEY

HS: Not at all. It looks like a paint shop or something. Chuy and Gustavo, they invested their own money, and I guess Peter Piech did an investment, and built the company for us in Tecamachalco. It was named after the city.

MA: More names. Jaime Torres.

HS: Ok. The number one is Bud Gourley.

MA: I was going to ask about him, too.

HS: Yeah. Bud was an American living in Mexico for many, many years in the film business. Bud ran the day to day working of the studio. He ran many situations. He handled customs. He had all the contacts and spoke perfect Spanish. He would sort out things with the government. Bud was really, really important. When Bud left eventually, Jaime Torres came in. He was a friend of Bud's and Jaime took over. Jaime lived, I believe with an American citizen, but he lived on both sides of the border. You want names of towns, or something?

MA: That's fine. Yeah.

HS: Reynosa. It was right opposite - it's a border town, really - I'll try to remember some of these names. It's a long time ago.

MA: You're doing pretty well.

HS: I'm trying to think of the town, but Jaime lived on both sides, and he knew everybody in politics. The word in Spanish is called the gordita. Have you heard of that word?

MA: Yes, I have.

HS: Ok, a gordita is a bike to get across the border at certain times of the day. If you write about that, you could get put in jail for that. A lot of it was illegal so that you could get the work done. So, Bud was number one. He left after he was with us for quite a few years. He left for the States and Jaime came in, and he ran the Mexican end of the studio. I ran the production end of it. In most of the books on the shows by Gamma, I don't credit for anything, basically, which is ok, but they wrote stories. They were interviewed by the author, but no one interviewed me except Darrell. The first person.

MA: I did talk about you in my book: "In 1964, Harvey Siegel became co-owner of Gamma with Jaime Torres and was the head of Gamma until it closed in 1970," which you could probably tell me if that's accurate.

HS: Yeah.

MA: I probably got most of my information from Roman Arambula, because I had a decent interview with him.

HS: I stayed on. I left in 1980. I stayed on. I got there in '59, and since I owned part of the company, I was put in charge of the production, actually. There's a book called *The Moose That Roared*. There's so many things in that book that are so wrong. I'm looking at the books I've got that were written, and the only one that's written that's worthwhile is Darrell's, as far as Gamma's concerned.

(1)

HI MARK

I'M SENDING THINGS OF INTEREST FOR YOUR ENJOYMENT.

IN GOING THROUGH YOUR WONDERFUL BOOK – I HAVE NOTED SOME ITEMS OF INTEREST AS WELL

I WENT TO MEXICO AS HEAD OF PRODUCTION BUT WORKED IN ALL AREAS. I PURCHASED FR $10,000 (TEN THOUSAND) LENARD KEYS SHARE IN THE BW SHOW AND WAS PART OWNER OF GAMMA FROM DAY ONE.

BOB SHLEH WAS MENTIONED AS NOT CARING TO WORK. NOT IN MY OPINION. BOB WAS THE CORNERSTONE AT VALIMAR AND GAMMA. A FANTASTIC TALENT IN ALL PHASES OF ANIMATION!!!

BUD GOURLEY WAS NOT SENT TO MEXICO. HE LIVED THERE WITH HIS WIFE AND SON FOR MANY YEARS. WE WERE BOTH INTERESTED IN FIRE-ARMS AND WERE CLOSE FRIENDS. WHEN HE LEFT MEXICO JAIME TORRES VASQUEZ TOOK OVER AS ADMINISTRATOR UNICO AND ALSO GREAT TO WORK WITH. HE KNEW THE INS & OUTS OF GETTING THINGS INTO MEXICO VIA AMIGOS AT THE BORDER.

I SOLD MY SHARES TO GORDON JOHNSON (VIA HOTCHKISS) AND IN RETURN WAS GIVEN ALL OF GAMMAS EQUIPMENT AND SHARES IN MEXICO. I BOUGHT CHUY MARTINEZ SHARES AND CREATED ANIMATION INTERNACIONAL.

WE WORKED FOR THE U.S. STATE DEPT, SESAME STREET, AND MANY OTHER AD AGENCYS.

ROGER CARLIN AND HIS SISTER CYNTHIA TRIED TO GET A 20 MINUTE SPOT ON THE AIR CALLED CHILDRENS PRAYERS. I PRODUCED SOME STORYBOARDS BUT NO SALES. RELIGION WAS A NO NO

MA: In my book, I do have a chapter on Gamma, and I mentioned things with a grain of salt, from *The Moose That Roared*, because the book starts off saying, "Oh yeah, they did these other cartoons like Underdog and Tennessee Tuxedo that weren't very good," and I said, "Hey, I like those cartoons! What is this?" I mean, they're not the same type of cartoon as Rocky and Bullwinkle, but I still enjoyed them.

HS: Yeah. The problem is that now all of the credit goes to the Jay Ward group. They take credit for everything. I mean everything. We never had a chance to even defend ourselves. A lot of it was just plain lies.

MA: So that was the purpose of my book. You definitely need a copy of my book because then you'll see what I wrote.

HS: Ok, great.

MA: And then you can embellish upon that. You can read it and say, "Oh, this is right. This is wrong. You need to add this."

(2)

I PRODUCED MANY COMMERCIALS FOR THE "MILLS": CY WAS A GOOD FRIEND AND I STAYED AT HIS HOME IN MINN. MANY TIMES. HIS WIFE HEATHER A LOVELY DOWN TO EARTH PERSON. IZZY KLIEN WAS CY'S ASST AT THE MILLS.

THE MILLS TRIED TO GET A NEW CEREAL OUT—CALLED 'KABOOM'. AND I DESIGNED THE BOX AND CHARACTERS. TROUBLE WAS— THE CEREAL WAS VERY COLORFUL (RED, PURPLE, GREEN, YELLOW) ECH!! AND COLORED THE MILK HORRIBLE LOOKING — SO IT FAILED

BETWEEN US— ANOTHER MONEY MAN BOB TRAVIS WAS INVOLVED ALONG WITH GORDON, I ATTENDED HIS DAUGHTERS WEDDING IN NYC.

GORDON JOHNSON HAD A HABIT OF MAKING SPIT BALLS AT SOME IMPORTANT MEETING.

I'LL SAY NOTHING ABOUT MONEY BEING PASSED AROUND.

TROUBLE WITH WARD— PAT BID ON THE PILOT (MOON MEN) USING VERY SIMPLE ANIMATION. WE WENT TO MEXICO WITH THAT IN MIND. JAY WANTED MORE AND MORE ANIMATION WHICH WE COULD NOT AT FIRST PRODUCE. NO MONEY AND LIMITED TALENT UNTIL MUCH LATER.

A GREAT BACKGROUND MAN — JOE MONTELL

SANDOVAL LOOKED LIKE MR WHOOPEE; NICE QUIET MAN.

CARLOS MANRIQUEZ RAN A TIGHT SHIP—INK & PAINT BUT FAILED IN THE CHECKING OF THE CELLS FOR INK CHIPPING AND WRONG COLORS.

HS: Most definitely. If I can't help you with the truth that's going on with the show itself. The people were wonderful. There's all these stories about Mexico like there was always a strike, because there was no toilet paper. There's stupid things like that. There was no toilet paper so they went on strike. It's a lie. It's so stupid. Then, of course, the building was broken because of the earthquake and divided the building in half.

MA: I left stuff like that out, because I felt that it sounded a little far-fetched.

HS: First of all, they were unionized and the government would have closed us down right away.

MA: Let me ask you about a few people who weren't down there, but you worked with like Gordon Johnson of General Mills. Did you work with him?

HS: Gordon Johnson was with Dancer Fitzgerald Sample.

MA: That's what I meant. Did you deal with him directly?

HS: Oh yeah, a lot. We were good friends. In fact, Gordon bought my share of the show. I was very naive about money, and I still am. Gordon knew what he was doing, so he came down one day and said, "Harvey, the show is going to be closing up soon, but I can buy it from you and you want to sell it?" And I said, "Ok." It was like $10,000 for seven years, but I wished I had kept some of it, anyway. He was in charge at Dancer Fitzgerald Sample. He was big. To me, he was the top man there.

MA: Of course, I interviewed all four owners of TTV - Buck Biggers, Joe Harris, Tread Covington and Chet Stover. I don't know if you have any memories about them.

HS: I met Tread and I loved him. He was a wonderful man. He got me and (at the time my wife) Eileen, I think it was tickets to *The Man of La Mancha*. I think it was one of the great shows in the New York scene. Tread was very good and nice to work with. A lot of these people from the Gamma group tried desperately to get work from Ward to help us out, and it was always a dead end. They don't believe it was all in LA. We had talent, but it was not #1. We'd try and I think the show proved it. It was weird stop action and characters shifting from scene to scene. I think, considering the pressure we were under and considering what we had, the show was still going strong, and it would go strong, Underdog included. We must have done something right.

MA: After Jay Ward pulled out after *Hoppity Hooper*, I guess you were still working on Klondike Kat, and what else was going on at Total TeleVision?

HS: We had Tooter Turtle, I believe, at one point.

MA: Yeah, and *The Beagles* was like the last series?

HS: I think Joe and Tread could give you the exact dates of the shows. Commander McBragg - I love that one!

MA: When it was just the Total TeleVision shows for like the last year or so?

HS: I think the characters Joe created, the characters are all his. He was there from the very beginning.

MA: Yes, but what I mean was, what was the studio like in the later days?

HS: We had a going studio at that time. We had about 125 people. We did a lot of work for the US government for International Development or AID. We did a lot of work on documentary films for them. I mentioned to you that we won a contest for 42,000 commercials. We were in the Top 100 of 1969. You can Google all this stuff, I believe. One of the Top 100 was a Trix commercial. I think it was called VOT - v - o - t - like voting. On the box was a ballot. The idea was to have the kids send in - cut the ballot out and send it in - to have the rabbit get Trix. The story was that he never gets the Trix. Trix are for kids. That was the idea. I think Nixon was running then. What I heard and what I remember, that more votes were cast for our character than for the President of the United States.

MA: That sounds about right. I do remember that. I was a kid when that came out. I was about five years old, so it could have been the 1972 election, or it could have been 1968.

(3)

GUSTAVO VALDEZ THREW FANTASTIC EXPENSIVE PARTYS A FEW TIME A YEAR AT HIS FANTASTC HOME IN THE "PEDRIGAL". A GENTLEMAN AND FRIEND-

VALMAR EXISTED PRIOR TO OUR COMING TO MEXICO. OFFICE WAS LOCATED IN AN OFFICE BUILDING ON ALVARO OBREGON STREET.

CHUY MARTINEZ WAS AN ARCHITECT AND HE DESIGN OUR NEW OFFICE BUILT BY GUSTAVO. THE BLDG HAD NO OTHER OFFICES NEAR US. THE PHOTO DARRELL HAS — LOOKS NOTHING LIKE WE HAD BUILT

AS FOR MYSELF I'M A DISABLED MARINE AND ARMY VET LIVING ON PAIN KILLERS SO PLEASE EXCUSE MY WRITINGS AS MY MIND IS DULLED BY PAIN KILLERS. I'M NOT AN ADDICT BUT USE PAIN KILLERS ON A MEDICAL ROUTINE ONLY. SO PLEASE FORGIVE MY TRYING TO GET MY POINTS TO YOU AS BEST I CAN.

IF YOU NEED ANYMORE INFO - PLEASE CONTACT ME.

BEST WISHES -

HARVEY

HS: I think it was 1969, because I got a letter from that time.

MA: Well, they might have rerun it in '72.

HS: Yeah. I got a letter from Cy congratulating me on winning the 100 Best Commercials. I got the letter. I still have it. I'll send you a copy of it in the mail. I'll get your address and all. I'll send you copies of the stuff I've got here.

MA: Now is that Cy Plattes you're talking about?

HS: Yes. Cy Plattes. Cy was a wonderful man. I keep saying "wonderful man", but they really were great people to work with.

MA: What was Cy like? The only thing that I really know is that he was one of the characters as a platypus, and they ended up putting him in a *Tennessee Tuxedo*. I don't know much about him beyond that.

HS: I stayed in his home in Minnesota. That's how close we were. He invited me up to General Mills. He was the head of marketing at General Mills. Heather, his wife, I met with her, and I stayed with him at his home in Minneapolis. That was for about a week in Minnesota. He was really a straight shooter and a wonderful man. They were really nice people. I couldn't say that about the Ward group.

MA: I got that impression, too, about TTV. Everyone I interviewed was very nice. The thing that was really strange was that it took me a while to track them down even like yourself. The only people that got credit were really the voice artists from Total TeleVision. I just knew the voices and that's it.

HS: Yeah, definitely.

MA: It says, "Animation: Gamma Productions". That's it.

HS: We had a hard time getting our name in the show titles. They made the titles up in LA and left us off the titles. Instead of saying, "Harvey Siegel,

BULLWINKLE...HECHO EN MEXICO

Harvey Siegel-Williams

Very few people realize that the Bullwinkle series that has developed such a cult following, was produced in Mexico City. I initially went to Mexico for a period of 18 months to produce "Rocky and his Friends," which later became "The Bullwinkle Show." So successful were those early efforts and so pleased was our sponsor -- General Mills -- with the results, that 18 months turned into more than 10 years of animation production in Mexico. And those 10 years expanded to 23 years, during which my animation company produced Underdog, King Leonardo, Hoppity Hooper and other animated films.

It all started in 1959, when Peter M. Peich, president of the "Producers Associates of Television" (PAT), asked me to view a new animated pilot created by Jay Ward. I watched the antics of a goofy moose and a flying squirrel and when the lights in the projection room came on, I agreed to join PAT and take charge of the animation studio that was to produce the Bullwinkle and Rocky series. I was so sure of Bullwinkle's success once we hit the air that I invested my money as well as my talent. Eventually, I came to own Gamma Productions, changed the name to Animation International, and produced other animation series, TV commercials, education films for the U.S. Department of State, and nearly 300 segments for Sesame Street.

Many people have great ideas for an animated series , but without financing, they remain just that... great ideas. Peter Peich was instrumental in securing the necessary financing, without which Rocky and Bullwinkle would probably have remained grounded.

Peter's role was in finding the major financing necessary to produce Jay Ward's concept. Peter interested General Mills in becoming the sponsor of "Rocky and his Friends." Cyril W. Plattes, then General Mills' division vice president and director of marketing, was our main contact at General Mills, and his assistance and support were invaluable.

At first, it was decided to produce the show in Japan, but because of logistics, Mexico was chosen. Because of both time and financial constraints in producing a weekly animated series, the animation was deliberately simple. In some ways, this simplicity contributed to the charm of the show. In no way does this take away from the talents of the Mexican team of animators I assembled, since that same team was capable of high quality full animation. In fact, we produced many commercials for General Mills, including one for Trix cereal which Advertising Age named one of the top 100 commercials of the year.

I arrived in Mexico City and was met by Bud Gourley, an

Head of Production", you never saw that, really, so all the credit went to them. Truly, the only guy I liked working with that was really tough was Sean Bohlman (?). Sean was very particular about what he liked and we tried to please him. It was difficult because the cameras wouldn't do what he wanted. We had an Oxford camera. Actually we had two cameras. We had one camera and that camera was a lemon. So when Peter built the camera, we didn't know what to look for so you couldn't do dissolves or fadeouts or fadeins. We eventually had to hire an engineer in Mexico to create for us, a camera that would work. I remember Gerard writing a letter to us, really angry, saying, "When I say 'Fade to black, I mean black!'" He'd bang his hand down on the table and say, "I mean black!" We couldn't do it. That was the problem. The camera wouldn't fade to black because it was a plain old Brownie camera.

MA: I just interviewed Gerard on Tuesday. He gave me a lot of information, but he never worked for Total TeleVision, did he?

HS: No, no.

MA: He did work for Jay Ward. I just did a book on DePatie-Freleng now and I forgot that he also worked there, so I talked to him a little about that. He did a couple of Dr. Seuss specials.

HS: Yeah, yeah. He is a very good director and a very good animator, but again he was part of Ward's group, and that was putting a knife in our back. Whenever they had a chance, they would do it. That was very unfortunate, because they helped us in the very beginning, and really helped us, not to come down there, and make speeches. They sent some of the animators down; some of the top guys - a guy named Hurtz, for instance.

MA: Oh, Bill Hurtz.

HS: Yeah, whom I hate. Some guys I love, Hurtz I hate. He did anything possible to kill us. Also, I was sitting at the table here at our house, and the book came out about the show. He took credit for opening the company and starting the company in Mexico City. He took all the credit for that, and it was one big lie, because the credit goes to Bud Gourley, Bob Schleh and myself. He never mentioned that. It was always Bill Hurtz, Bill Hurtz, Bill Hurtz. He took credit for everything.

MA: I think I got the story straight in my book.

HS: It's unfortunate, really, because I could have been so helpful in the beginning. He went down to Mexico to see if he could help us out a bit, but it was any way they could kill us. So when they came down for trips, three or four of them from Ward's group, they never once asked us, "Can we bring you something? Can we bring you paint? Can we bring you ink? Brushes? A camera? Iodide? Special lamps that you used for the cameras to get the correct Kelvin rating?" We had our own Kelvin rating and it would be wrong. They're small and tiny and they came down as tourists and they would not get searched. We would get searched. They would come down and they could have said, "Can you use something? Can you use some Scotch tape? Anything?" Never once did they help us with that. Never once. That just shows you what we were up against. It was tough the first few years with shows going. I was not happy at the beginning because we had to train people who literally knew nothing about animation. They came off the street, went to art school and brought in trained people in the beginning. It got going and eventually became very commercial. In fact, the letter I have from Cy Plattes says, "We'll give Harvey more work when he gets the thing going." That's how Cy felt about us. He was a wonderful man. He retired from General Mills and then he made his living in Helene right now. I lost track. I lost track of him.

MA: I think he's gone too, but I don't know.

HS: He was a really nice person and professional. He was very happy with the shows.

MA: You were talking about Jay Ward, and the whole purpose of why Total TeleVision started was that General Mills and Dancer Fitzgerald Sample were having troubles with Jay Ward. They said, "What is all this? We want a kids show, not stuff with spies, espionage and stuff like that. We want a simple kids show," and that's why they created Total TeleVision, in order to make simpler shows.

HS: That's right.

MA: That was always their plan. For a while it kind of worked that they had them both going out of Hollywood and New York.

HS: Absolutely. If you're familiar with Tiffany Ward and so on, and he asked me to show her the first pilot show. I think it was a 3½ minute - 4 minute pilot. The shows themselves, they would have been so much easier to deal with or to accomplish our goal if we helped one another. They just didn't. If you look at the pilot, have you seen the pilot?

MA: I've seen frames from it, but I haven't seen the actual film.

HS: Well, try to get a hold of that. That's what we bid on and that's what we were doing, and they complained, "No, no, we want more animation and more this and more that." Well, that's not

American expatriate who was to handle the business side of the animation studio while I directed the production. PAT had bought into a small Mexican animation studio called "Val-Mar." We changed the name to "Gamma Productions," brought in animation cameras, equipment, and as the show progressed, American animation talent. Mexico at that time had no training programs in animation, and we literally took youngsters off the street and trained them. Before long, our Mexican staff grew from around 20 artists to well over 125.

The association of Jay Ward and Producers Associates of Television (Ward-PAT) was now ready to go into production. Typically, Ward's group in California would send us sound-tracks, story boards and some direction on each of the segments.

We had many problems with this system of production, one of which was the difference in pronunciation between Spanish and English (for example, the English "i" sound -- as in "kick" would be pronounced "ee" -- or "keek" in Spanish). To ensure that the characters' mouth action matched the dialogue, we had to re-write the sound track phonetically.

When the show went into full production, which included Dudley Do-Right, Fractured Fairy Tales and Aesop's Fables, we were producing approximately 18.5 minutes of animation a week. During the many years we produced the Bullwinkle series and other shows for General Mills, I am proud to say, Gamma Productions never missed a deadline or an air date.

Aficionados of the series may have noticed the changes the characters of Bullwinkle and Rocky underwent as the show progressed. I redesigned Rocky and Bullwinkle to make them more appealing.

Among the talent within the Gamma Productions animation team were several former Disney artists, Tex Henson (of Chip and Dale fame) and Carlos Manriquez, who headed our ink and paint department. Other members of my animation team included Sal Fallaice, Sammy Kai, George Singer, and Bob Schleh. Joe Montell worked closely with the talented Mexican background design team. Other key Mexican artists included Carlos Sandoval and Ernie Terrazas. After a few years, Bud Gourley left to return to the U.S., and Jaime Torres took over as business manager. Eventually, when the series came to an end, a number of our Mexican staff went on to work with Hanna-Barberra and others started their own animation studios.

I have yet to see any article or film dealing with the history of Bullwinkle that gives credit to the team that brought Bullwinkle to life. The recent documentary, "Of Moose and Men" is a case in point. There has never been any mention of this highly skilled group of artists and animators who worked with me at Gamma to bring the series to the TV screen. I feel that the time has come for those involved in the production of the show to get the credit they deserve...credit which has been exclusively claimed by the California-based Ward group.

MARK - I DO NOT KNOW IF THIS WOULD BE OF INTEREST TO YOU. IT WAS FOR A WRITE UP FOR A NEWSPAPER ARTICLE.

SORRY ABOUT NO MENTION OF TTV - All THEY WANTED WAS WARD AND BW

what we bid on, also on General Mills and P.A.T. He got a very great, primitive looking show. It was very, very simple and that's what we were turning out, but he wanted more and more and more, and better, better, better work. That's not what I signed on to do. If you look at the first show, with Cloyd and Gidney, the moonmen, with the pilot of going to the moon, you look, that's what we bid on. It was paper cut outs, basically. So, when they ordered more and more and more, we didn't have anybody to do that more and more and more. That's where we didn't fail. Personally, I've said, we gave them what they wanted. I said that we didn't have the talent to do that, and there were major problems. I do believe with *Underdog*, we did much better.

MA: Well yeah, I always say that the best series was *Underdog* and *Tennessee Tuxedo* for Total TeleVision, and where you did best for Jay Ward was probably *Hoppity Hooper*, even though nobody remembers it.

HS: That was a great show, by the way.

MA: I love *Hoppity Hooper*. I wish they would put out a proper release of it on home video.

HS: I don't know why they held it up. I have no idea really.

MA: I don't, either. I've asked about it. I used to go to the Dudley Do-Right Emporium in LA and ask, "What happened to Hoppity Hooper?" They'd say, "Oh, Classic Media owns it." Then, I would call the people at Classic Media and they'd say, "Oh, Jay Ward owns it." They didn't know.

HS: Very strange. It was a funny show. Jay Ward's stuff, let's put it that way, you could have had, in my opinion, a blank screen, and just have the characters speaking. You would have had a show. It was so funny, really.

R. F. Bodeau 4WW
1/29/69
C. W. Plattes 4NW

Nit-picking is no way to judge a commercial's impact over-all. You will recall how pleased I was with the TRIX Election commercial. I was delighted to see AD AGE rate it very high and, in fact, give it an award.

When we look at a commercial, we have got to look at the action and animation first. Right now the color on the Cheerios O Man and O Boy is excellent but the commercials are duds as far as animation and action.

I hope that when Harvey Siegel gets his business established down there so that he will control it and can give us some good prices, you will consider giving him some commercials; because I regard Harvey as a tremendous technician and a great creative talent.

NOT WRITING ABOUT US.

CWP/kjl

bcc: Harvey Siegel

WE DID GET MANY COMMERCIALS FOR THE 'MILLS' INCLUDING CHEERIOS, COCOA PUFFS, LUCKY CHARMS AND SO ON.

MA: So the later Total TeleVision show I mentioned. I don't know if you remember it, was *The Beagles*. It was about two dogs and they went around and they sang songs and things like that. Do you remember anything about that?

HS: I really don't remember *The Beagles* at all.

MA: Yeah. It wasn't a big success, but Gamma did animate it. Once you see my book, you might remember it from the pictures or something. It's kind of one of those weird shows also, that is now kind of lost.

HS: It sounds familiar, yet it doesn't sound familiar.

MA: There were two dogs, one was tall and played a guitar, and one was short, and played a standup bass.

HS: I can't remember that at all. I remember *Tennessee Tuxedo* because that was more of an educational show.

MA: *Tennessee* was on for three years and *Underdog* was on for three years. *The Beagles* was only a year, so that might be why.

HS: Yeah. I remember Joe Menfield, who was our background man, did a lot of the backgrounds on the *Tennessee Tuxedo* shows. I'm thinking right now. I remember the pistons of the automobile going up and down. Joe figured out how to show that on a black and white background and it worked out really, really nicely. He's a terrific background artist. Joe Menfield. He passed away, also.

MA: One person I didn't get a chance to interview, and you might know him, and he did storyboards. Gerry Ray?

HS: Gerry was in Mexico when I got down there. He was already in Mexico working for a company called Tompkins. I forget his first name, but Tompkins had an animation studio. Gerry really worked for Tompkins. He never worked for Gamma. He worked through Ward, I believe.

MA: I have him at TV Spots. I think Joe Harris got Gerry to do storyboards sometimes, and those were sent down to Gamma. I think that's what it was.

HS: Possibly, yeah. I don't believe that Gamma hired him. At least he wasn't on my payroll.

MA: In the back of my book, I have a Who's Who of Total TeleVision. You can go through it and see if I got everybody.

HS: Why don't I do that? I can go through the names. I'm sure Sammy Timerg worked on this, on the *Underdog* series, I believe.

MA: Here's a storyboard artist also - Gerry Mooney. He worked with Joe Harris.

HS: Yeah, yeah. Joe Harris, yes.

MA: Joe mentioned that he went down to see you guys once during. It was like in 1965 or something. He said that was his one visit to Mexico. He thought everything ran pretty smoothly.

HS: It was a different category. They were very helpful [TTV]. Hopefully, they liked what we did. People still know Underdog.

MA: In the interviews I did, nobody on the Total TeleVision side ever said any bad words about Gamma. They didn't really work when it was Val-Mar, if there were problems back then. By the time Total TeleVision came in, everything was pretty much established. They thought it worked pretty well. The only thing that was a shock to them, initially, was that General Mills said that they had to use Gamma. They weren't sure, but General Mills said that that was part of the deal, and so they said, "Ok," and that was it.

HS: Yeah, yeah. Well, they were with us for quite a while after that.

MA: Back then, Terrytoons was still there in New York, and Paramount was still in New York. They thought that this would be done in New York.

HS: I guess we were cheaper. I don't know the financial part of the deal of how much it cost and so on, but the cost I know in Mexico was much cheaper than in the States. That's why a lot of work was done down in Mexico.

MA: Right. So, I've heard that Gamma kind of closed up or at least stopped doing the series animation in 1967. Is that correct?

HS: I have to get my papers, because they changed the name from Gamma. They changed it to Animation International.

MA: This is the story I know, and you can correct me, is that you stopped doing series animation in 1967, you closed the doors to Gamma and changed the name in 1970.

HS: What I'm going to do, I'm going to send you some paperwork that says when we closed and the exact dates. It's some Mexican credentials proving that I did that. I have a drawer full of things here and see what I've got. I've got paperwork with exactly the date that we closed our doors. I've got it all, so let me write it all down.

3 King Leonardo and his Short Subjects

by Mark Arnold

Since *Created and Produced by Total TeleVision productions* was published in 2009, DVD sets of *Tennessee Tuxedo and his Tales* and *The Underdog Show* have been released, complete with input by me. But why no *King Leonardo and his Short Subjects* DVD set? The answer lies in the proverbial music rights issues. These same music issues keep some of the early Hanna-Barbera cartoon series like *Ruff and Reddy* and *Quick Draw McGraw* from being released. The return on investment is predicted to be so low that no one wants to pay for the music rights in order to get these cartoons a proper release. The alternative (which has been done before) is to reissue the cartoons with brand new music cues. The problem with that is that for animation purists, it is akin to sacrilege to alter the music cues that the fans grew up with. A couple of good examples of where this was done was when *The Gumby Show* and *The Casper Show* were reissued in the 1990s. Both shows were given a music makeover with updated synthesized 1990s-type music that just went against the grain of virtually all fans. The powers-that-be claimed that this updating would make the cartoons appear fresh and new, but to everyone else, it made watching the cartoon a trying experience because the digitally clear sounds didn't correspond with the sometimes grainy cartoon images. Sometimes, like in the case of *The Mr. Magoo Show,* character voices were also replaced in order to make them more politically correct.

You may ask why a good amount of *King Leonardo* episodes did make it onto the *Tennessee Tuxedo* set from Shout Factory. The answer is that the later *King Leonardo* cartoons that were animated by Gamma dispensed with the older music cues and were replaced by new ones that were created especially for TTV shows rather than relying on the typical Winston Sharples music cue library and others.

I will say that there are ways of getting bootleg copies of the entire *King Leonardo* series, which may irk the major labels, but hey, major labels, find a way to issue this stuff, or this is where we turn.

One of the reviews I got on Amazon for my original TTV book was that I made no mention of Mr. Mad in the book. At the time I was writing the original book, I had no access to the later Gamma-animated episodes of *King Leonardo,* and it is these episodes that originally featured this character. Mr. Mad is kind of an animated-looking version of the Dracula character in the Francis Ford Coppola version of the film. I still don't have much to say about Mr. Mad, except that he appeared in at least one episode (#79, "Introducing Mr. Mad"), he was voiced by Norman Rose (even though I mistakenly attributed him to Kenny Delmar in my earlier book) and I'll show a picture of him in this book.

King Leonardo and his Short Subjects was syndicated as *The King and Odie Show*. Similar to how *The Rocky Show* was syndicated from *Rocky and his Friends, The King and Odie Show* was designed to be shown in either a 15-minute or a half-hour format.

Early in the series' NBC run, selected Columbia Pictures theatrical cartoons were aired on the program, some featuring The Fox and the Crow and Li'l Abner.

These shorts were added to fill time when production of the early shows was delayed. The Columbia cartoons were featured during NBC showings of Hanna-Barbera's *Ruff and Reddy*, but not included in subsequent syndicated versions of the series.

Another segment of the original *King Leonardo* show was Twinkles (an orange elephant), which simultaneously appeared as a feature on Jay Ward's *Rocky and his Friends* [over Ward's objections; after a brief period, it was seen on *King Leonardo* exclusively]. The title character served as the mascot of Twinkles Cereal, a product of the show's chief sponsor, General Mills. The 90-second Twinkles segments continued to air in syndication during the 1960s, and were presented in a 15-minute format under the title *The King and Odie*, but later phased out after a firefighter character replaced the elephant as the cereal's mascot. The segments also appeared during some NBC network rebroadcasts of *Underdog*. The Twinkles segments were not included when *King Leonardo and his Short Subjects* was syndicated in a half-hour format during the 1980s.

Updated episode listing:

* - episodes available on DVD

\+ - listed on packaging, but not on DVD due to issues of the cartoons not having available audio.

King Leonardo and his Short Subjects (39 shows)

Adjustments to the original air dates as provided by David R. Dunsford. These dates are accurate as to what the *TV Guide* published from 1960-1963 in regards to TTV shows that aired on NBC. It does prove that creating perfect TTV show combinations are not possible as repeat segments were commonly combined with new segments. Plus, theatrical cartoons of Columbia's Fox and the Crow series were added at times for contractual reasons. Those episodes without a confirmed original airdate are designated with a (?). In some cases, the original airdate is missing, but the repeat airdate is listed from the *TV Guide* listings.

Original *King Leonardo* shows from 1960-1963 consisted of a King and Odie segment each week, an alternating Tooter Turtle or Hunter segment each week, a Twinkles segment each week, and a Columbia Screen Gems cartoon or a second King and Odie segment each week.

"The King & Odie" (104 episodes)

First Season: 10/15/60-5/20/61, NBC (32 episodes, 1 per show)

King & Odie #1 Riches to Rags (10/15/60; 5/27/61; 5/5/62)

*King & Odie #2 Nose for the Noose (10/22/60; 6/3/61; 5/12/62)

King & Odie #3 Drumming Up the Bongos (10/29/60; 6/10/61; 5/19/62)

King & Odie #4 How High is Up? (11/5/60; 6/17/61; 5/26/62)
King & Odie #5 Royal Amnesia (11/12/60; 6/24/61; 6/2/62)
King & Odie #6 Loon from the Moon (11/19/60; 7/1/61; 6/9/62)
King & Odie #7 Dim Gem (11/26/60; 7/8/61; 6/16/62)
King & Odie #8 The Clanking Castle Caper (12/3/60; 7/15/61; 6/23/62)
King & Odie #9 Duel to the Dearth (12/10/60; 7/22/61; 6/30/62)
King & Odie #10 Ringside Riot (12/17/60; 7/29/61; 7/7/62)
King & Odie #11 Trial of the Traitors (12/24/60; 8/5/61)
King & Odie #12 Battle-Slip (12/31/60; 8/12/61)
King & Odie #13 Paris Pursuit (1/7/61; 8/19/61)
King & Odie #14 The Awful Tower (1/14/61; 8/26/61)
King & Odie #15 The Sport of Kings (1/21/61; 9/2/61)
*King & Odie #16 Black is White (1/28/61; 9/9/61)
King & Odie #17 Fatal Fever (2/4/61; 12/16/61; 9/1/62)
King & Odie #18 Pulling the Mane Switch (2/11/61; 12/16/61)
*King & Odie #19 Sticky Stuff (2/18/61; 12/30/61; 9/15/62)
King & Odie #20 Am I Glue (2/25/61; 12/30/61; 9/15/62)
King & Odie #21 The King and Me (3/4/61; 12/9/61; 9/22/62)
King & Odie #22 The Loves of Lynetta Lion (3/11/61; 12/9/61; 9/22/62)
King & Odie #23 Heroes are Made...With Salami (3/18/61; 1/20/62)
King & Odie #24 The Big Freeze (3/25/61; 1/20/62)
King & Odie #25 De-Based Ball (4/1/61; 2/3/62)
*King & Odie #26 Bats in the Ballpark (4/8/61; 2/10/62)
King & Odie #27 True Blue Blues (4/15/61; 2/17/62)
King & Odie #28 My Dog has Fleas (4/22/61; 2/24/62)
King & Odie #29 The Legend of Leonardo the Neat (4/29/61; 3/10/62)
*King & Odie #30 Home Neat Home (5/6/61; 3/17/62)
King & Odie #31 Perfume Panic (5/13/61; 3/24/62)
King & Odie #32 Style Awhile (5/20/61; 3/31/62)

Second Season: 9/16/61-3/3/62, NBC (26 episodes, 2 per show)

*King & Odie #33 Lead Foot Leonardo (9/16/61; 4/7/62)
King & Odie #34 The Rat Race (9/23/61; 4/14/62)
King & Odie #35 Long Lost Lennie (9/30/61; 4/21/62)
King & Odie #36 Ghosts Guests (10/7/61; 4/28/62)
King & Odie #37 The Obey Ball (10/14/61)
King & Odie #38 Out of the Depths (10/21/61)
*King & Odie #39 Double Trouble (10/28/61; 7/14/62)

King & Odie #40 Switcheroo Ruler (11/4/61; 7/21/62)
King & Odie #41 No Bong Bongos (11/11/61; 7/28/62)
King & Odie #42 The Ad Game (11/18/61; 8/4/62)
King & Odie #43 If at First you Don't Succeed (11/25/61; 8/11/62)
King & Odie #44 Try, Try Again (12/2/61; 8/18/62)
King & Odie #45 The Loco Play (8/25/62)
King & Odie #46 Romeo and Joliet (?)
*King & Odie #47 Long Laugh Leonardo (12/23/61; 9/8/62)
*King & Odie #48 He Who Laughs Last (12/23/61)
King & Odie #49 Beatnik Boom (1/13/62; 9/29/62)
King & Odie #50 Call Out the Kids (1/13/62; 9/29/62)
King & Odie #51 Royal Bongo War Chant (3/3/62)
King & Odie #52 Showdown at Dhyber Pass (3/3/62)

Third Season: 10/6/62-3/30/63, NBC (26 episodes, 1 per show)

*King & Odie #53 East Side West Side (10/6/62; 4/6/63)
King & Odie #54 Coney Island Calamity (10/13/62; 4/13/63)
*King & Odie #55 An Ode in Code (10/20/62; 4/20/63)
*King & Odie #56 Two Beneath the Mast (10/27/62; 4/27/63)
*King & Odie #57 Hunting a Hobby (11/3/62; 5/4/63)
*King & Odie #58 Teeing Off (11/10/62; 5/11/63)
*King & Odie #59 The Tourist Trade (11/17/62; 5/18/63)
King & Odie #60 Bye Bye Bicycle (11/24/62; 5/25/63)
King & Odie #61 Back to Nature (12/1/62; 6/1/63)
*King & Odie #62 My Vine is your Vine (12/8/62; 6/8/63)
*King & Odie #63 Fortune Feller (12/15/62; 6/15/63)
*King & Odie #64 Wild and Wobbly (12/22/62; 6/22/63)
King & Odie #65 Bringing in Biggy (12/29/62; 6/29/63)
King & Odie #66 Confound it! Confusion (1/5/63; 7/6/63)
*King & Odie #67 Smarty Gras (1/12/63; 7/13/63)
King & Odie #68 Bayou Blues (1/19/63; 7/20/63)
*King & Odie #69 Hip Hip Hypnosis (1/26/63; 7/27/63)
*King & Odie #70 Odie Hit the Roadie (2/2/63; 8/3/63)
King & Odie #71 Uranium Cranium (2/9/63; 8/10/63)
King & Odie #72 Mistaked Claim (2/16/63; 8/17/63)
King & Odie #73 The Trail of the Lonesome Mine (2/23/63; 8/24/63)
King & Odie #74 The Treasure of Sierra Bongo (3/2/63; 8/31/63)
King & Odie #75 Stage Struck (3/9/63; 9/7/63)

King & Odie #76 One Way Ticket to Venus (3/16/63; 9/14/63)
King & Odie #77 Chicago Shenanigans (3/23/63; 9/21/63)
King & Odie #78 Loop the Loop (3/30/63; 9/28/63)

Fourth Season, 9/28/63-3/21/64, CBS (as part of Tennessee Tuxedo and his Tales*) (26 episodes)*

*King & Odie #79 Introducing Mr. Mad (9/28/63)
*King & Odie #80 Falling Asleep (10/5/63)
King & Odie #81 Hup-2-3-Hike (10/12/63)
King & Odie #82 Spring Along with Itch (10/19/63)
*King & Odie #83 Left Alone Leonardo (10/26/63)
*King & Odie #84 A Tour de Farce (11/2/63)
*King & Odie #85 Get 'Em Up Scout (11/9/63)
King & Odie #86 The King Camps Out (11/16/63)
*King & Odie #87 Offensive Defensive (11/23/63)
*King & Odie #88 A Long Long Trail A-Binding (11/30/63)
King & Odie #89 Treasure Train (12/7/63)
*King & Odie #90 Handcar Heroes (12/14/63)
*King & Odie #91 Honey Business (12/21/63)
+King & Odie #92 Bye Bye Bees (12/28/63)
*King & Odie #93 The Royal Race (1/4/64)
*King & Odie #94 The Shifty Sail (1/11/64)
King & Odie #95 Asleep on the Deep (1/18/64)
King & Odie #96 An Ace for a King (1/25/64)
King & Odie #97 Odie Takes a Dive (2/1/64)
King & Odie #98 Go and Catch a Falling King (2/8/64)
*King & Odie #99 Royal Rodeo (2/15/64)
*King & Odie #100 Ride 'em Cowboy (2/22/64)
*King & Odie #101 S.O. Essex Calling (2/29/64)
*King & Odie #102 The Big Falling Out (3/7/64)
*King & Odie #103 Long Day's Journey Into Fright (3/14/64)
*King & Odie #104 Making A Monkey Shine (3/21/64)

"Tooter Turtle" (39 episodes)

First Season: 10/15/60-4/8/61, NBC (as part of King Leonardo and his Short Subjects*) (26 episodes)*

Tooter Turtle #1 Two Gun Turtle (6/17/61; 5/26/62)
*Tooter Turtle #2 Tailspin Tooter (Plane Failure) (7/29/61; 7/7/62)
Tooter Turtle #3 Sea Haunt (2/25/61; 12/23/61)

*Tooter Turtle #4 Highway Petrol or Road Blockhead (6/3/61)

Tooter Turtle #5 Knight of the Square Table or the Joust and the Unjoust (7/1/61; 6/9/62)

*Tooter Turtle #6 Mish-Mash-Mush Panting For Gold (1/13/62)

+Tooter Turtle #7 The Unteachables (or) The Lawless Years (7/15/61; 6/23/62)

*Tooter Turtle #8 Kink Of Swat (Babe Rube) (4/22/61; 2/24/62)

*Tooter Turtle #9 One Trillion B.C. (Dinosaur Dope) (8/26/61)

*Tooter Turtle #10 Olimping Champion (Weak-Greek) (2/10/62)

*Tooter Turtle #11 Stuper Man Muscle Bounder (3/3/62)

*Tooter Turtle #12 Buffaloed Bill or Custard's Last Stand ()

Tooter Turtle #13 Moon Goon (Space Head) (12/31/60)

*Tooter Turtle #14 Robin Hoodwink or Thimple Thief (12/16/61)

*Tooter Turtle #15 Steamboat Stupe or Captains Outrageous (12/2/61)

*Tooter Turtle #16 Souse Painter Brush-Boob (9/9/61)

Tooter Turtle #17 Railroad Engineer or Stupefied Jones (5/20/61; 3/31/62)

*Tooter Turtle #18 Quarterback Hack or (Pigskinned) (11/4/61; 7/21/62)

*Tooter Turtle #19 Drafthead or (Overwhere?) (12/30/61; 9/15/62)

Tooter Turtle #20 Lumber-Quack Topped (2/11/61; 12/9/61; 8/25/62)

Tooter Turtle #21 Jerky Jockey or (Kenducky Derby) (9/29/62)

Tooter Turtle #22 Fired Fireman or Hook and Batter (10/21/61)

*Tooter Turtle #23 Sky Diver or Jump, Jerk, Jump..! (?)

*Tooter Turtle #24 Tuesday Turtle (Private Pie) (3/17/62)

*Tooter Turtle #25 Snafu Safari or Trackdown Tooter (10/7/61; 4/28/62)

*Tooter Turtle #26 Anti-Arctic or (North Pole Nuisance) (11/18/61; 8/4/62)

Second Season: 10/13/62-3/30/63, NBC (as part of King Leonardo and his Short Subjects*) (13 episodes)*

*Tooter Turtle #27 The Master Builder or Rivet Riot (10/13/62; 4/13/63)

*Tooter Turtle #28 Taxi Turtle or (My Flag is Down) (12/8/62; 6/8/63)

*Tooter Turtle #29 Canned Camera or (Peek a Boob) (10/27/62; 4/27/63)

*Tooter Turtle #30 Muddled Mountie or "One, Two, Buckle My Snowshoe" (2/16/63; 8/17/63) (aka Snowshoe Mountie)

*Tooter Turtle #31 Duck Haunter or Decoy Drip (?)

*Tooter Turtle #32 Bull Fright or (Olay Down) (3/2/63; 8/31/63)

Tooter Turtle #33 News Nuisance or (Sub Scribe) (12/22/62; 6/22/63)

Tooter Turtle #34 The Sheep of Araby or Beau Geste Goes West (1/5/63; 7/6/63)

Tooter Turtle #35 Waggin' Train or California Bust (1/19/63; 7/20/63)

Tooter Turtle #36 Anchors Awry or Nautical Nut (2/2/63; 8/3/63)

Tooter Turtle #37 Vaudevillain or Song and Dunce Man (11/24/62; 5/25/63)

Tooter Turtle #38 Rod and Reeling or (Field & Scream) (11/10/62)

Tooter Turtle #39 The Man in the Blue Denim Suit (or Hay! Hay!) (3/30/63; 9/28/63)

"The Hunter" (65 episodes)

First Season: 10/15/60-4/8/61, NBC (as part of King Leonardo and his Short Subjects) (26 episodes) (airdates 10/3/64 and later are part of The Underdog Show on CBS.)

*The Hunter #1 Brookloined Bridge (5/27/61; 10/9/65)

*The Hunter #2 Counterfeit Wants (7/8/61; 6/16/62)

*The Hunter #3 Haunted Hunter (1/21/61; 7/3/65; 3/19/66)

*The Hunter #4 Fort Knox Fox (1/13/62)

The Hunter #5 Stealing a March (9/22/62; 3/20/65)

*The Hunter #6 Horn-a-Plenty (4/15/61; 2/17/62)

The Hunter #7 Concrete Crook (3/3/62; 10/17/64)

The Hunter #8 Subtracted Submarine (2/18/61; 12/23/61; 9/8/62; 7/10/65)

The Hunter #9 Risky Ransom (2/4/61; 12/9/61)

The Hunter #10 Unfaithful Old Faithful (4/1/61)

The Hunter #11 The Armored Car Coup (12/30/61; 9/15/62)

The Hunter #12 Telephone Poltergeist (1/7/61; 8/19/61; 10/10/64)

The Hunter #13 Sheepish Shamus (11/11/61; 7/28/62)

The Hunter #14 Rustler Hustler (8/11/62; 12/5/64)

The Hunter #15 The Case of the Missing Muenster (?)

The Hunter #16 The Great Train Robbery (6/10/61; 9/30/61)

The Hunter #17 Florida Fraud (6/24/61)

The Hunter #18 The Great Plane Robbery (7/17/65)

The Hunter #19 Girl Friday (7/22/61; 6/30/62; 10/24/64)

The Hunter #20 Stamp Stickup (3/10/62)

*The Hunter #21 Statue of Liberty Play (8/5/61)

*The Hunter #22 Frankfurter Fix (4/7/62)

The Hunter #23 The Case of the Missing Mowers (5/1/65)

*The Hunter #24 Fancy Fencing (7/14/62; 7/24/65)

*The Hunter #25 Racquet Racket (12/16/61; 9/1/62)

The Hunter #26 Seeing Stars (1/20/62; 4/3/65)

Second Season: 9/29/62-12/23/61, NBC (as part of King Leonardo and his Short Subjects) (13 episodes)

*The Hunter #27 Elevator Escapade (12/1/62; 6/1/63)

The Hunter #28 Hula Hoop Havoc (10/6/62; 12/15/62; 4/6/63; 6/15/63; 4/10/65)

*The Hunter #29 The Counterfeit Newspaper Caper (10/13/62; 11/17/62; 5/18/63; 7/31/65)

*The Hunter #30 Diamond Dither (10/20/62; 4/20/63; 8/7/65)

+The Hunter #31 Grand Canyon Caper (11/3/62)

The Hunter #32 Borrowed Beachland (8/14/65)

The Hunter #33 Peek-a-Boo Pyramids (1/12/63; 7/13/63)

+The Hunter #34 Lincoln Tunnel Caper (2/9/63; 8/10/63; 8/28/65)

*The Hunter #35 TV Terror (12/29/62; 6/29/63; 9/4/65)

*The Hunter #36 Bye Bye Bell (1/26/63; 7/27/63; 9/11/65)

*The Hunter #37 Time Marches Out (2/23/63; 8/24/63)

*The Hunter #38 The Fox's Foul Play (3/9/63; 9/7/63; 9/18/65)

*The Hunter #39 Bow Wow Blues (3/23/63; 9/21/63)

Third Season, 9/28/63-3/21/64, CBS (as part of Tennessee Tuxedo and his Tales) (26 episodes)

The Hunter #40 Breaking in Big (9/28/63; 3/27/65; 3/26/66)

*The Hunter #41 The Bank Dicks (10/5/63; 10/31/64)

*The Hunter #42 Eye on the Ball (10/12/63; 11/7/64)

*The Hunter #43 Breakout at Breakrock (10/19/63; 11/14/64)

*The Hunter #44 Getting the Business (10/26/63)

*The Hunter #45 "An Uncommon Cold" (11/2/63; 11/28/64)

The Hunter #46 The Pickpocket Pickle (11/9/63)

*The Hunter #47 Goofy Guarding (11/16/63)

+The Hunter #48 The Big Birthday Blast (11/23/63; 12/12/64)

*The Hunter #49 Under the Spreading Treasure Tree (11/30/63; 12/19/64)

The Hunter #50 School Days, Fool Days (12/7/63)

The Hunter #51 Fall of the House of the Hunter (12/14/63; 12/26/64)

The Hunter #52 Oyster Stew (12/21/63; 1/2/65)

The Hunter #53 The Stolen Spoon Saga (12/28/63; 1/9/65)

*The Hunter #54 Under Par (1/4/64; 1/16/65)

*The Hunter #55 Chew Gum Charlie (1/11/64)

*The Hunter #56 Using the Ole Bean (1/18/64; 1/23/65)

*The Hunter #57 The Case of the Hunted Hunter (1/25/64; 1/30/65)

*The Hunter #58 The Purloined Piano Puzzle (2/1/64; 2/6/65)
+The Hunter #59 Record Rocket (2/8/64; 2/13/65)
The Hunter #60 The Hunter's Magic Lamp (2/15/64; 2/20/65)
The Hunter #61 Hunter Goes Hollywood (2/22/64; 2/27/65)
*The Hunter #62 Two for the Turkey Trot (2/29/64; 11/21/64)
*The Hunter #63 Captain Horatio Hunter (3/7/64; 3/6/65)
*The Hunter #64 The Horn of the Lone Hunter (3/14/64; 3/13/65)
The Hunter #65 Little Boy Blues (3/21/64)

"Twinkles"

Twinkles and the Missing Fish (4/1/61)
Twinkles and the Carousel (5/20/61; 2/24/62)
Twinkles and the Big Fan (5/27/61)
Twinkles and the Bananas (6/17/61)
Twinkles and the Haunted House (7/1/61)
Twinkles and the Horse Show (7/15/61; 6/23/62)
Twinkles and the Mountain Climb (10/21/61; 11/10/62)
Twinkles and the Little Toy (11/18/61)
Twinkles and the Falling Leaves (12/23/61)
Twinkles and the Soap Boat (12/31/61)
Twinkles and the Parachute (1/23/62)
Twinkles and the Baby Sitter (1/20/62)
Twinkles and the Volunteer Firemen (2/10/62)
Twinkles and the Gold Mine (2/17/62)
Twinkles and the Tractor (3/3/62)
Twinkles and the Honey Bee (4/7/62)
Twinkles and the Sailboat (10/6/62)
Twinkles and the Carnival (11/3/62)
Twinkles and the Swimming Pool (12/22/62)
Twinkles and the Musical Band (12/29/62)

"The Fox and the Crow" (Columbia Pictures cartoons and not TTV) NBC (as part of King Leonardo and his Short Subjects) (5 known episodes)

Land of Fun (4/1/61)
Mr. Moocher (5/27/61; 12/1/62)
Sighed, Sealed and Clobbered (2/17/62)
Foxy Flatfoot (8/18/62)
The Fox and Grapes (10/6/62)

King Leonardo and his Short Subjects Gallery

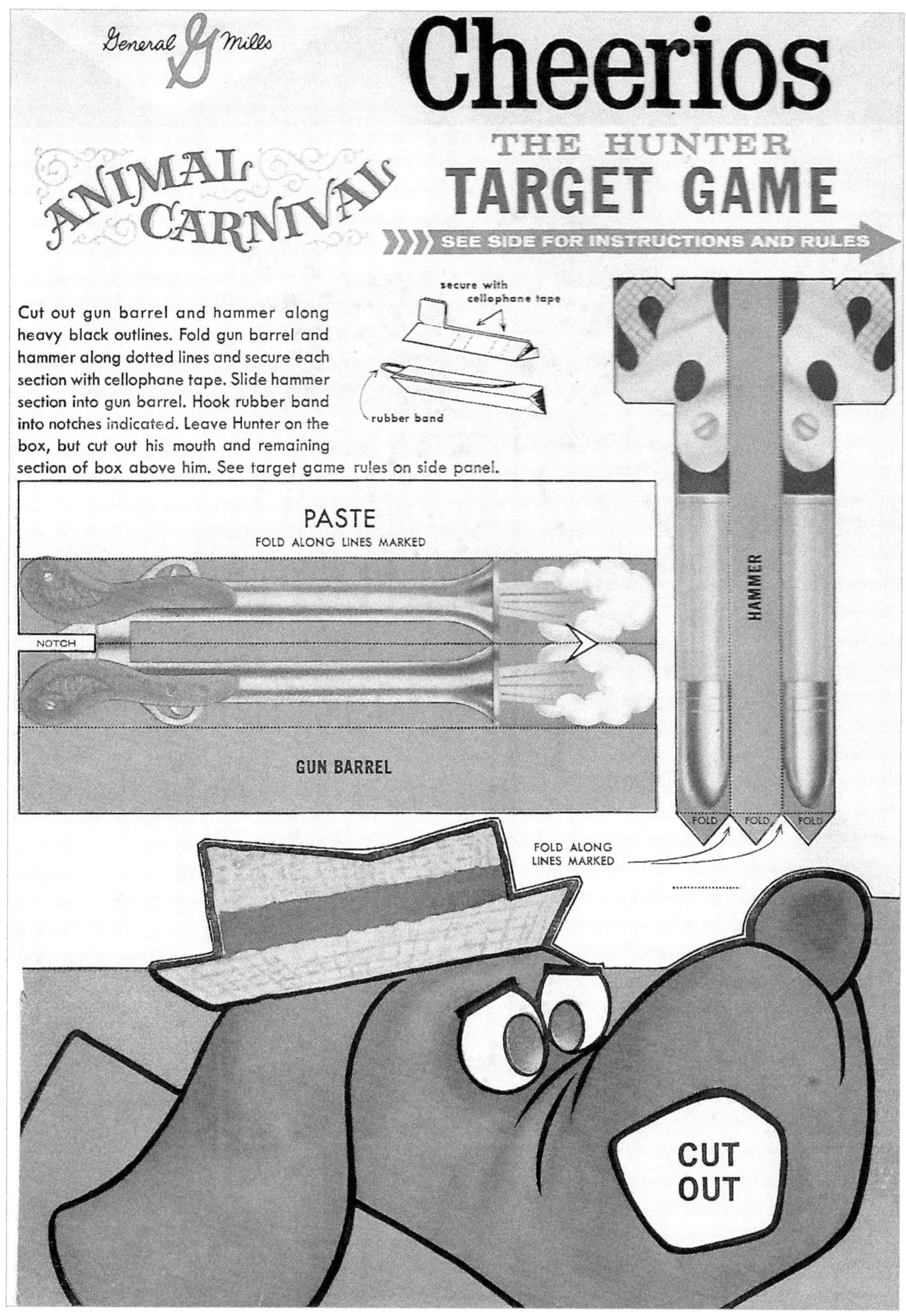

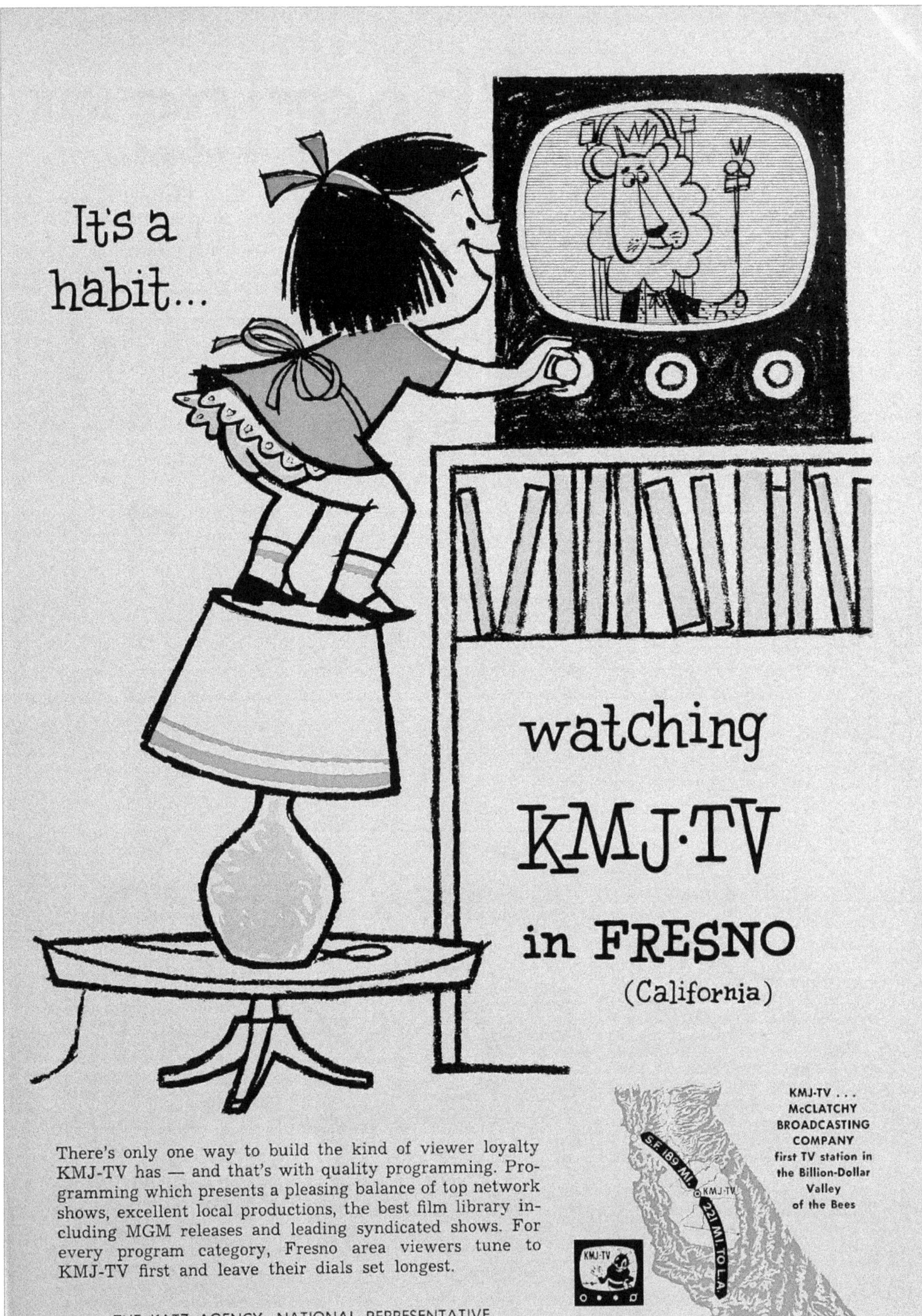
It's a habit...
watching
KMJ-TV
in FRESNO
(California)
There's only one way to build the kind of viewer loyalty KMJ-TV has — and that's with quality programming. Programming which presents a pleasing balance of top network shows, excellent local productions, the best film library including MGM releases and leading syndicated shows. For every program category, Fresno area viewers tune to KMJ-TV first and leave their dials set longest.
THE KATZ AGENCY, NATIONAL REPRESENTATIVE
KMJ-TV . . . McCLATCHY BROADCASTING COMPANY first TV station in the Billion-Dollar Valley of the Bees
S.F. 189 MI.
KMJ-TV
221 MI. TO L.A.

BIGGY RAT
model

General Mills
cocoa puffs
FREE! ACTION GAME FOR YOUR CARTOON CARNIVAL
COLLECT ALL EIGHT and HAVE A CARNIVAL of FUN • EVERYDAY
GAME RULES:
One player places fish face down on game booth ledge. Other player uses "Odie Colognie" to hook the fish of his choice. If he hooks the winning fish he scores a point. Players change turns. The first player to score 15 points wins.
PUNCH STRING HOLE IN ODIE
Attach a 2 foot piece of string.
...WATCH FOR "KING LEONARDO and ODIE" ON YOUR LOCAL TELEVISION STATIONS
PLACE FISH HERE FACE DOWN
PLACE FISH HERE FACE DOWN
CUT ON ALL RED DOTTED LINES
FOLD ON ALL BLUE DOTTED LINES
FOLD THIS FLAP DOWN
PLAY KING LEONARDO and ODIE'S "FISH 'N WIN"!
BIG CARTOON CARNIVAL

General Mills
Cheerios
ANIMAL CARNIVAL
Bullwinkle's
CARD TOSS GAME
See side for rules
CUT OUT CARDS ALONG DOTTED LINES

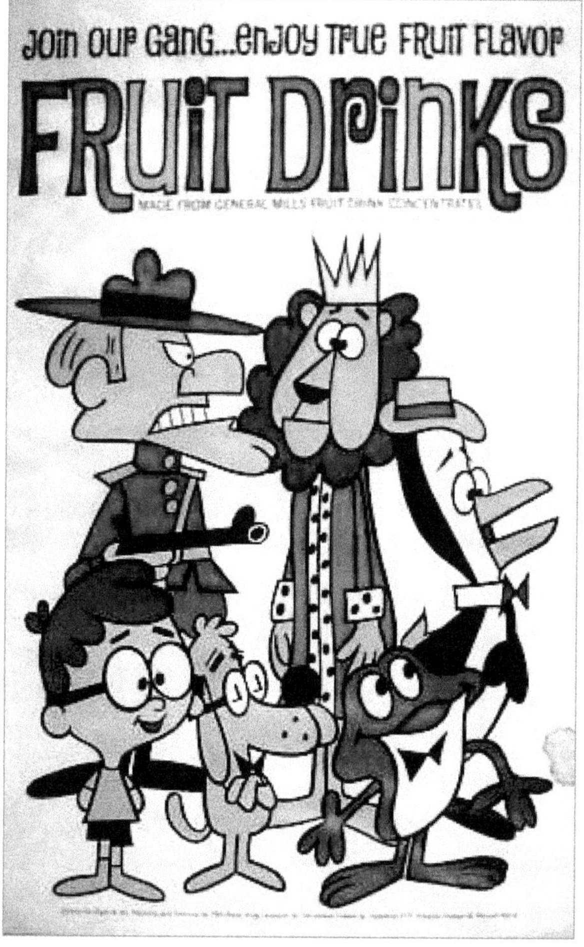
Join our Gang...enjoy True Fruit Flavor
FRUIT DRINKS

General Mills
ANIMAL CARNIVAL
FREE CUT-OUT
ON BACK
KING LEONARDO MASK
Cheerios
Goodness IN TOASTED OAT CEREAL
NET WT. 15 OZ FAMILY ECONOMY SIZE

General Mills
Cheerios
ANIMAL CARNIVAL
KING LEONARDO MASK

CARTOON CARNIVAL
KING LEONARDO
SUPERCAR
21
VIEW-MASTER
stereo pictures

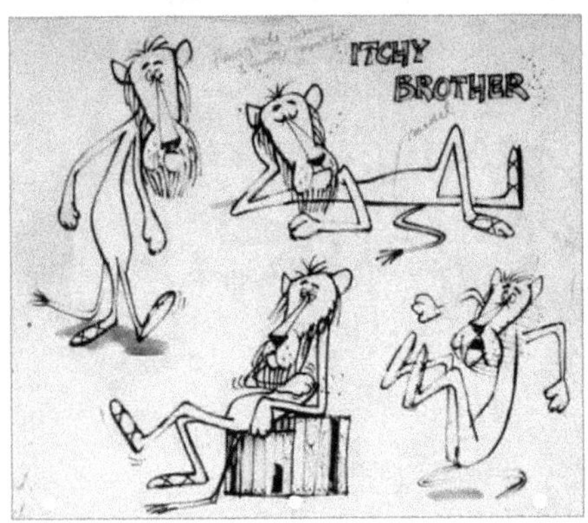
ITCHY BROTHER

BARNEY
King LEONARDO LION

Odie Cologne

Want More Ideas For Cooking Fun?

YOU'LL FIND THEM HERE IN BETTY CROCKER'S NEW BOYS AND GIRLS COOK BOOK

More than 275 recipes and bright food ideas, all specially chosen by boys and girls and tested by them in their own homes, are just waiting for you to try in this beautiful, big picture cookbook. In bookstores everywhere.

RECIPES FROM Betty Crocker

Follow these Kitchen Tips

When you cook, be sure to choose a time when you won't be in your mother's way. Wash your hands. Wear an apron to keep your clothes clean.

Read your recipe and all directions in it very carefully. Set out all ingredients on a tray. Then place each one aside as you use it. Take out all utensils and pans you'll need before you begin to cook.

When you have finished, read your recipe again to be sure you haven't left out anything. Wash pans and utensils and put everything away. Leave the kitchen spic and span. Then your mother will be glad to have you cook again!

"Kitchen-tested" (R) recipes from Betty Crocker
GENERAL MILLS, INC.

Cereal Snack Surprises

© Leonardo Prod. P. A. T.

"CHUMLEY'S" CRUNCHY-O'S

Melt 2 to 4 tablespoons butter in heavy skillet. Add 4 cups Cheerios; stir over medium heat about 5 minutes. Sprinkle with ½ teaspoon salt. Cool (Cheerios will become crisp.) Serve like popcorn.

CHOCOLATE CLACKERS CRUNCH

¼ cup butter
1/3 cup brown sugar (packed)
2 tablespoons light corn syrup
1 square (1 ounce) semisweet chocolate, cut up
3 cups Clackers cereal

Measure butter, sugar and corn syrup into large saucepan. Stirring constantly, heat to boiling and boil gently 2 minutes. Add chocolate; stir over low heat until chocolate is melted. Remove from heat; fold in Clackers cereal until evenly coated. Spread mixture on baking sheet. When cool, break into pieces. Makes about 4 cups.

Breakfast with Bullwinkle

MENU

Sparkling Orange Juice
Scrambled Eggs with Bac*Os
"The Hunter's" Hidden Jewel Muffins
Easy Stir-up Hot Chocolate

SPARKLING ORANGE JUICE

Pour orange juice into glass until 2/3 full; fill with chilled lemon-lime carbonated beverage. Serve at once.

SCRAMBLED EGGS WITH BAC*OS

2 eggs
2 tablespoons milk
1/8 teaspoon salt
1 or 2 teaspoons butter
2 tablespoons Bac*Os

Break eggs into bowl. Add milk and salt. Beat with fork. Heat butter in small heavy skillet. Pour in egg mixture. Cook slowly over low heat, turning gently with broad spatula as mixture starts to set at bottom of pan. When eggs are cooked through, but are still moist and shiny, stir in Bac*Os and serve. Makes 1 or 2 servings.

"THE HUNTER'S"
HIDDEN JEWEL MUFFINS

Heat oven to 400°. Grease 16 medium muffin cups or line with paper baking cups. Prepare Betty Crocker Corn Muffin Mix as directed on package except -- fill muffin cups ½ full. Top each with scant teaspoonful cherry (or your favorite) fruit preserves. Bake 15 to 20 minutes. Makes 16.

EASY STIR-UP HOT CHOCOLATE

Measure 1 tablespoon Betty Crocker Chocolate Ready-to-Spread Frosting into each cup. Fill cup with hot milk; stir until frosting is dissolved.

"HOPPITY HOOPER'S"
CEREAL HITS

Place one of the following in a tall glass or small pitcher. Fill with milk and stir thoroughly. Pour over bowl of Clackers. Serve immediately.

Honey-Orange Blossom: 1 tablespoon honey and 1 tablespoon orange juice concentrate.

Banana Special: ½ banana, mashed.

Maple Smoothie: 2 tablespoons maple-flavored syrup.

Soups and Sandwiches with Sherman

SOUP-ER THRILLS

Just before serving, sprinkle 1 teaspoon Bac*Os over each bowl of tomato, cream of mushroom, bean or vegetable soup.

Just before serving, float Pizza Spins on hot cream of tomato soup.

SILHOUETTE SANDWICHES

Spread two slices of bread with butter; top each with slice of luncheon meat. With cookie cutter, cut diamond, heart, dog or gingerbread boy shape from center of slice of process American cheese. Place cutout cheese on one slice of meat. Place cheese outline on second slice. (Meat shows through cheese, making silhouette.)

SNACK-A-BOB FRANKS

Place cooked frankfurters in buns. On wooden picks, alternate cubes of cheese and pickle chunks with Pizza Spins and New Daisy*s. Insert 2 or 3 Snack-a-Bobs in top of each warm frankfurter bun.

BAC*OS-WICHES

Honey-Peanut Butter: In small bowl, blend ½ cup peanut butter and ½ cup honey. Stir in ¼ cup Bac*Os. Spread peanut butter mixture over 4 slices bread; top with remaining 4 slices. Cut each in half diagonally.

Grilled Cheese: Spread 2 slices bread lightly with butter. Place 1 slice process American cheese between bread slices and sprinkle with 1 teaspoon Bac*Os. Spread outside of sandwich generously with butter. In skillet, brown lightly over low heat on both sides until cheese melts. Cut sandwich in half diagonally to serve.

Lettuce and Tomato: For each sandwich, spread slice of toast with mayonnaise; sprinkle with 1 tablespoon Bac*Os. Top with tomato slices, lettuce and a second slice of toast. Cut in half diagonally to serve.

MAKE-AHEAD HAPPY FACE HAMBURGERS

Cook hamburger patties (1 pound ground beef makes 4 to 5 patties). Place in sliced hamburger buns. Make a "face" on top of each bun with slices of pimiento-stuffed olive for eyes and nose and a strip of carrot for mouth. Wrap in aluminum foil and refrigerate. To reheat, place wrapped in 350° oven for 15 minutes. Serve in foil.

Cake Mix Tricks

ORANGE POLKA-DOT COOKIES

1 package Betty Crocker Sunkist* Orange Cake Mix
1/3 cup butter or margarine, softened
½ cup shortening
2 egg yolks
1 teaspoon vanilla
1 package (6 ounces) semisweet chocolate pieces

Heat oven to 350°. In bowl, combine half the cake mix, the butter, shortening, egg yolks and vanilla; mix thoroughly. Blend in remaining cake mix. (If dough does not hold together, mix in 1 to 1½ teaspoons water.) Stir in chocolate pieces. Shape dough by teaspoonfuls into balls; place on ungreased baking sheet. Bake 8 to 10 minutes. Cool cookies slightly before removing from baking sheet. Makes 5 dozen.

CHEERY CHERRY CRUNCH

½ cup butter or margarine
1 package Betty Crocker Yellow Cake Mix
2 cans (1 pound 5 ounces each) cherry pie filling
½ cup chopped walnuts

Heat oven to 350°. Cut butter into cake mix (dry mix) with fork until mixture resembles coarse crumbs; reserve 1 cup. Pat remaining mixture lightly into ungreased oblong pan, 13x9x2 inches, building up ½-inch edge. Spread pie filling over cake mixture to within ½ inch of pan edge. Mix walnuts and the 1 cup reserved mixture; sprinkle over top. Bake 45 to 50 minutes. 12 to 15 servings.

*T. M. Sunkist Growers, Inc.

Brownie 'n Ice Cream Treats

"QUICK TRICK" BROWNIES

Bake Betty Crocker Fudge Brownie Mix (1 pound) as directed on package. Remove from oven; immediately place about 12 chocolate-covered mint patties (each about 1½ inches in diameter) on top. Allow mints to soften; spread evenly over brownies. Cool. Cut into squares.

© Leonardo Prod. P. A. T.

"TOOTER'S" SLOWPOKES

1 package (1 pound) Betty Crocker Fudge Brownie Mix
¼ cup water
1 egg
Walnut or pecan halves
1 can Betty Crocker Ready-to-Spread Chocolate Frosting

Heat oven to 375°. In mixer bowl, blend brownie mix, water and egg. (Dough will be stiff.) For each cookie, place 3 walnut halves with ends touching in center on greased baking sheet. Drop dough by level teaspoonfuls onto center of each group of nuts. Bake 10 minutes. Cool slightly before removing from baking sheet. Finish cooling and frost. Makes about 4 dozen.

"TENNESSEE TUXEDO'S" TOPPERS

In saucepan, combine 1 can Betty Crocker Dark Dutch Fudge or Butterscotch Ready-to-Spread Frosting, 1 tablespoon corn syrup and 1 tablespoon milk. Heat over low heat, stirring often. Spoon warm sauce over ice cream. Store leftover sauce covered in refrigerator. Makes 1 3/4 cups.

Mr. Peabody's Party Delights

© Jay Ward Prod. P.A.T.

ROCKY ROAD PUDDING

In bowl, mix 1 can Betty Crocker Chocolate Fudge or Butterscotch Pudding and 1½ cups miniature marshmallows; pour into serving dishes. Refrigerate at least 2 hours. If desired, top with whipped cream and maraschino cherries. 6 servings.

"FILLMORE'S" FROSTY FUDGIES

Spoon Betty Crocker Chocolate or Chocolate Fudge Pudding into 4-ounce paper drinking cups, paper baking cups or other small molds. Insert flat wooden stick in each. Place in baking pan or tray; freeze until firm. Remove from paper cup or mold; eat like lollipop.

© Hooper Prod. P. A. T.

CUPCAKE CONES

Heat oven to 400°. Prepare any flavor Betty Crocker Layer Cake Mix except Marble as directed on package. Pour scant ¼ cup batter into each of 30 flat-bottom waffle ice-cream cones, filling each a scant ½ full. (If cones are filled more than ½ full, batter will run over top.) Place cones in oblong baking pan; bake as directed on package for cupcakes. Frost cones; decorate with candles, tiny multi-colored candies or colored sugars.

BALLOON CAKE

Bake any flavor Betty Crocker Layer Cake Mix in oblong pan, 13x9x2 inches, as directed on package. Cool. Frost with Betty Crocker Classic Creamy White Frosting Mix. Arrange pastel mint wafers in a cluster to resemble balloons at upper left corner of cake. Cut thin strips of gumdrops or use shoestring licorice for balloon strings. Bring all strings to one point at lower left edge of cake. Insert candles. If desired, place cake pan in wicker basket; light candles and serve.

"LION'S" ZOO CAKE

Bake any flavor Betty Crocker Layer Cake Mix in oblong pan, 13x9x2 inches, as directed on package. Cool 10 minutes. Remove from pan and cool thoroughly. Prepare Betty Crocker Chocolate Fudge Frosting Mix as directed on package. Frost sides and top of cake (frosting on top should be about 1/4 inch thick). To decorate, stand animal crackers upright around top edge of cake, alternating with colored gumdrops. Press more animal crackers and gumdrops around sides of cake. Decorate with candles.

Twinkles Gallery

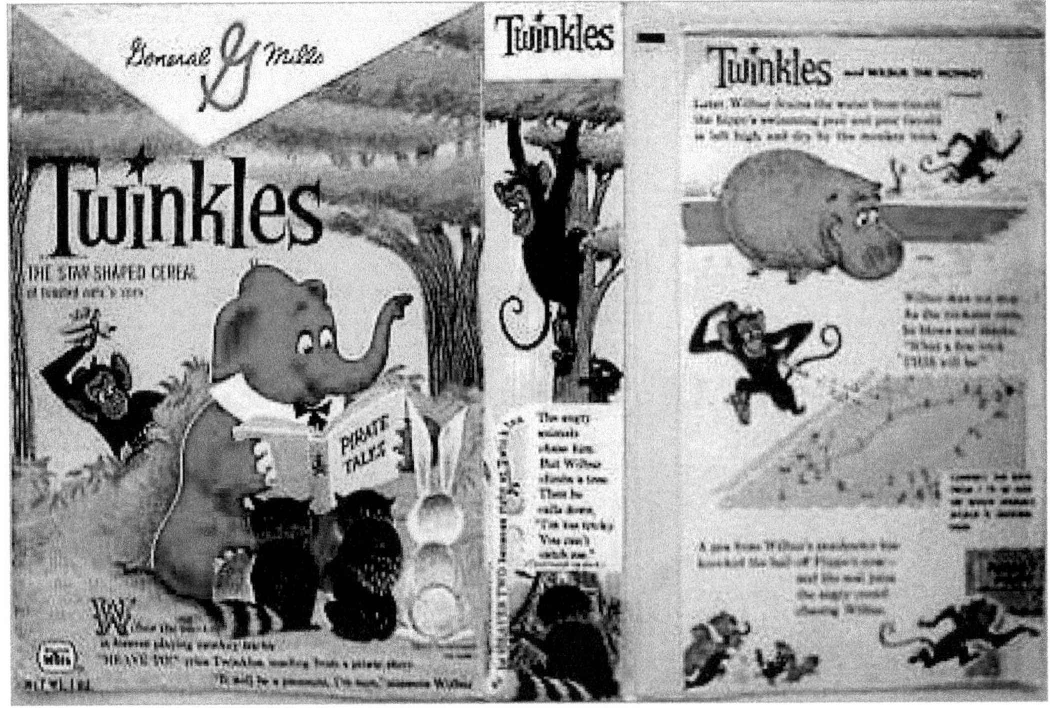

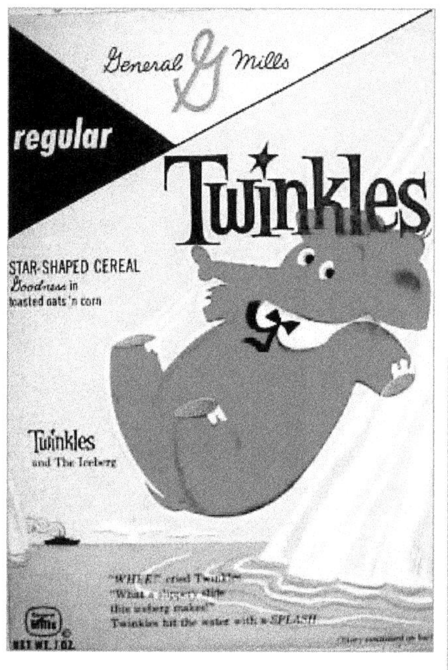
General Mills
regular
Twinkles
STAR-SHAPED CEREAL
Goodness in
toasted oats 'n corn
Twinkles
and The Iceberg
Twinkles hit the water with a SPLASH
Mills
NET WT. 7 OZ.

General Mills
"STORY BOOK PACKAGE"
Twinkles
STAR-SHAPED CEREAL
Goodness in
toasted oats 'n corn
Twinkles
and THE SCHOOL BELOW THE SEA
Have you ever heard of Twinkles' visit
to the school below the sea?
Mills
NET WT. 7 OZ.
It was a very special

General Mills
sugar
sparkled
Twinkles
STAR-SHAPED CEREAL
Goodness in
toasted oats 'n corn
Twinkles
and The Platypus
Twinkles and his friends stared at the strange
thing. It had a beak. But its body was furry.
And its webbed feet looked like paddles.
"What is it?" wondered Twinkles.
Mills
NET WT. 9½ OZ.
(Story continued on back)

General Mills
"STORY BOOK PACKAGE"
Twinkles
STAR-SHAPED CEREAL
Goodness in
toasted oats 'n corn
Twinkles
and THE TEDDY BEAR
Once a little koala bear came to the zoo.
Twinkles cradled him gently in his trunk and said,
"Has anyone ever told you that you look
Mills
NET WT. 7 OZ.
(Story continued on side)

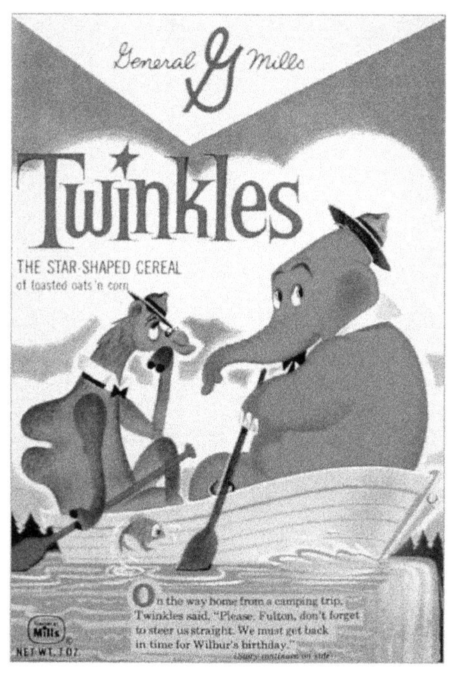
General Mills
Twinkles
THE STAR-SHAPED CEREAL
of toasted oats 'n corn
On the way home from a camping trip,
Twinkles said, "Please, Fulton, don't forget
to steer us straight. We must get back
in time for Wilbur's birthday."
Mills
NET WT. 7 OZ.

General Mills
Twinkles
THE STAR-SHAPED CEREAL
of toasted oats 'n corn
(Story continued on side)
Fulton the camel
is a very sad inventor.
Twinkles says,
"Cheer up, Fulton.
Some day one of your
inventions will work."
At this moment,
Wilbur the monkey
Mills
NET WT. 7 OZ.

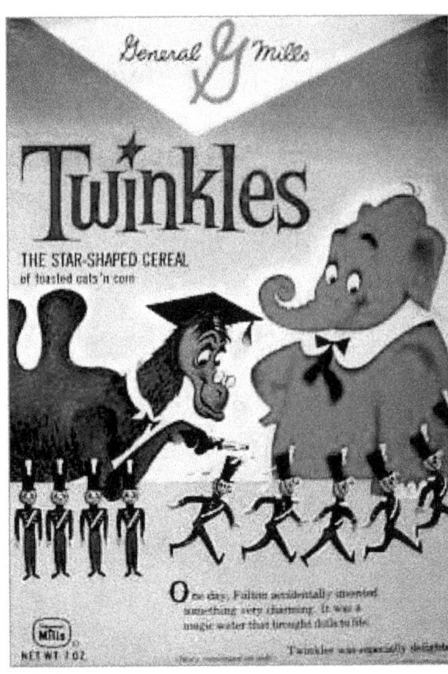
General Mills
Twinkles
THE STAR-SHAPED CEREAL
of toasted oats 'n corn
Mills

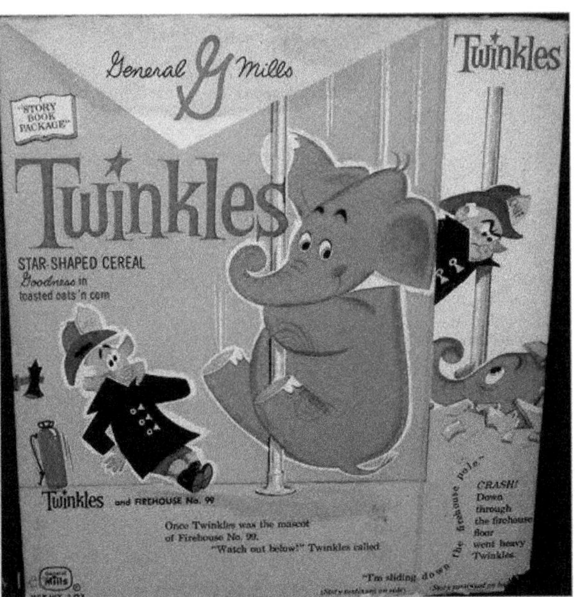
General Mills
"STORY BOOK PACKAGE"
Twinkles
STAR-SHAPED CEREAL
Goodness in toasted oats 'n corn
Twinkles and FIREHOUSE No. 99
Once Twinkles was the mascot of Firehouse No. 99.
"Watch out below!" Twinkles called.
CRASH! Down through the firehouse floor went heavy Twinkles.
Mills

Twinkles
General Mills
Twinkles
STAR-SHAPED CEREAL
OPEN THE MAGIC PAGE FOR MORE FUN WITH TWINKLES!
Twinkles and THE MAGIC LAMP
Once Wilbur rubbed a magic lamp.
A cloud of smoke poured out—
and there stood a giant genie.
PRICE
Twinkles AND THE MAGIC LAMP

General Mills
sugar sparkled
Twinkles
STAR-SHAPED CEREAL
Goodness in sweetened toasted oats 'n corn
What a show! We'll have the audience glued to their seats!
TWINKLES—HIS FRIENDS PRESENT
A FUN FILLED CARNIVAL
FREE GRATIS
FOR ALL CHILDREN
AT THE ZOO
TOMORROW
Great! That ought to hold 'em!
Twinkles and THE ONE ELEPHANT CARNIVAL

General Mills
NEW
sugar sparkled
Twinkles
Goodness in sweetened toasted oats 'n corn
FUN-TIME PACKAGE
HOW TO
MAKE A
BIG TREE!
PLUS 3 PAGES OF FUN
NET WT. 9.5 OZ.

LGR 557
LITTLE GOLDEN RECORD 29¢
78 RPM
Twinkles and his Pals
The Hide and Seek Game
The Parade
©1961 GENERAL MILLS, INC.

Tennessee Tuxedo and his Tales

by Mark Arnold

One of the quibbles about the *Tennessee Tuxedo Complete* and the *Underdog Complete* DVD sets is that all of the episodes are separate and not really "shows" in the traditional sense. Reasons for this are numerous. First, repeat episodes commonly appeared with new TTV episodes during their original runs. General Mills, when they made these shows, allotted a certain amount of episodes for a particular series, and when that allotment was made, except in rare circumstances, that was it. No more episodes were made. This created some nightmares of compilation as some series had more episodes than another series, creating a need for repeats along with the new episodes. This, coupled with the fact that crazy things like leftover Columbia Pictures cartoons aired in some shows due to contractual obligations created a confusing mess. Since the first version of my book, more information has come to light, but the Shout Factory DVD sets were based upon my original book information and not later information.

Later reruns of *Tennessee Tuxedo and His Tales* are quite different from the original network series, like most cartoon series produced by Total TeleVision. The first 34 Tennessee Tuxedo cartoons were incorporated into syndicated prints of *The Underdog Show*. That syndicated package actually was a revised version of another earlier (mid-1960s) syndicated series called *Cartoon Cut-Ups* which initially featured first season segments of Underdog, Tennessee Tuxedo, and Commander McBragg. In fact, the syndicated *Underdog Show* includes some artifacts such as the *Cartoon Cut-Ups* closing, combining portions of the original *Tennessee Tuxedo* and *Underdog Show* closing titles, effectively eliminating the punch line of the visual "Post No Bills" joke in the original *Underdog Show* closing. It also includes the final teaser at the end of the show in which announcer George S. Irving says, "Looks like this is the end...but don't miss our next *Cartoon Cut-Ups* show!" (The line was redubbed to say "Underdog" instead of "Cartoon Cut-Ups".)

The episodes "That is Horse" and "Ponda That Moose" are erroneous.

Since my original book came out, new short episodes of *Tennessee Tuxedo and Chumley* were created in 2014 for YouTube by Chuck Gammage Animation in Toronto, and Cartoon Lagoon Studios in New York. Sponsored by Trix cereal, they resided on sillychannel.com. They feature the voice talent of Chris Phillips as Tennessee Tuxedo, Robb Pruitt as Yakkety Yak and Ashley Paige Albert as Mrs. Baldy, and released through DreamWorks Classics.

Updated episode listing:

* - episodes available on DVD

Tennessee Tuxedo and his Tales (70 shows)

This section appears identical to what was listed in *Created and Produced by Total TeleVision*, as David R. Dunsford said that *TV Guide* did not provide episode listings from 1963-1966 in regards to TTV shows that aired on CBS. It is possible that the original air dates are off by a week or so due to some unknown preemptions or repeats, but essentially this is what aired in each season and roughly when they originally aired. Again, creating perfect TTV show combinations are not possible as repeat segments were commonly combined with new segments. The first season of TTT consisted of a Tennessee Tuxedo segment, a Tennessee Tuxedo riddle, a new King and Odie segment and a new Hunter segment. Repeat Tooter Turtle segments also aired as well as repeats of King and Odie and Hunter. Later shows also incorporated Commander McBragg and Go Go Gophers and quite possibly (read probably) had some Jay Ward segments thrown into the mix.

"Tennessee Tuxedo" (70 episodes)

First Season: 9/28/63-3/21/64, CBS (26 episodes)

*Tennessee Tuxedo #1 Mixed-Up Mechanics (9/28/63)

*Tennessee Tuxedo #2 The Rain Makers (10/5/63) (aka The Rainmakers)

*Tennessee Tuxedo #3 The Lamplighters (10/12/63)

*Tennessee Tuxedo #4 Telephone Terrors or Dial "M" For Mayhem (10/19/63)

*Tennessee Tuxedo #5 Giant Clam (10/26/63) (aka The Giant Clam Caper)

*Tennessee Tuxedo #6 Tick Tock (11/2/63)

*Tennessee Tuxedo #7 Scuttled Sculptor (11/9/63)

*Tennessee Tuxedo #8 Snap That Picture! (11/16/63)

*Tennessee Tuxedo #9 Zoo's News (11/23/63)

*Tennessee Tuxedo #10 Aztec Antics (11/30/63)

*Tennessee Tuxedo #11 Coal Minors (12/7/63)

*Tennessee Tuxedo #12 Hot Air Heroes (12/14/63)

*Tennessee Tuxedo #13 Irrigation Irritation (12/21/63)

*Tennessee Tuxedo #14 T.V. Testers (12/28/63)

*Tennessee Tuxedo #15 "By the Plight of the Moon" (1/4/64)

*Tennessee Tuxedo #16 Lever Levity (1/11/64)

*Tennessee Tuxedo #17 The Bridge Builders (1/18/64)

*Tennessee Tuxedo #18 Howl, Howl the Gang's All Here! (1/25/64)

*Tennessee Tuxedo #19 Sail Ho! (2/1/64) (aka Sail On, Sail On)

*Tennessee Tuxedo #20 Tell-Tale Telegraph (2/8/64)

*Tennessee Tuxedo #21 Rocket Ruckus (2/15/64)

*Tennessee Tuxedo #22 "All Steamed Up" (2/22/64) (aka Getting Steamed Up)

*Tennessee Tuxedo #23 Tale of a Tiger (2/29/64)

*Tennessee Tuxedo #24 "Dog Daze" (3/7/64)

*Tennessee Tuxedo #25 Brushing Off a Toothache (3/14/64)

*Tennessee Tuxedo #26 Funny Honey (3/21/64)

Second Season: 9/12/64-2/20/65, CBS (24 episodes)

*Tennessee Tuxedo #27 The Treasure of Jack the Joker (9/12/64)

*Tennessee Tuxedo #28 Wreck of a Record (9/19/64)

*Tennessee Tuxedo #29 Miner Forty-Niner (9/26/64)

*Tennessee Tuxedo #30 Helicopter Hi-Jinx (10/3/64) (aka Helicopter Hi-Jinks)

*Tennessee Tuxedo #31 Oil's Well (10/10/64)

*Tennessee Tuxedo #32 Parachuting Pickle (10/17/64)

*Tennessee Tuxedo #33 Wish Wash (10/24/64)

*Tennessee Tuxedo #34 Telescope Detectives (10/31/64)

*Tennessee Tuxedo #35 "The Eyes Have It" (11/7/64)

*Tennessee Tuxedo #36 Mad Movie Makers (11/14/64)

*Tennessee Tuxedo #37 "Snow Go" (11/21/64)

*Tennessee Tuxedo #38 The Big Question (11/28/64)

*Tennessee Tuxedo #39 Brain Strain (12/5/64)

*Tennessee Tuxedo #40 Rocky Road to Diamonds (12/12/64)

*Tennessee Tuxedo #41 X-Ray X-Perts (12/19/64)

*Tennessee Tuxedo #42 Food Feud (12/26/64)

*Tennessee Tuxedo #43 How Does Your Garden Grow (1/2/65)

*Tennessee Tuxedo #44 Perils of a Platypus (1/9/65)

*Tennessee Tuxedo #45 Hail to the Chief (1/16/65)

*Tennessee Tuxedo #46 "Physical Fatness" (1/23/65)

*Tennessee Tuxedo #47 Playing it Safe (1/30/65)

*Tennessee Tuxedo #48 House Painters (2/6/65)

*Tennessee Tuxedo #49 Admiral Tennessee (2/13/65)

*Tennessee Tuxedo #50 Three Ring Circus (2/20/65)

Third Season: 10/2/65-2/12/66, CBS (20 episodes)

*Tennessee Tuxedo #51 The Big Drip (10/2/65)

*Tennessee Tuxedo #52 Boning Up on Dinosaurs (10/9/65)

*Tennessee Tuxedo #53 Smilin' Yak's Sky Service (10/16/65)

*Tennessee Tuxedo #54 "Teddy Bear Trouble" (10/23/65) (aka Koala Caper)

*Tennessee Tuxedo #55 Sword Play (10/30/65)

*Tennessee Tuxedo #56 "Phunnie Munnie" (11/6/65)

*Tennessee Tuxedo #57 Romance of Plymouth Rock (11/13/65)

*Tennessee Tuxedo #58 The Zoolympics (11/20/65)

*Tennessee Tuxedo #59 The Tree Trimmers (11/27/65)

*Tennessee Tuxedo #60 Goblins Will Get You (12/4/65)
*Tennessee Tuxedo #61 The Cheap Skates (12/11/65)
*Tennessee Tuxedo #62 Going Up (12/18/65)
*Tennessee Tuxedo #63 Monster from Another Planet (12/25/65)
*Tennessee Tuxedo #64 Signed and Sealed (1/1/66)
*Tennessee Tuxedo #65 The Barbers (1/8/66)
*Tennessee Tuxedo #66 Catch a Falling Hammock (1/15/66)
*Tennessee Tuxedo #67 Peace and Quiet (1/22/66)
*Tennessee Tuxedo #68 Robot Revenge (1/29/66)
*Tennessee Tuxedo #69 There Auto Be a Law (2/5/66)
*Tennessee Tuxedo #70 Samantha (2/12/66)

"Tennessee Tuxedo and Chumley" (5 episodes)

Tennessee Tuxedo and Chumley #1 Go South (2014)
Tennessee Tuxedo and Chumley #2 Be Like Baldy (2014)
Tennessee Tuxedo and Chumley #3 Dinner Party (2014)
Tennessee Tuxedo and Chumley #4 Catch the Cable Man (2014)
Tennessee Tuxedo and Chumley #5 Yakkety Yak (2014)

Is that a bra in Tennessee Tuxedo's trash?

✶ TV CHARACTERS ✶ PLAYING CARDS AND 2 GAMES

SET #1

GO GOPHER (For 2 Players)

Deal out three cards to a player. Put the deck in the middle. The object is to get two of a kind by asking for a card you already have in your hand. If your opponent has that card he has to give it to you. If he doesn't you pick up one card from the deck and put it in your hand. If it is the card you have asked for, you go again. Otherwise he goes. Put all pairs in front of you on table. The first person to get rid of all his cards wins.

SNYDLEY'S BOOBY TRAP (For 2 Players)

Deal out all the cards. The object is to make pairs. You hold your hand up and your opponent chooses a card unseen from your hand. When you get a pair, take them out of your hand. The player left with Snydley at the end wins the Booby prize.

Look for *different TV Playing Cards and Games on Kix and Jets. Collect a complete 3-set pack—45 cards in all! See side of package for game you can play with two or three set pack!*

ALL NEW!
Twinkles Scramble-Up GAME
Just cut out the pieces and make 'em up the funniest way you can!
L. C. LEPRECHAUN
BULLWINKLE
TENNESSEE TUXEDO
HOPPITY HOOPER
MAKE LOTS OF FUNNY COMBINATIONS
Like This

FREE! ACTION GAME FOR YOUR CARTOON CARNIVAL

COLLECT ALL EIGHT and HAVE A CARNIVAL of FUN • EVERYDAY

CUT ON ALL RED DOTTED LINES FOLD ON ALL BLUE DOTTED LINES

The Top 10 Things We Love This Week

The MUST LIST

(From left) Kristen Wiig, Jon Hamm, Adam Scott, and Jennifer Westfeldt

1 FRIENDS WITH KIDS

How about a smart, witty relationship comedy that's got a mini-*Bridesmaids* reunion to boot? Costar Jennifer Westfeldt directs a sterling ensemble that includes Kristen Wiig and Jon Hamm. *(Rated R)*

2 TENNESSEE TUXEDO, the complete collection Discover the escapades of Tennessee the penguin and Chumley the walrus with all 70 episodes of the classic 1960s cartoon, most of them out on DVD for the first time.

3. ARCADIA, by Lauren Groff When the utopian commune Bit Stone calls home disintegrates around him, he's forced to venture into the "Outside." Groff's sensitive, ambitious novel follows Bit, forever shaped by his idealistic upbringing, as he tackles the challenges of an ever-changing world.

4 BREAK IT YOURSELF, Andrew Bird This gorgeous violin-plucking opus trades Bird's usual whimsy for something far more rootsy but just as lovely. Don't worry—there's still plenty of whistling to be had.

Illustration by JESSE LENZ

March 16, 2012 EW.COM | 11

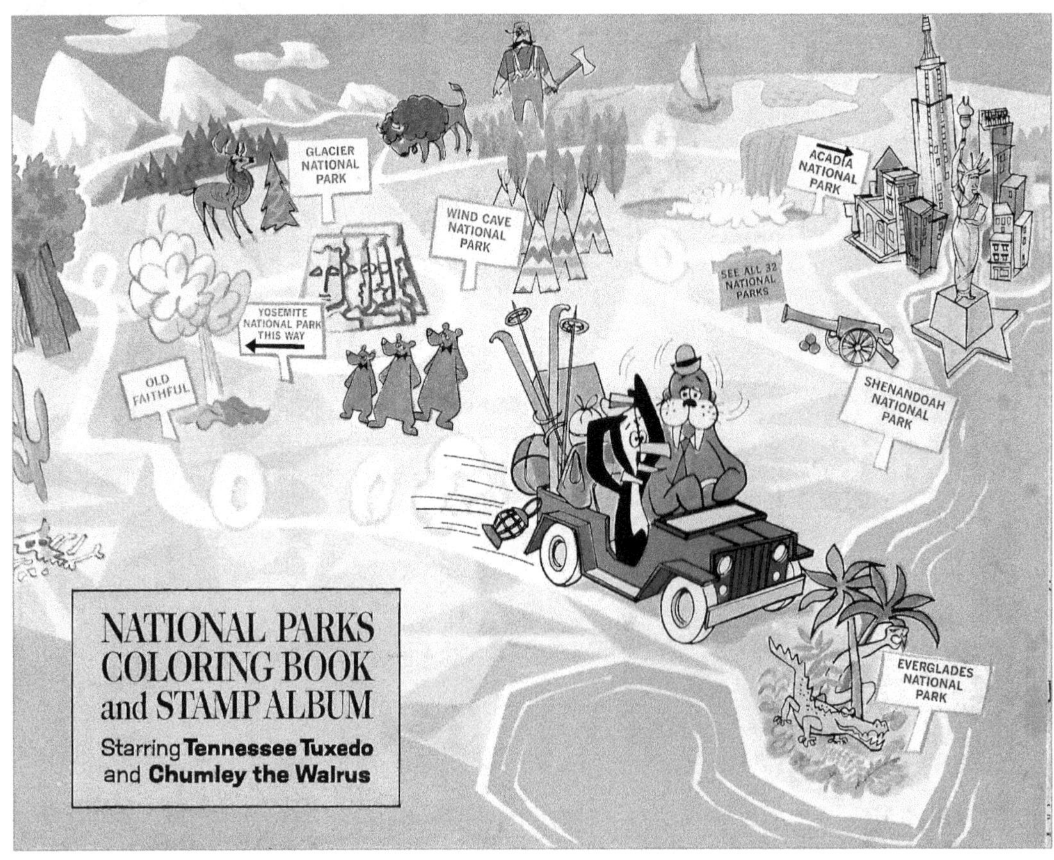

Tennessee Tuxedo never had a comic book published by Gold Key.

191 Broadway-Apt. #6H
Dobbs Ferry, N. Y. 10522
February 13, 2008

ark Arnold
5291 Norton Road
aratoga, CA 95070

ark:

I forgot to mention in my interview there was a period in which I was pro-
ucing radio commercials,for local sponsors. I would write, produce and announce
ll the spots. It was a one man operation and for awhile it was quite lucrative.
ost of the spots were light and funny. One spot was for a local podiatrist and
he commercial was aabout a tap dancing centipede who had foot trouble big
ime. It got quite a response and the doctor picked up quite a few patients.

My writing today is limited to letters to the editor. So far I have a 1.000
atting average. Every letter I have sent has been printed with the exception
f one. It referred to President Bush's colonoscopy last year. I related how
he examining physician stated that it was the easiest colonoscopy he had ever
erformed. He further said,"Of course, you have to realize that I was working
ith the world's biggest asshole." You tell me, why didn't the local paper
rint it?

I look forward to seeing my interview and some of the above published.
ood luck on the bookand be sure to let me know how you are progressing and also
end me a few copies.

As requested, attached is an autographed picture taken a few years back.
 am a little thinner now, not that I was interested in losing weight. Frankly,
he only things that age well are: wine, whisky and violins. Everything else turns
o shit.

truly
Bradley Bolke
Bradley Bolke

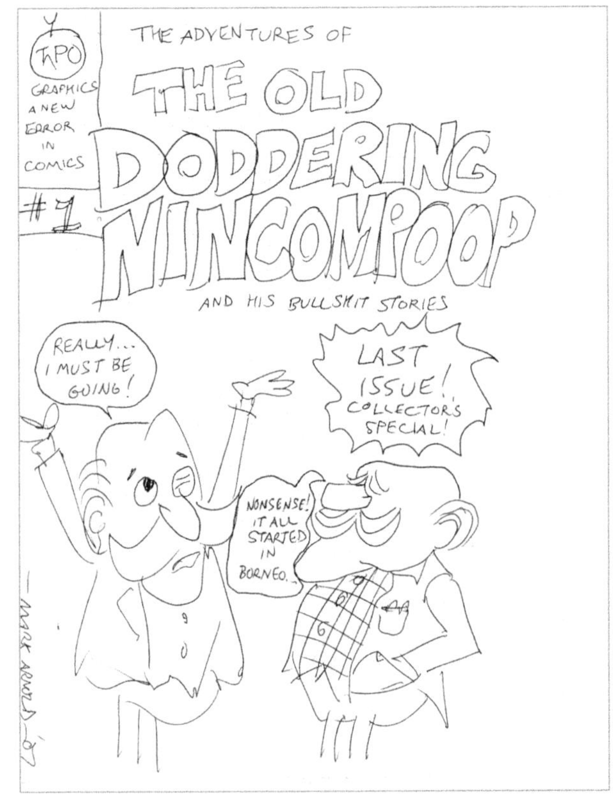

5 The Underdog Show

by Mark Arnold

Many mistakes in *Created and Produced by Total TeleVision productions* were made due to me literally guessing about the original air dates of TTV shows. One that was partially correct was that *The Underdog Show* aired a special Thanksgiving episode on Thanksgiving 1965. What I reported in the previous book is that only two episodes of the four episode story of "Simon Says, 'No Thanksgiving'" aired on Thanksgiving Day in 1965, when in actuality all four episodes aired that day. The Underdog balloon made its debut in the *Macy's Thanksgiving Day Parade* as well as a street float. Such was the excitement given this first horizontal balloon that he was featured (along with Bullwinkle) in a cartoon cover on *The New Yorker* in 1966.

I discussed the Underdog balloon in the previous book to some extent, but for this edition, I have consulted Bob Smith, who is a *Macy's Thanksgiving Day Parade* aficionado. In fact, he works for the company that supplies the balloons. I also mentioned Underdog balloon appearances in commercials and on TV shows like *Friends*, but I forgot to mention the real Underdog balloon's appearance in the 1984 Woody Allen comedy *Broadway Danny Rose.*

Since my original book came out, new short episodes of *Tennessee Tuxedo and Chumley* were created in 2014 for YouTube by Chuck Gammage Animation in Toronto, and Cartoon Lagoon Studios in New York. While creating these episodes, the studio took a stab at a new Underdog episode called *Underdog: The Adventure Continues* in 2013. This episode was not completed, but one can view the results on YouTube.

Updated episode listing:

* - episodes available on DVD

The Underdog Show (52 shows)

Adjustments to the original air dates as provided by David R. Dunsford. These dates are accurate as to what the *TV Guide* published from 1964-1973 in regards to TTV shows that aired on NBC. It does prove that creating perfect TTV show combinations are not possible as repeat segments were commonly combined with new segments. Those episodes without a confirmed original airdate are designated with a (?). In some cases, the original airdate is missing, but the repeat airdate is listed from the *TV Guide* listings.

Original *Underdog Shows* from 1964-1966 consisted of two Underdog segments each week (one at the beginning of the show and one at the end of the show), a Go Go Gophers segment, a Commander McBragg segment, and a Hunter segment each week. For the 1965 summer rerun months, there were two Underdog segments each week (one at the beginning of the show and one at the end of the show), a Jay Ward Aesop and Son segment, a Commander McBragg segment, and a Hunter segment each week. The 1966-1967 season consisted of two Underdog segments each week (one at the beginning of the show and one at the end of the show), a Go Go Gophers segment, a Commander McBragg segment, and a Klondike Kat segment each week. When Underdog went into reruns beginning in fall 1967 through 1970, the show consisted of four Underdog episodes to form a complete story. Presumably, a repeat Commander McBragg (or similar length segment like Jay Ward's Bullwinkle's Corner or Mr. Know-it-All) was also part of the show.

Following all of this, the 62 episode syndicated *Underdog Show* series that ran from approximately 1973 through 1995 through the DFS Program Exchange. This version also incorporated Tennessee Tuxedo episodes, plus added the originally unaired pilots of Gene Hattree and Cauliflower Cabby from 1964 and the three Sing-a-long Family segments that originally aired on *The Beagles*.

"Underdog" (124 episodes)

First Season: 10/3/64-4/10/65, NBC (52 episodes, 2 per show)

*Underdog #1 Zot Part 1 (10/3/64; 12/26/64; 10/18/69; 5/2/70)

*Underdog #2 Zot Part 2 (10/3/64; 12/26/64; 10/18/69; 5/2/70)

*Underdog #3 Zot Part 3 (10/10/64; 1/2/65; 10/18/69; 5/2/70)

*Underdog #4 Zot Part 4 (10/10/64; 1/2/65; 10/18/69; 5/2/70)

*Underdog #5 (Safe Waif) (pilot cartoon; no on-screen title shown) (10/17/64; 4/17/65)

*Underdog #6 March of the Monsters (10/17/64; 4/17/65)

*Underdog #7 "Go Snow" Part 1 (10/24/64; 4/24/65; 12/25/65; 6/18/66; 1/10/70; 7/25/70)

*Underdog #8 "Go Snow" Part 2 (10/24/64; 4/24/65; 12/25/65; 6/18/66; 1/10/70; 7/25/70)

*Underdog #9 "Go Snow" Part 3 (10/31/64; 5/1/65; 1/1/66; 6/25/66; 1/10/70; 7/25/70)

*Underdog #10 "Go Snow" Part 4 (10/31/64; 5/1/65; 1/1/66; 6/25/66; 1/10/70; 7/25/70)

*Underdog #11 The Great Gold Robbery Part 1 (11/7/64; 5/8/65; 12/27/69; 7/11/70)

*Underdog #12 The Great Gold Robbery Part 2 (11/7/64; 5/8/65; 12/27/69; 7/11/70)

*Underdog #13 The Great Gold Robbery Part 3 (11/14/64; 5/15/65; 12/27/69; 7/11/70)

*Underdog #14 The Great Gold Robbery Part 4 (11/14/64; 5/15/65; 12/27/69; 7/11/70)

*Underdog #15 Fearo Part 1 (11/21/64; 5/22/65; 12/6/69; 6/20/70)

*Underdog #16 Fearo Part 2 (11/21/64; 5/22/65; 12/6/69; 6/20/70)

*Underdog #17 Fearo Part 3 (11/28/64; 5/29/65; 12/6/69; 6/20/70)

*Underdog #18 Fearo Part 4 (11/28/64; 5/29/65; 12/6/69; 6/20/70)

*Underdog #19 The Big Shrink Part 1 (12/5/64; 6/5/65; 10/11/69; 4/25/70) (aka Shrinking Water)

*Underdog #20 The Big Shrink Part 2 (12/5/64; 6/5/65; 10/11/69; 4/25/70)

*Underdog #21 The Big Shrink Part 3 (12/12/64; 6/12/65; 10/11/69; 4/25/70)

*Underdog #22 The Big Shrink Part 4 (12/12/64; 6/12/65; 10/11/69; 4/25/70)

*Underdog #23 The Bubbleheads Part 1 (12/19/64; 6/19/65; 11/1/69; 5/16/70)

*Underdog #24 The Bubbleheads Part 2 (12/19/64; 6/19/65; 11/1/69; 5/16/70)

*Underdog #25 The Bubbleheads Part 3 (1/9/65; 6/26/65; 11/1/69; 5/16/70)

*Underdog #26 The Bubbleheads Part 4 (1/9/65; 6/26/65; 11/1/69; 5/16/70)

*Underdog #27 From Hopeless to Helpless Part 1 (1/16/65; 7/3/65; 1/25/69; 2/21/70; 8/29/70)

*Underdog #28 From Hopeless to Helpless Part 2 (1/16/65; 7/3/65; 1/25/69; 2/21/70; 8/29/70)

*Underdog #29 From Hopeless To Helpless Part 3 (1/23/65; 7/10/65; 4/2/66; 1/25/69; 2/21/70; 8/29/70)

*Underdog #30 From Hopeless To Helpless Part 4 (1/23/65; 7/10/65; 4/2/66; 1/25/69; 2/21/70; 8/29/70)

*Underdog #31 Tricky Trap by Tap Tap (1/30/65; 7/17/65)

*Underdog #32 Simon Says (1/30/65; 7/17/65)

*Underdog #33 The Witch of Pickyoon Part 1 (2/6/65; 7/24/65; 7/2/66; 1/3/70; 7/18/70)

*Underdog #34 The Witch of Pickyoon Part 2 (2/6/65; 7/24/65; 7/2/66; 1/3/70; 7/18/70)

*Underdog #35 The Witch of Pickyoon Part 3 (2/13/65; 7/31/65; 7/9/66; 1/3/70; 7/18/70)

*Underdog #36 The Witch of Pickyoon Part 4 (2/13/65; 7/31/65; 7/9/66; 1/3/70; 7/18/70)

*Underdog #37 Weathering the Storm Part 1 (2/20/65; 8/7/65)

*Underdog #38 Weathering the Storm Part 2 (2/20/65; 8/7/65)

*Underdog #39 Weathering the Storm Part 3 (2/273/65; 8/14/65)

*Underdog #40 Weathering the Storm Part 4 (2/27/65; 8/14/65)

*Underdog #41 The Gold Bricks Part 1 (3/6/65; 8/21/65; 1/17/70; 8/1/70)

*Underdog #42 The Gold Bricks Part 2 (3/6/65; 8/21/65; 1/17/70; 8/1/70)

*Underdog #43 The Gold Bricks Part 3 (3/13/65; 8/28/65; 1/17/70; 8/1/70)

*Underdog #44 The Gold Bricks Part 4 (3/13/65; 8/28/65; 1/17/70; 8/1/70)

*Underdog #45 The Magnet Men Part 1 (3/20/65; 9/4/65; 1/11/69; 2/7/70; 8/22/70)

*Underdog #46 The Magnet Men Part 2 (3/20/65; 9/4/65; 1/11/69; 2/7/70; 8/22/70)

*Underdog #47 The Magnet Men Part 3 (3/27/65; 9/11/65; 1/11/69; 2/7/70; 8/22/70)

*Underdog #48 The Magnet Men Part 4 (3/27/65; 9/11/65; 1/11/69; 2/7/70; 8/22/70)

*Underdog #49 The Phoney Booths Part 1 (4/3/65; 9/18/65; 11/29/69; 6/13/70) (aka The Phoney Booth Ring)

*Underdog #50 The Phoney Booths Part 2 (4/3/65; 9/18/65; 11/29/69; 6/13/70)

*Underdog #51 The Phoney Booths Part 3 (4/10/65; 9/25/65; 11/29/69; 6/13/70)

*Underdog #52 The Phoney Booths Part 4 (4/10/65; 9/25/65; 11/29/69; 6/13/70)

Second Season: 10/2/65-3/19/66, NBC (36 episodes, 2 per show)

*Underdog #53 "Pain Strikes Underdog" Part 1 (10/2/65; 4/9/66; 1/4/69; 1/31/70; 8/15/70)

*Underdog #54 "Pain Strikes Underdog" Part 2 (10/2/65; 4/9/66; 1/4/69; 1/31/70; 8/15/70)

*Underdog #55 "Pain Strikes Underdog" Part 3 (10/9/65; 4/16/66; 1/4/69; 1/31/70; 8/15/70)

*Underdog #56 "Pain Strikes Underdog" Part 4 (10/9/65; 4/16/66; 1/4/69; 1/31/70; 8/15/70)

*Underdog #57 The Molemen Part 1 (10/16/65; 4/23/66; 11/8/69; 5/23/70)

*Underdog #58 The Molemen Part 2 (10/16/65; 4/23/66; 11/8/69; 5/23/70)

*Underdog #59 The Molemen Part 3 (10/23/65; 4/30/66; 11/8/69; 5/23/70)

*Underdog #60 The Molemen Part 4 (10/23/65; 4/30/66; 11/8/69; 5/23/70)

*Underdog #61 The Flying Sorcerers Part 1 (10/30/65; 5/7/66; 9/27/69; 4/11/70)

*Underdog #62 The Flying Sorcerers Part 2 (10/30/65; 5/7/66; 9/27/69; 4/11/70)

*Underdog #63 The Flying Sorcerers Part 3 (11/6/65; 5/14/66; 9/27/69; 4/11/70)

*Underdog #64 The Flying Sorcerers Part 4 (11/6/65; 5/14/66; 9/27/69; 4/11/70)

*Underdog #65 "The Forget-Me-Net" Part 1 (11/13/65; 5/21/66; 1/24/70; 8/8/70)

*Underdog #66 "The Forget-Me-Net" Part 2 (11/13/65; 5/21/66; 1/24/70; 8/8/70)

*Underdog #67 "The Forget-Me-Net" Part 3 (11/20/65; 5/28/66; 1/24/70; 8/8/70)

*Underdog #68 "The Forget-Me-Net" Part 4 (11/20/65; 5/28/66; 1/24/70; 8/8/70)

*Underdog #69 Simon Says..No Thanksgiving Part 1 (11/25/65; 8/13/66; 12/13/69; 6/27/70)

*Underdog #70 Simon Says..No Thanksgiving Part 2 (11/25/65; 8/13/66; 12/13/69; 6/27/70)

*Underdog #71 Simon Says..No Thanksgiving Part 3 (11/25/65; 8/20/66; 12/13/69; 6/27/70)

*Underdog #72 Simon Says..No Thanksgiving Part 4 (11/25/65; 8/20/66; 12/13/69; 6/27/70)

*Underdog #73 Whistler's Father Part 1 (11/27/65; 6/4/66; 9/6/69; 3/21/70) (aka Guerilla Warfare)

*Underdog #74 Whistler's Father Part 2 (11/27/65; 6/4/66; 9/6/69; 3/21/70)

*Underdog #75 Whistler's Father Part 3 (12/4/65; 6/11/66; 9/6/69; 3/21/70)

*Underdog #76 Whistler's Father Part 4 (12/4/65; 6/11/66; 9/6/69; 3/21/70)

*Underdog #77 The Silver Thieves Part 1 (12/11/65; 7/16/66)

*Underdog #78 The Silver Thieves Part 2 (12/11/65; 7/16/66)

*Underdog #79 The Silver Thieves Part 3 (12/18/65; 7/23/66)

*Underdog #80 The Silver Thieves Part 4 (12/18/65; 7/23/66)

*Underdog #81 Riffraffville Part 1 (2/12/66; 7/30/66)

*Underdog #82 Riffraffville Part 2 (2/12/66; 7/30/66)

*Underdog #83 Riffraffville Part 3 (2/19/66; 8/6/66)

*Underdog #84 Riffraffville Part 4 (2/19/66; 8/6/66)

*Underdog #85 The Tickle Feather Machine Part 1 (3/12/66; 8/27/66; 2/1/69; 10/25/69; 2/28/70; 5/9/70)

*Underdog #86 The Tickle Feather Machine Part 2 (3/12/66; 8/27/66; 2/1/69; 10/25/69; 2/28/70; 5/9/70)

*Underdog #87 The Tickle Feather Machine Part 3 (3/19/66; 9/3/66; 2/1/69; 10/25/69; 2/28/70; 5/9/70)

*Underdog #88 The Tickle Feather Machine Part 4 (3/19/66; 9/3/66; 2/1/69; 10/25/69; 2/28/70; 5/9/70)

Third Season: 9/10/66-1/21/67, CBS (36 episodes, 2 per show)

*Underdog #89 Underdog vs. Overcat Part 1 (9/10/66; 10/4/69; 4/18/70)

*Underdog #90 Underdog vs. Overcat Part 2 (9/10/66; 10/4/69; 4/18/70)

*Underdog #91 Underdog vs. Overcat Part 3 (9/17/66; 10/4/69; 4/18/70)

*Underdog #92 Underdog vs. Overcat Part 4 (9/17/66; 10/4/69; 4/18/70)

*Underdog #93 The Big Dipper Part 1 9/24/66; 11/15/69; 5/30/70)

*Underdog #94 The Big Dipper Part 2 (9/24/66; 11/15/69; 5/30/70)

*Underdog #95 The Big Dipper Part 3 (10/1/66; 11/15/69; 5/30/70)

*Underdog #96 The Big Dipper Part 4 (10/1/66; 11/15/69; 5/30/70)

*Underdog #97 The Just in Case Part 1 (10/8/66; 11/22/69; 6/6/70)

*Underdog #98 The Just in Case Part 2 (10/8/66;11/22/69; 6/6/70)

*Underdog #99 The Just in Case Part 3 (10/15/66; 11/22/69; 6/6/70)

*Underdog #100 The Just in Case Part 4 (10/15/66; 11/22/69; 6/6/70)

*Underdog #101 The Marble Heads Part 1 (10/22/66; 12/20/69; 7/4/70)

*Underdog #102 The Marble Heads Part 2 (10/22/66; 12/20/69; 7/4/70)

*Underdog #103 The Marble Heads Part 3 (10/29/66; 12/20/69; 7/4/70)

*Underdog #104 The Marble Heads Part 4 (10/29/66; 12/20/69; 7/4/70)

*Underdog #105 Simon Says Be My Valentine Part 1 (11/5/66)

*Underdog #106 Simon Says Be My Valentine Part 2 (11/5/66)

*Underdog #107 Simon Says Be My Valentine Part 3 (11/12/66)

*Underdog #108 Simon Says Be My Valentine Part 4 (11/12/66)

*Underdog #109 Round and Round Part 1 (11/19/66; 1/18/69; 2/14/70; 9/5/70)

*Underdog #110 Round and Round Part 2 (11/19/66; 1/18/69; 2/14/70; 9/5/70)

*Underdog #111 Round and Round Part 3 (11/26/66; 1/18/69; 2/14/70; 9/5/70)

*Underdog #112 Round and Round Part 4 (11/26/66; 1/18/69; 2/14/70; 9/5/70)

*Underdog #113 A New Villain Part 1 (12/3/66)

*Underdog #114 A New Villain Part 2 (12/3/66)

*Underdog #115 A New Villain Part 3 (12/10/66)

*Underdog #116 A New Villain Part 4 (12/10/66)

*Underdog #117 Batty Man Part 1 (12/17/66; 9/13/69; 3/28/70)

*Underdog #118 Batty Man Part 2 (12/17/66; 9/13/69; 3/28/70)

*Underdog #119 Batty Man Part 3 (1/7/67; 9/13/69; 3/28/70)

*Underdog #120 Batty Man Part 4 (1/7/67; 9/13/69; 3/28/70)

*Underdog #121 The Vacuum Gun Part 1 (1/14/67; 9/20/69; 4/4/70)

*Underdog #122 The Vacuum Gun Part 2 (1/14/67; 9/20/69; 4/4/70)

*Underdog #123 The Vacuum Gun Part 3 (1/21/67; 9/20/69; 4/4/70)

*Underdog #124 The Vacuum Gun Part 4 (1/21/67; 9/20/69; 4/4/70)

"Go Go Gophers" (48 episodes)

First Season: 10/3/64-3/27/65, NBC (as part of The Underdog Show) (13 episodes)

*Go Go Gophers #1 Moon Zoom (10/3/64; 12/26/64; 7/3/65; 3/26/66)

*Go Go Gophers #2 "Trojan Totem" (10/10/64; 1/9/65; 7/10/65; 3/19/66)

*Go Go Gophers #3 Introducing General Nuisance (10/17/64; 1/16/65; 7/17/65)

*Go Go Gophers #4 Gatling Gophers (10/24/64; 1/23/65; 7/24/65)

*Go Go Gophers #5 "Mesa Mess" (10/31/64; 2/13/65; 8/14/65)

*Go Go Gophers #6 "Medicine Men" (11/7/64; 2/6/65; 8/7/65)

*Go Go Gophers #7 The "Cleveland Indians" (11/14/64; 1/30/65; 7/31/65)

*Go Go Gophers #8 "Termite Terror" (11/21/64; 2/20/65; 8/21/65) (aka Termite Trainers)

*Go Go Gophers #9 "Who's a Dummy?" (11/28/64; 2/27/65; 8/28/65) (aka Who's the Dummy?)

*Go Go Gophers #10 Tapping the Telegraph (12/5/64; 3/6/65; 9/4/65)

*Go Go Gophers #11 Bold as Gold (12/12/64; 3/13/65; 9/11/65)

*Go Go Gophers #12 Up in the Air (12/19/64; 3/20/65; 9/18/65)

*Go Go Gophers #13 The Big Banger (1/2/65; 3/27/65; 9/25/65)

Second Season: 10/2/65-2/5/66, NBC (as part of The Underdog Show) (16 episodes)

*Go Go Gophers #14 He's For The Berries (10/2/65)

*Go Go Gophers #15 "Swamped" (10/9/65)

*Go Go Gophers #16 "Tanks to the Gophers" (10/16/65)

*Go Go Gophers #17 "Indian Treasure" (10/23/65)

*Go Go Gophers #18 The Carriage Trade (10/30/65) (aka The Horseless Carriage Trade)

*Go Go Gophers #19 Honey Fun (11/6/65)

*Go Go Gophers #20 The Colonel Cleans Up (11/13/65)

*Go Go Gophers #21 "The Raw Recruits" (11/20/65)

*Go Go Gophers #22 "Tenshun!" (11/27/65)

*Go Go Gophers #23 "Cuckoo Combat" (12/4/65)

*Go Go Gophers #24 "Kitchen Capers" (12/11/65)

*Go Go Gophers #25 The Great White Stallion (12/18/65)

*Go Go Gophers #26 "Blankety-Blank Blanket" (1/8/66)

*Go Go Gophers #27 "The Ironclad" (1/15/66) (aka The Unsinkable Ironclad)

*Go Go Gophers #28 "Crash Diet" (1/22/66) (aka Losing Weight)

*Go Go Gophers #29 Wild Wild Flowers (1/29/65)

Third Season: 10/9/66-2/5/66, CBS (as part of Tennessee Tuxedo and his Tales) (19 episodes)

*Go Go Gophers #30 Look Out! Here Comes Aunt Flora (10/9/65)

*Go Go Gophers #31 Root Beer Riot (10/16/65)

*Go Go Gophers #32 Amusement Park (10/23/65)

*Go Go Gophers #33 Tricky Teepee Trap (10/30/65)

*Go Go Gophers #34 3-Ring Circus (11/6/65)

*Go Go Gophers #35 Don't Fence Me In (11/13/65)

*Go Go Gophers #36 Locked Out (11/20/65)

*Go Go Gophers #37 Hotel Headaches (11/25/65)

*Go Go Gophers #38 Choo Choo Chase (11/27/65)

*Go Go Gophers #39 Rocket Ruckus (12/4/65)

*Go Go Gophers #40 Go Go Gamblers (12/11/65)

*Go Go Gophers #41 Radio Raid (12/18/65)

*Go Go Gophers #42 Steam Roller (12/25/65)

*Go Go Gophers #43 Mutiny a Go-Go (1/1/66)

*Go Go Gophers #44 Marooned on Cannibal Island (1/8/66)

*Go Go Gophers #45 The Indian Giver (1/15/66)

*Go Go Gophers #46 The Big Pow-Wow (1/22/66)

*Go Go Gophers #47 Back to the Indians (1/29/66)

*Go Go Gophers #48 California Here We Come (2/5/66)

"Commander McBragg" (48 episodes)

First Season: 10/3/64-3/27/65, NBC (as part of The Underdog Show) (26 episodes)

*Commander McBragg #1 "Over the Falls" (10/3/64)

*Commander McBragg #2 "Fish Story" (10/10/64)

*Commander McBragg #3 "The Himalayas" (10/17/64)

*Commander McBragg #4 "The North Pole" (10/24/64)

*Commander McBragg #5 "Khyber Pass" (10/31/64)

*Commander McBragg #6 "Ace Of Aces" (11/7/64)
*Commander McBragg #7 Niagara Falls (11/14/64)
*Commander McBragg #8 Dodge City Dodge (11/21/64)
*Commander McBragg #9 Football By Hex (11/28/64)
*Commander McBragg #10 "Rabelasia" (12/5/64)
*Commander McBragg #11 Okefenokee Swamp (12/12/64)
*Commander McBragg #12 The Flying Machine (12/19/64)
*Commander McBragg #13 The Giant Elephant (12/26/64)
*Commander McBragg #14 "The Great Bird" (1/2/65)
*Commander McBragg #15 "Chicago Mobster" (1/9/65)
*Commander McBragg #16 The Monster Bear (1/16/65)
*Commander McBragg #17 "The Kangaroo" (1/23/65)
*Commander McBragg #18 The Giant Mosquito (1/30/65)
*Commander McBragg #19 The Black Knight (2/6/65)
*Commander McBragg #20 "The Flying Pond" (2/13/65)
*Commander McBragg #21 The Old Ninety-Two (2/20/65)
*Commander McBragg #22 Our Man in Manhattan (2/27/65)
*Commander McBragg #23 Oyster Island (3/6/65)
*Commander McBragg #24 The Steam Car (3/13/65)
*Commander McBragg #25 Swimming the Atlantic (3/20/65)
*Commander McBragg #26 Fort Apache (3/27/65)

Second Season: 9/18/65-2/5/66, NBC (as part of The Underdog Show)
(22 episodes)

*Commander McBragg #27 The Flying Trapeze (9/18/65)
*Commander McBragg #28 Around the World (9/25/65)
*Commander McBragg #29 Indianapolis Speedway (10/2/65)
*Commander McBragg #30 The Rhino Charge (10/9/65)
*Commander McBragg #31 Mystifying McBragg (10/16/65)
*Commander McBragg #32 Mamouth Cavern (10/23/65) (aka Mammoth Cavern)
*Commander McBragg #33 The Astronaut (10/30/65)
*Commander McBragg #34 Dam Break (11/6/65)
*Commander McBragg #35 The Eclipse (11/13/65)
*Commander McBragg #36 Ship of the Desert (11/20/65)
*Commander McBragg #37 Egypt (11/25/65)
*Commander McBragg #38 The Singing Cowboy (11/27/65)
*Commander McBragg #39 The Lumberjack (12/4/65)
*Commander McBragg #40 The Bronco Buster (12/11/65)
*Commander McBragg #41 Echo Canyon (12/18/65)

*Commander McBragg #42 Tightrope (12/25/65)
*Commander McBragg #43 Lake Tortuga (1/1/66)
*Commander McBragg #44 Coney Island (1/8/66)
*Commander McBragg #45 Rainbow Island (1/15/66)
*Commander McBragg #46 The Insect Collector (1/22/66)
*Commander McBragg #47 Lost Valley (1/29/66)
*Commander McBragg #48 The Orient Express (2/5/66)

"Klondike Kat" (26 episodes)

First Season: 9/10/66-12/10/66, CBS (as part of The Underdog Show) (14 episodes)

*Klondike Kat #1 Honor at Steak (9/10/66)
*Klondike Kat #2 Secret Weapon (9/17/66)
*Klondike Kat #3 The Big Fromage (9/24/66)
*Klondike Kat #4 Hard To Guard (10/1/66)
*Klondike Kat #5 The Candy Mine (10/8/66)
*Klondike Kat #6 Rotten to the Core (10/15/66)
*Klondike Kat #7 Trap Baiting (10/22/66) (aka Baiting the Trap)
*Klondike Kat #8 Gravy Train (10/29/66)
*Klondike Kat #9 Cream Puff Buff (11/5/66)
*Klondike Kat #10 Plane Food (11/12/66)
*Klondike Kat #11 Banana Skinned (11/19/66)
*Klondike Kat #12 Up a Tree (11/26/66)
*Klondike Kat #13 Pie Fly (12/3/66)
*Klondike Kat #14 Jail Break (12/10/66)

Second Season: 9/10/66-11/26/67, CBS (as part of The Beagles) (12 episodes)

Klondike Kat #15 Fort Frazzle Frolics (9/10/66)
*Klondike Kat #16 Sticky Stuff (9/17/66)
*Klondike Kat #17 Who's a Pill (9/24/66)
*Klondike Kat #18 Getting the Air (10/1/66) (aka Getting in the Air)
Klondike Kat #19 If I'd-a Known you was Comin' (10/8/66)
*Klondike Kat #20 The Big Race (10/15/66)
Klondike Kat #21 Date on the Desert (10/22/66)
*Klondike Kat #22 Klondike Goes to Town (10/29/66)
Klondike Kat #23 Motorcycle Mountie (11/5/66)
Klondike Kat #24 Island in the Sky (11/12/66)
Klondike Kat #25 The Island Hideout (11/19/66)
Klondike Kat #26 The Kat Napper (11/26/66)

"Aesop and Son" (aired during summer repeats of The Underdog Show. This is a Jay Ward-produced segment.) Known airdates:

Aesop and Son The Lion and the Mouse (4/3/65)

Aesop and Son The Fox and the Stork (4/10/65)

Aesop and Son The Hare and the Hound (5/1/65)

Syndicated Underdog Shows (62 episodes)

Episode 301

- Underdog #1 (Episode 1: Safe Waif) (pilot cartoon; no on-screen title shown)
- Tennessee Tuxedo #2 (The Rain Makers) (902, 972)
- The Sing-A-Long Family #1 (Picnic) (Sing-A-Long Family cartoon titles are unofficial and do not appear on screen) (also appears in syndicated shows #328, 355)
- Underdog #2 (Episode 2: The March Of The Monsters)

Episode 302

- Underdog #3 (Episode 3: Simon Says)
- Tennessee Tuxedo #4 (Telephone Terrors or Dial M For Mayhem) (904, 974)
- The Sing-A-Long Family #2 (Skating) (also appears in syndicated shows #329, 356)
- Underdog #32 (Episode 4: Tricky Trap By Tap Tap) (Note: Tricky Trap By Tap Tap is the epilogue of the four-episode serial From Hopeless To Helpless, which is featured later in the series in shows #315 and #316.)

Episode 303

- Underdog #4 (Go Snow/Episode 1)
- Tennessee Tuxedo #5 (Giant Clam) (not The Giant Clam Caper) (905, 975)
- The Sing-A-Long Family #3 (Fair) (also appears in syndicated shows #330, 357)
- Underdog #5 (Go Snow/Episode 2)

Episode 304

- Underdog #6 (Go Snow/Episode 3)
- Tennessee Tuxedo #6 (Tick Tock) (906, 976)
- Commander McBragg #4 (The North Pole)
- Underdog #7 (Go Snow/Episode 4)

Episode 305

- Underdog #8 (Zot/Episode 1)
- Tennessee Tuxedo #7 (Scuttled Sculptor) (907, 977)
- Commander McBragg #5 (Khyber Pass)
- Underdog #9 (Zot/Episode 2)

Episode 306
- Underdog #10 (Zot/Episode 3)
- Tennessee Tuxedo #8 (Snap That Picture!) (908, 978)
- Commander McBragg #6 (Ace Of Aces)
- Underdog #11 (Zot/Episode 4)

Episode 307
- Underdog #12 (The Great Gold Robbery/Episode 1)
- Tennessee Tuxedo #9 (Zoo's News) (909, 979)
- Commander McBragg #7 (Niagara Falls)
- Underdog #13 (The Great Gold Robbery/Episode 2)

Episode 308
- Underdog #14 (The Great Gold Robbery/Episode 3)
- Tennessee Tuxedo #10 (Aztec Antics) (910, 980)
- Commander McBragg #8 (Dodge City Dodge)
- Underdog #15 (The Great Gold Robbery/Episode 4)

Episode 309
- Underdog #16 (Fearo/Episode 1)
- Tennessee Tuxedo #11 (Coal Miners) (not Coat Minors) (911, 981)
- Commander McBragg #9 (Football By Tex Hex)
- Underdog #17 (Fearo/Episode 2)

Episode 310
- Underdog #18 (Fearo/Episode 3)
- Tennessee Tuxedo #12 (Hot Air Heroes) (912, 982)
- Commander McBragg #10 (Rabelasia)
- Underdog #19 (Fearo/Episode 4)

Episode 311
- Underdog #20 (The Big Shrink/Episode 1) (not Shrinking Water)
- Tennessee Tuxedo #13 (Irrigation Irritation) (913, 983)
- Commander McBragg #11 (Okefenokee Swamp)
- Underdog #21 (The Big Shrink/Episode 2)

Episode 312
- Underdog #22 (The Big Shrink/Episode 3)
- Tennessee Tuxedo #14 (TV Testers) (914, 984)
- Commander McBragg #12 (The Flying Machine)
- Underdog #23 (The Big Shrink/Episode 4)

Episode 313
- Underdog #24 (The Bubbleheads/Episode 1)
- Tennessee Tuxedo #15 (By The Plight Of The Moon) (915, 985)

- Commander McBragg #13 (The Giant Elephant)
- Underdog #25 (The Bubbleheads/Episode 2)

Episode 314

- Underdog #26 (The Bubbleheads/Episode 3)
- Tennessee Tuxedo #17 (Bridge Builders) (917, 987)
- Commander McBragg #14 (The Great Bird) (not The Giant Bird)
- Underdog #27 (The Bubbleheads/Episode 4)

Episode 315

- Underdog #28 (From Hopeless To Helpless/Episode 1)
- Tennessee Tuxedo #16 (Lever Levity) (916, 986)
- Commander McBragg #15 ("Chicago" Mobster)
- Underdog #29 (From Hopeless To Helpless/Episode 2)

Episode 316

- Underdog #30 (From Hopeless To Helpless/Episode 3)
- Tennessee Tuxedo #18 (Howl, Howl, The Gang's All Here) (918, 988)
- Commander McBragg #16 (The Monster Bear)
- Underdog #31 (From Hopeless To Helpless/Episode 4)

Episode 317

- Underdog #33 (The Witch Of Pickyoon/Episode 1) (not The Wicked Witch Of Pickyoon)
- Tennessee Tuxedo #19 (Sail Ho!) (not Sail On, Sail On) (919, 989)
- Commander McBragg #17 (The Kangaroo)
- Underdog #34 (The Witch Of Pickyoon/Episode 2)

Episode 318

- Underdog #35 (The Witch Of Pickyoon/Episode 3)
- Tennessee Tuxedo #20 (Tell-Tale Telegraph) (920, 990)
- Commander McBragg #18 (The Giant Mosquito)
- Underdog #36 (The Witch Of Pickyoon/Episode 4)

Episode 319

- Underdog #37 (Weathering The Storm/Episode 1)
- Tennessee Tuxedo #21 (Rocket Ruckus) (921, 991)
- Commander McBragg #19 (The Black Knight)
- Underdog #38 (Weathering The Storm/Episode 2)

Episode 320

- Underdog #39 (Weathering The Storm/Episode 3)
- Tennessee Tuxedo #22 (All Steamed Up) (not Getting Steamed Up) (922, 992)
- Commander McBragg #20 (The Flying Pond)
- Underdog #40 (Weathering The Storm/Episode 4)

Episode 321

- Underdog #41 (The Gold Bricks/Episode 1)
- Tennessee Tuxedo #23 (Tale Of A Tiger) (923, 993)
- Commander McBragg #21 (The Old Ninety-Two)
- Underdog #42 (The Gold Bricks/Episode 2)

Episode 322

- Underdog #43 (The Gold Bricks/Episode 3)
- Tennessee Tuxedo #24 (Dog Daze) (Sequel to Tennessee Tuxedo #18/ Howl, Howl, The Gang's All Here) (924, 994)
- Commander McBragg #22 (Our Man In Manhattan) (not Secret Agent In New York)
- Underdog #44 (The Gold Bricks/Episode 4)

Episode 323

- Underdog #45 (The Magnet Men/Episode 1)
- Tennessee Tuxedo #25 (Brushing Off A Toothache) (925, 995)
- Commander McBragg #23 (Oyster Island)
- Underdog #46 (The Magnet Men/Episode 2)

Episode 324

- Underdog #47 (The Magnet Men/Episode 3)
- Tennessee Tuxedo #26 (Funny Honey) (926, 996)
- Commander McBragg #24 (The Steam Car)
- Underdog #48 (The Magnet Men/Episode 4)

Episode 325

- Underdog #49 (The Phoney Booths/Episode 1)
- Tennessee Tuxedo #1 (Mixed-Up Mechanics) (901, 971)
- Commander McBragg #25 (Swimming The Atlantic)
- Underdog #50 (The Phoney Booths/Episode 2)

Episode 326

- Underdog #51 (The Phoney Booths/Episode 3)
- Tennessee Tuxedo #3 (The Lamplighters) (903, 973)
- Commander McBragg #26 (Fort Apache)
- Underdog #52 (The Phoney Booths/Episode 4)

Episode 327

- Underdog #53 (Pain Strikes Underdog/Episode 1)
- Go Go Gophers #1 (Moon Zoom)
- Klondike Kat #1 (Honor At Steak)
- Commander McBragg #27 (The Flying Trapeze)
- Underdog #54 (Pain Strikes Underdog/Episode 2)

Episode 328

- Underdog #55 (Pain Strikes Underdog/Episode 3)
- Go Go Gophers #2 (Trojan Totem)
- Klondike Kat #2 (Secret Weapon)
- The Sing-A-Long Family #1 (Picnic) (also appears in syndicated shows #301, 355)
- Underdog #56 (Pain Strikes Underdog/Episode 4)

Episode 329

- Underdog #57 (The Molemen/Episode 1)
- Go Go Gophers #3 (Introducing General Nuisance)
- Klondike Kat #3 (The Big Fromage)
- The Sing-A-Long Family #2 (Skating) (also appears in syndicated shows #302, 356)
- Underdog #58 (The Molemen/Episode 2)

Episode 330

- Underdog #59 (The Molemen/Episode 3)
- Tennessee Tuxedo #27 (The Treasure Of Jack The Joker) (not The Treasure Of Jack And The Joker) (927, 997)
- The Sing-A-Long Family #3 (Fair) (also appears in syndicated shows #303, 357)
- Underdog #60 (The Molemen/Episode 4)

Episode 331

- Underdog #61 (The Flying Sorcerers/Episode 1) (not The Flying Sorceress)
- Go Go Gophers #4 (Gatling Gophers)
- Klondike Kat #4 (Hard To Guard)
- Commander Mc Bragg #31 (Mystifying McBragg)
- Underdog #62 (The Flying Sorcerers/Episode 2)

Episode 332

- Underdog #63 (The Flying Sorcerers/Episode 3)
- Go Go Gophers #5 (The Cleveland Indians)
- Klondike Kat #5 (The Candy Mine)
- Commander Mc Bragg #32 (Mammouth Cavern)
- Underdog #64 (The Flying Sorcerers/Episode 4)

Episode 333

- Underdog #65 (The Forget-Me-Net/Episode 1)
- Go Go Gophers #6 (Medicine Men)
- Klondike Kat #6 (Rotten To The Core)
- Commander Mc Bragg #33 (The Astronaut) (also appears in syndicated show #358)
- Underdog #66 (The Forget-Me-Net/Episode 2)

Episode 334

- Underdog #67 (The Forget-Me-Net/Episode 3)
- Tennessee Tuxedo #28 (Wreck Of A Record) (928, 998)
- Commander Mc Bragg #34 (Dam Break) (also appears in syndicated show #359)
- Underdog #68 (The Forget-Me-Net/Episode 4)

Episode 335

- Underdog #69 (Whistler's Father/Episode 1) (not Guerilla Warfare)
- Go Go Gophers #7 (Mesa Mess)
- Klondike Kat #7 (The Trap Baiting) (not Baiting The Trap)
- Commander Mc Bragg #35 (The Eclipse) (also appears in syndicated show #360)
- Underdog #70 (Whistler's Father/Episode 2)

Episode 336

- Underdog #71 (Whistler's Father/Episode 3)
- Go Go Gophers #8 (Termite Terror) (not Termite Trainers)
- Klondike Kat #8 (Gravy Train)
- Commander Mc Bragg #36 (Ship Of The Desert) (also appears in syndicated show #361)
- Underdog #72 (Whistler's Father/Episode 4)

Episode 337

- Underdog #73 (Simon Says "No Thanksgiving"/Episode 1)
- Go Go Gophers #9 (Who's A Dummy)
- Klondike Kat #9 (Cream Puff Buff)
- Commander Mc Bragg #37 (Egypt)
- Underdog #74 (Simon Says "No Thanksgiving"/Episode 2)

Episode 338

- Underdog #75 (Simon Says "No Thanksgiving"/Episode 3)
- Tennessee Tuxedo #29 (Miner Forty-Niner) (929, 999)
- Commander Mc Bragg #38 (The Singing Cowboy)
- Underdog #76 (Simon Says "No Thanksgiving"/Episode 4)

Episode 339

- Underdog #77 (The Silver Thieves/Episode 1)
- Go Go Gophers #10 (Tapping The Telegraph)
- Klondike Kat #10 (Plane Food)
- Commander Mc Bragg #39 (The Lumberjack)
- Underdog #78 (The Silver Thieves/Episode 2)

Episode 340

- Underdog #79 (The Silver Thieves/Episode 3)
- Go Go Gophers #11 (Bold As Gold)

- Klondike Kat #11 (Banana Skinned)
- Commander Mc Bragg #40 (The Bronco Buster)
- Underdog #80 (The Silver Thieves/Episode 4)

Episode 341

- Underdog #81 (Riffraffville/Episode 1)
- Go Go Gophers #12 (Up In The Air)
- Klondike Kat #12 (Up A Tree)
- Commander Mc Bragg #41 (Echo Canyon)
- Underdog #82 (Riffraffville/Episode 2)

Episode 342

- Underdog #83 (Riffraffville/Episode 3)
- Tennessee Tuxedo #30 (Helicopter Hi-Jinks) (930, 1000)
- Commander Mc Bragg #42 (Tightrope)
- Underdog #84 (Riffraffville/Episode 4)

Episode 343

- Underdog #85 (The Tickle Feather Machine/Episode 1)
- Go Go Gophers #13 (The Big Banger)
- Klondike Kat #13 (Pie Fly)
- Commander Mc Bragg #43 (Lake Tortuga)
- Underdog #86 (The Tickle Feather Machine/Episode 2)

Episode 344

- Underdog #87 (The Tickle Feather Machine/Episode 3)
- Go Go Gophers #14 (He's For The Berries)
- Klondike Kat #14 (Jail Break)
- Commander Mc Bragg #44 (Coney Island)
- Underdog #88 (The Tickle Feather Machine/Episode 4)

Episode 345

- Underdog #89 (Underdog Vs. Overcat/Episode 1) (not Underdog Vs. Overcoat)
- Go Go Gophers #15 (Swamped)
- Klondike Kat #15 (Fort Frazzle Frolics)
- Commander Mc Bragg #45 (Rainbow Island)
- Underdog #90 (Underdog Vs. Overcat/Episode 2)

Episode 346

- Underdog #91 (Underdog Vs. Overcat/Episode 3)
- Tennessee Tuxedo #31 (Oil's Well) (931, 1001)
- Commander Mc Bragg #46 (The Insect Collector)
- Underdog #92 (Underdog Vs. Overcat/Episode 4)

Episode 347
- Underdog #93 (The Big Dipper/Episode 1)
- Go Go Gophers #16 (Tanks To The Gophers/Blankety Blank Blanket)
- Klondike Kat #16 (Sticky Stuff)
- Commander Mc Bragg #47 (Lost Valley)
- Tooter Turtle #1 (Nuisance/Subscribe)
- Underdog #94 (The Big Dipper/Episode 2)

Episode 348
- Underdog #95 (The Big Dipper/Episode 3)
- Go Go Gophers #17 (Indian Treasure)
- Klondike Kat #17 (Who's A Pill)
- Commander Mc Bragg #48 (The Orient Express)
- Underdog #96 (The Big Dipper/Episode 4)

Episode 349
- Underdog #97 (Just In Case/Episode 1)
- Go Go Gophers #18 (The Carriage Trade) (not The Horseless Carriage Trade)
- Commander Mc Bragg #1 (Over The Falls)
- Underdog #98 (Just In Case/Episode 2)

Episode 350
- Underdog #99 (Just In Case/Episode 3)
- Tennessee Tuxedo #32 (Parachuting Pickle) (932, 1002)
- Commander Mc Bragg #2 (Fish Story)
- Underdog #100 (Just In Case/Episode 4)

Episode 351
- Underdog #101 (The Marble Heads/Episode 1)
- Go Go Gophers #19 (Honey Fun)
- Klondike Kat #19 (If I'd-A Known You Was Comin')
- Commander Mc Bragg #3 (The Himalayas)
- Underdog #102 (The Marble Heads/Episode 2)

Episode 352
- Underdog #103 (The Marble Heads/Episode 3)
- Go Go Gophers #20 (The Colonel Cleans Up)
- Klondike Kat #20 (The Big Race)
- Commander Mc Bragg #28 (Around The World)
- Underdog #104 (The Marble Heads/Episode 4)

Episode 353
- Underdog #105 (Simon Says "Be My Valentine"/Episode 1)
- Go Go Gophers #21 (The Raw Recruits)

- Klondike Kat #21 (Date On The Desert)
- Commander Mc Bragg #29 (Indianapolis Speedway)
- Underdog #106 (Simon Says "Be My Valentine"/Episode 2)

Episode 354

- Underdog #107 (Simon Says "Be My Valentine"/Episode 3)
- Tennessee Tuxedo #33 (Wish Wash) (933, 1003)
- Commander Mc Bragg #30 (The Rhino Charge)
- Underdog #108 (Simon Says "Be My Valentine"/Episode 4)

Episode 355

- Underdog #109 (Round And Round/Episode 1)
- Go Go Gophers #22 (Tenshun!)
- Klondike Kat #22 (Klondike Goes To Town)
- The Sing-A-Long Family #1 (Picnic) (also appears in syndicated shows #301, 328)
- Underdog #110 (Round And Round/Episode 2)

Episode 356

- Underdog #111 (Round And Round/Episode 3)
- Go Go Gophers #23 (Cuckoo Combat)
- Klondike Kat #23 (Motorcycle Mountie)
- The Sing-A-Long Family #2 (Skating) (also appears in syndicated shows #302, 329)
- Underdog #112 (Round And Round/Episode 4)

Episode 357

- Underdog #113 (A New Villain/Episode 1)
- Go Go Gophers #24 (Kitchen Capers)
- Klondike Kat #24 (Island In The Sky)
- The Sing-A-Long Family #3 (Fair) (also appears in syndicated shows #303, 330)
- Underdog #114 (A New Villain/Episode 2)

Episode 358

- Underdog #115 (A New Villain/Episode 3)
- Tennessee Tuxedo #34 (Telescope Detectives) (934, 1004)
- Commander McBragg #33 (The Astronaut) (also appears in syndicated show #333)
- Underdog #116 (A New Villain/Episode 4)

Episode 359

- Underdog #117 (Batty-Man/Episode 1)
- Go Go Gophers #25 (The Great White Stallion)
- Klondike Kat #25 (The Island Hideout)

- Commander McBragg #34 (Dam Break) (also appears in syndicated show #334)
- Underdog #118 (Batty-Man/Episode 2)

Episode 360
- Underdog #119 (Batty-Man/Episode 3)
- Go Go Gophers #26 (Blankety-Blank Blanket)
- Klondike Kat #26 (The Kat Napper)
- Commander McBragg #35 (The Eclipse) (also appears in syndicated show #335)
- Underdog #120 (Batty-Man/Episode 4)

Episode 361
- Underdog #121 (The Vacuum Gun/Episode 1)
- Cauliflower Cabbie (Introducing The Champion!)
- Commander McBragg #36 (Ship Of The Desert) (also appears in syndicated show #336)
- Underdog #122 (The Vacuum Gun/Episode 2)

Episode 362
- Underdog #123 (The Vacuum Gun/Episode 3)
- Gene Hattree (The Trap)
- Go Go Gophers #27 (The Ironclad) (not The Unsinkable Iron Clad)
- Underdog #124 (The Vacuum Gun/Episode 4)

Underdog (2007)

Underdog: The Adventure Continues (2013)

The Underdog Show Gallery

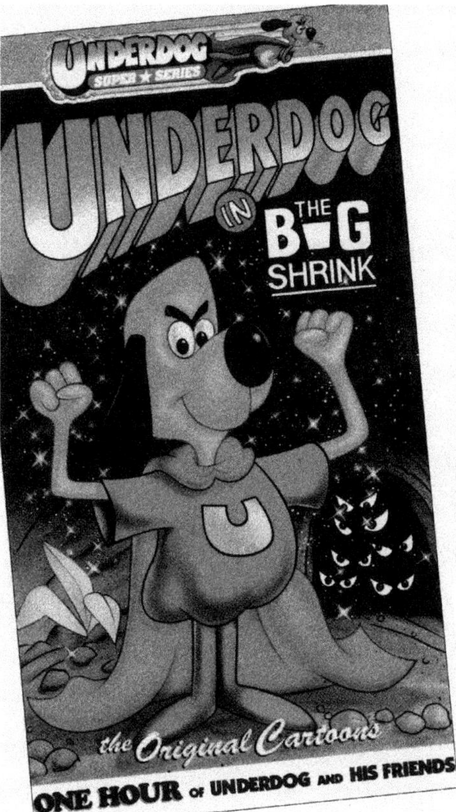

Topic: **Animation**
Title: UNDERDOG IN THE BIG SHRINK
1967 (60 minutes—color)
Manufacturer: **United American Video**
Price: **$9.95 VHS**

Description: There's no shortage of animated super-heroes ready to do battle on your home video screens. Now, that super crime-fighting canine Underdog can be added to the list.

This tape (the first in a series of nine) finds Underdog battling his archenemy, the evil Simon Barsinister, who has invented a liquid substance that can shrink a six-foot man to the size of his thumb. With everyone turned to lilliputian size, the diminutive Simon would realize his goal of becoming "the biggest man in the world." One of his victims is WTTV ace reporter Sweet Polly Purebreed, and it's up to Underdog to rescue her and also rid the nation of the harmful liquid.

The tape also includes other characters from the Leonardo Productions/Total Television team: Tooter Turtle, Klondike Kat, King Leonardo and Odie Colognie, the Go-Go Gophers, Commander McBragg and The Hunter are all featured in their own animated shorts. Most cartoon fans know that Wally Cox, TV's Mr. Peepers, provided the voice for Underdog. But, pay close attention to the man supplying The Hunter's voice, actor Kenny Delmar. Delmar was the voice of Senator Claghorn on radio's "Fred Allen Show," the inspiration for Mel Blanc's voice of Foghorn Leghorn in the Warner Bros. cartoons.

While Underdog may not possess the martial arts skill and contemporary speech of the Teenage Mutant Ninja Turtles, this tape provides an hour of super-hero cartoon fun for both kids and their parents.

Marshall Fish
San Mateo, CA

Marshall Fish is an assistant bookkeeper and collector of music and vintage TV videos. He's still waiting for "George of the Jungle" to be released on tape.

"Looks like this is the end..."

LOS ANGELES
COMIC BOOK AND SCIENCE FICTION CONVENTION

SPECIAL COLLECTORS
CERTIFICATE

This Certificate commemorates the personal appearance by Buck Biggers, the Co-Creator and Writer of the Underdog Cartoon Series, at the Los Angeles Comic Book and Science Fiction Convention on September 10, 2006 for the release of the Underdog Vinyl Figure by Dark ~~Horse~~ Entertainment.

No. 054

Signed by BUCK BIGGERS, the Co-Creator/ Writer of UNDERDOG

This is to certify that the above signed is a full-fledged member of the official Underdog fan club.

Underdog
President

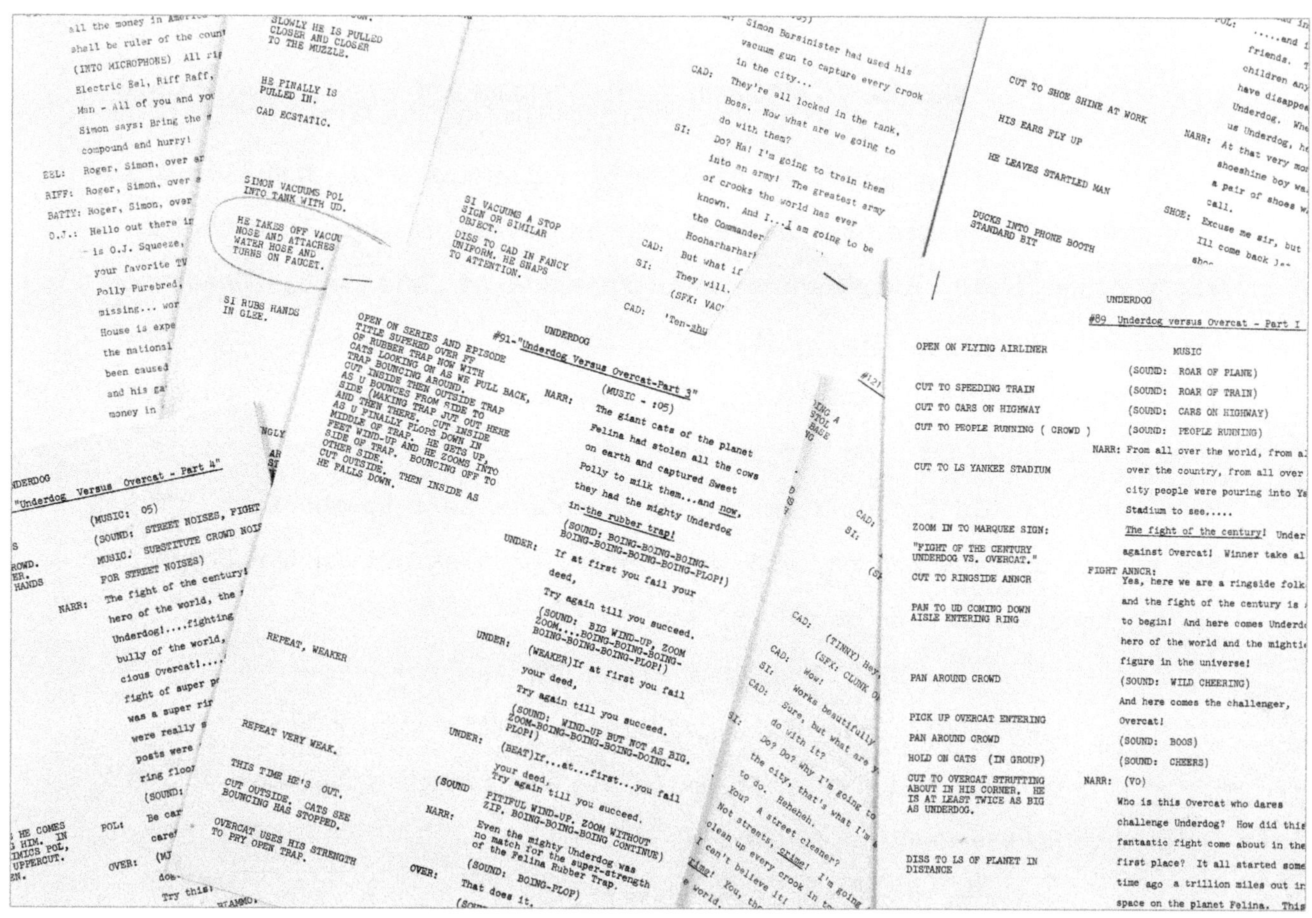
UNDERDOG

#89 Underdog versus Overcat - Part I

OPEN ON FLYING AIRLINER	MUSIC
	(SOUND: ROAR OF PLANE)
CUT TO SPEEDING TRAIN	(SOUND: ROAR OF TRAIN)
CUT TO CARS ON HIGHWAY	(SOUND: CARS ON HIGHWAY)
CUT TO PEOPLE RUNNING (CROWD)	(SOUND: PEOPLE RUNNING)
CUT TO LS YANKEE STADIUM	NARR: From all over the world, from all over the country, from all over city people were pouring into Ya Stadium to see.....
ZOOM IN TO MARQUEE SIGN: "FIGHT OF THE CENTURY UNDERDOG VS. OVERCAT."	The fight of the century! Under against Overcat! Winner take al
CUT TO RINGSIDE ANNCR	FIGHT ANNCR: Yes, here we are a ringside folk and the fight of the century is to begin! And here comes Underd hero of the world and the mighti figure in the universe!
PAN TO UD COMING DOWN AISLE ENTERING RING	
PAN AROUND CROWD	(SOUND: WILD CHEERING)
PICK UP OVERCAT ENTERING	And here comes the challenger, Overcat!
PAN AROUND CROWD	(SOUND: BOOS)
HOLD ON CATS (IN GROUP)	(SOUND: CHEERS)
CUT TO OVERCAT STRUTTING ABOUT IN HIS CORNER. HE IS AT LEAST TWICE AS BIG AS UNDERDOG.	NARR: (VO) Who is this Overcat who dares challenge Underdog? How did this fantastic fight come about in the first place? It all started some time ago a trillion miles out in space on the planet Felina. This
DISS TO LS OF PLANET IN DISTANCE	

UNDERDOG

#91-"Underdog Versus Overcat-Part 3"

OPEN ON SERIES AND EPISODE TITLE SUPERED OVER FF OF RUBBER TRAP NOW WITH CATS LOOKING ON AS WE PULL BACK, TRAP BOUNCING AROUND. CUT INSIDE THEN OUTSIDE TRAP AS U BOUNCES FROM SIDE TO SIDE (MAKING TRAP JUT OUT HERE AND THEN THERE. CUT INSIDE AS U FINALLY FLOPS DOWN IN MIDDLE OF TRAP. HE GETS UP, FEET WIND-UP AND HE ZOOMS INTO SIDE OF TRAP. BOUNCING OFF TO OTHER SIDE. CUT OUTSIDE. THEN INSIDE AS HE FALLS DOWN.	(MUSIC - :05) NARR: The giant cats of the planet Felina had stolen all the cows on earth and captured Sweet Polly to milk them...and now, they had the mighty Underdog in-the rubber trap! (SOUND: BOING-BOING-BOING-BOING-BOING-BOING-BOING-FLOP!) UNDER: If at first you fail your deed, Try again till you succeed. (SOUND: BIG WIND-UP, ZOOM ZOOM...BOING-BOING-BOING-BOING-BOING-BOING-FLOP!)
REPEAT, WEAKER	UNDER: (WEAKER)If at first you fail your deed, Try again till you succeed. (SOUND: WIND-UP BUT NOT AS BIG. ZOOM-BOING-BOING-BOING-BOING-FLOP!)
REPEAT VERY WEAK.	UNDER: (BEAT)If...at...first...you fail your deed, Try again till you succeed.
THIS TIME HE'S OUT. CUT OUTSIDE. CATS SEE BOUNCING HAS STOPPED.	(SOUND: PITIFUL WIND-UP, ZOOM WITHOUT ZIP, BOING-BOING-BOING CONTINUE) NARR: Even the mighty Underdog was no match for the super-strength of the Felina Rubber Trap.
OVERCAT USES HIS STRENGTH TO PRY OPEN TRAP.	OVER: (SOUND: BOING-FLOP) That does it.

NOV 10 REC'D October 27, 1964

UNDERDOG GUARDS TRAIN CARRYING GOLD

Our hero, Underdog (voiced by Wally Cox) is assigned to guard the train carrying a large gold shipment across country, in Part I of "The Great Gold Robbery" on "Underdog" Saturday, Nov. 7 (NBC colorcast, 10 a.m. EST). In Part II, the notorious criminal, Riff Raff, sets Sweet Polly Purebred adrift in a balloon to force Underdog to abandon his vigil on the gold train. In "Medicine Men" on "Go Go Gophers," Colonel Coyote believes Ruffled Feather and Running Board are casting a spell on him that will cause him great injury. Horrors calls on "The Hunter" to play on the Golden Gulch Galloping Gophers baseball team, in "Eye on the Ball."

-----o-----

'UNDERDOG' FACES A SEA MONSTER

O. J. Squeeze, Sweet Polly's boss, sends her on a special ship to a deserted island to do a story on Fearo, a ferocious giant, in Part One of "Fearo" on "Underdog" Saturday, Nov. 21 (NBC-TV colorcast 10 a.m. EST). A sea monster attacks the ship, and Shoeshine, who has stowed away, triumphantly emerges as Underdog. In Part Two, Polly and Captain Coward are attacked by a Stegosaurus. In "Termite Trainers," the Go Go Gophers decide to drive the Army out of their territory. In "Two for the Turkey Trot," the Hunter and Horrors go into the woods to get their Thanksgiving turkey in the old-fashioned way.

NBC-TV PROGRAM HIGHLIGHT NOV. 21

UNDERDOG -- Underdog locks paws with a ferocious sea monster. (Color.)

-----o-----

PRESS DEPARTMENT, NATIONAL BROADCASTING COMPANY, 30 ROCKEFELLER PLAZA, NEW YORK 20, NEW YORK

'UNDERDOG' BATTLES GIANT OCTOPUS AND CLAM DEC 29 REC'D

The leader tries to save Sweet Polly and Prof. Moby Von Ahab from the Bubble-Heads, but he seems to be losing his battle with the giant octopus and the giant clam, in Part III of "The Bubble-Heads" on "Underdog" Saturday, Jan. 9 (NBC-TV colorcast, 10 a.m. EST). In Part IV, revived by his vitamin ring, Underdog must still destroy the tidal wave machinery. In "The Trojan Totem," Ruffled Feather and Running Board use the old Trojan Horse trick to gain access to the fort. The Fox steals all the spoons, and the Hunter, on a safari in the Bongo Congo, hurries back to the U. S. A. 'STOLEN SPOON SAGA'

NBC-TV PROGRAM HIGHLIGHT JAN. 9

UNDERDOG: Underdog wages fierce battle with a giant octopus and a giant clam in his encounters with the Bubble-Heads. (Color.)

-----o-----

VITAMIN RING GIVES 'UNDERDOG' POWER OVER FOES

JUN 9 REC'D

In his struggle with the underwater people, our Hero is attacked by a giant octopus and a huge clam, in Part Three of "The Bubble-Heads" in the color cartoon series "Underdog" Saturday, June 26 on NBC-TV (10-10:30 a.m. EDT). In Part Four, U. D. is revived by his vitamin ring and conquers all. In "Chew Gum Charlie," the Hunter is finally stuck with the solution of the missing chewing gum. Then he leaps right into the "Grand Canyon Caper."

NBC-TV PROGRAM HIGHLIGHT JUNE 26

UNDERDOG: Our Hero, attacked by a giant octopus and clam, is finally revived by his vitamin ring. (Color.)

-----o-----

NBC COLOR TELEVISION NEWS

October 28, 1965

UNDERDOG GETS TOPDOG HOLIDAY TREATMENT WITH A THANKSGIVING COLOR SPECIAL ON NBC-TV, RIGHT AFTER MACY PARADE APPEARANCE

Underdog, NBC Television Network's super-canine (who is title star of the Saturday color cartoon series), will have a busy Thanksgiving Day this year. First, Underdog, along with Sweet Polly Purebred and Simon Barsinister, will take part in Macy's Thanksgiving Day Parade (NBC-TV colorcast, Nov. 25, 10 a.m.-12 noon EST). As soon as that's over, the whole group launches a half-hour color Thanksgiving special on the network (12 noon-12:30 p.m. EST).

This "Underdog" show, entitled "No Thanksgiving," will consist of four episodes (instead of the usual two), with the story being completed in the one day. Sponsors of "No Thanksgiving" are General Mills,Inc. and the De Luxe Reading Corporation. Agency is Dancer-Fitzgerald-Sample Inc. for both sponsors.

The storyline concerns the efforts of Simon Barsinister, the mad scientist, to stop a Thanksgiving Day parade and thereby capture an entire city. His method is to use a "time machine" to return in history to the day before the first Thanksgiving, stirring up enough bad feelings between the Pilgrims and Indians so that nobody has anything to be thankful for.

But Underdog thwarts those evil plans by his usual ingenuity, skill, finesse, and clean-living sneakiness. Of course, his super powers come in handy, too.

(more)

'Underdog' - 2

In the Macy's Thanksgiving Day Parade, Underdog takes the form of a giant balloon, suspended over the second largest float in the parade. Below him Sweet Polly Purebred is held captive in chains on top of a medieval castle while below her Simon Barsinister, seen in his evil-looking laboratory, clutches an atomic gun. Barsinister's aim is to destroy Underdog and the whole Thanksgiving Day parade -- and to keep Sweet Polly for his own.

Part of the attraction of the float is the taped dialogue among the three characters. "I shall wipe out the entire parade," Barsinister shouts as he points the atomic gun to his left and right. A huge cloud of smoke belches from the gun. "No, no," Polly cries.

Suddenly, Barsinister and Polly both see something above them. "It's a plane! It's a boid! It's a frog!" Barsinister yells.

"It's not a plane! It's not a boid! It's not a frog! It's just little old me," comes the answer from the sky. And the parade -- and Polly -- are saved. Underdog's reward is Polly's gratitude. "Oh, Underdog, you saved us," she coos.

Both the half-hour special and the design for the float were produced by Total TV Productions and Leonardo TV Productions. Macy's constructed the float, and the Goodyear Tire and Rubber Co. created the giant Underdog balloon.

NBC-TV PROGRAM HIGHLIGHT NOV. 25

'UNDERDOG' (Holiday Special): "No Thanksgiving" -- Right after appearing in Macy's Thanksgiving Day Parade, Underdog brings his super powers to bear in a half-hour Thanksgiving special. (Color.)

-----o-----

NBC-New York, 10/28/65

NBC FEATURE

June 24, 1965

AN ANIMATED CONVERSATION WITH PETER PIECH,

EXECUTIVE PRODUCER OF 'UNDERDOG' SERIES

"There is no set pattern or guidelines for writing humor for children, particularly in cartoons. The only thing we are concerned about is producing a good cartoon sequence."

So states Peter Piech, executive producer of NBC-TV's color cartoon series, "Underdog" (Saturdays, 10-10:30 a.m. EDT).

One of the most experienced men in cartoon productions, Pete has produced approximately 3,000 minutes of cartoons since 1959, more, he claims, than any other animation studio in the world. Among his creations are "Rocky," "Tennessee Tuxedo," "Leonardo the Lion," "The Hunter," and "Go Go Gophers."

Pete believes that both children and adults are fascinated by the supernatural and super powers; "Underdog" fits into both of these categories because of his super abilities and the supernatural powers of his enemies.

While he feels that there are no guidelines for writing humor for children, Piech is quick to add that there are definite elements that a cartoon should have to capture their interest and imagination.

"Children are paradoxical in that they are captivated by both the familiar and the unknown," says Pete. "They know, for instance, that Underdog is always going to catch the bad guy and bring him to justice in the end. They also know that he is going to rescue the heroine, Polly, from the teeth of a whirling circular saw or from the beam of villain Simon Barsinister's snow gun. The fact that they know this doesn't make the final rescue any less exciting."

(more)

PRESS DEPARTMENT, NATIONAL BROADCASTING COMPANY, 30 ROCKEFELLER PLAZA, NEW YORK, NEW YORK 10020

2 - Underdog

Kids love repetition, according to Piech, "but a producer can't just come up with one formula and then keep using it indefinitely. However, repetition is important, because it takes a while for a child to identify with a personality, whether he is live or animated."

Pete also maintains that children appreciate the same elements of humor that make adults laugh. They love Wally Cox as the voice of Underdog because it is very comical to hear such a meek voice coming from such a super-powered hero. They also like the unexpected situation that pops up, and this too is an element in all forms of humor.

Says Piech, "Children today are much more sophisticated than they used to be, and demand more from cartoons than they used to, because they want to use their knowledge more. It's no longer enough, to give them a 'Felix the Cat' or a 'Farmer Brown' musical cartoon with singing flowers and cows that kick over milk buckets. Today's kids are science-oriented and they want to use this knowledge. They can do this while watching Underdog fight the underwater Bubble-Heads and their tidal wave machine, but they can't if all they see is Felix trying to catch a mouse.

Pete is adamant in his feelings that there are many topics that cannot be animated, and anything that can be done using live actors and live situations should not be done in cartoon form. In cartoons, everything is much bigger than life, very exaggerated.

"Can you imagine Underdog being played by a real dog, like Lassie?" asks Pete. "It would be impossible! And it would be just as ridiculous if Mr. Novak was a cartoon instead of a live person."

-----o-----

NBC-New York, 6/24/65

THERE'S NO NEED TO FEAR...
The Complete Underdog Collection Is Finally Here!!
When the city is in trouble, humble and lovable Shoeshine Boy turns into his alter ego Underdog to stop a series of villains, including the evil Simon Bar Sinister and Riff Raff. Often, TV reporter Sweet Polly Purebred ends up getting into a dangerous situation and must be saved by her hero, Underdog!
Now you can enjoy the 1960s cartoon canine superhero in this complete collection that includes all three seasons of the classic series. Each of the nine discs features Underdog's greatest adventures along with all of the original shorts from Go Go Gophers, Klondike Kat and Commander McBragg.
Get ready for hours of heroic fun!
SPECIAL FEATURES:
COMPLETE COLLECTOR'S EDITION
UNDERDOG
9-DVD SET
COMPLETE COLLECTOR'S EDITION
UNDERDOG
THERE'S NO NEED TO FEAR...
9-DVD SET
COMPLETE COLLECTOR'S EDITION
UNDERDOG

© T. TV. & L. T. P., Inc.
U

© T. TV. & L. T. P., Inc.

© T. TV. & L. T. P., Inc.

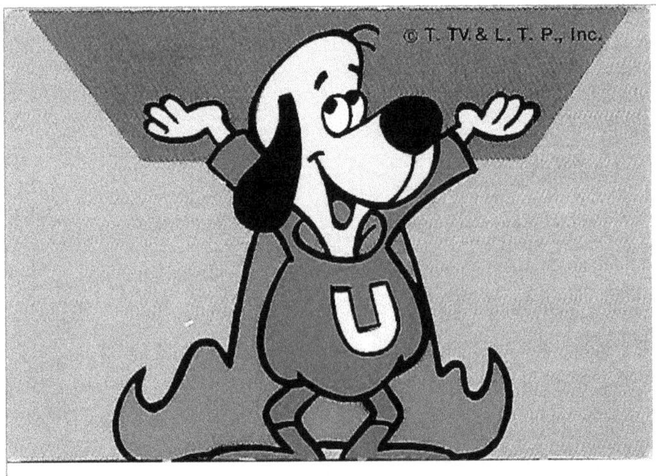

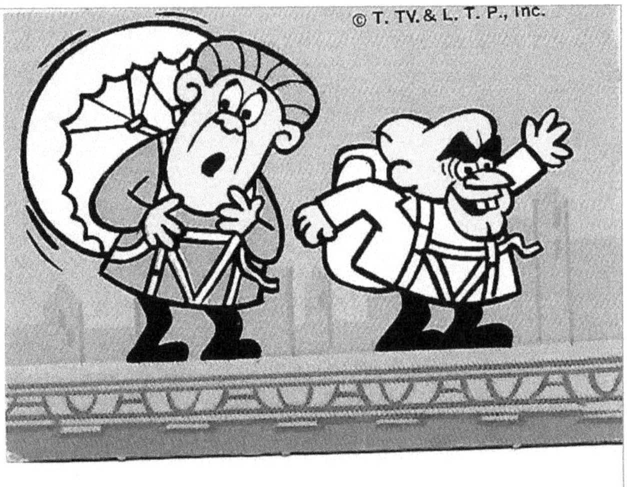

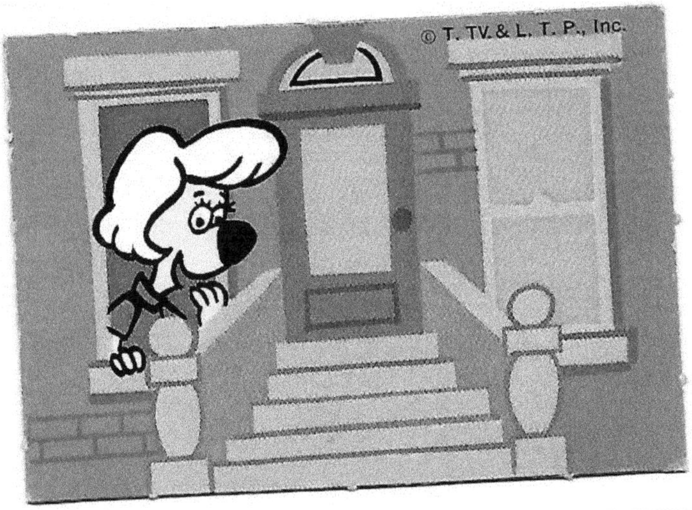

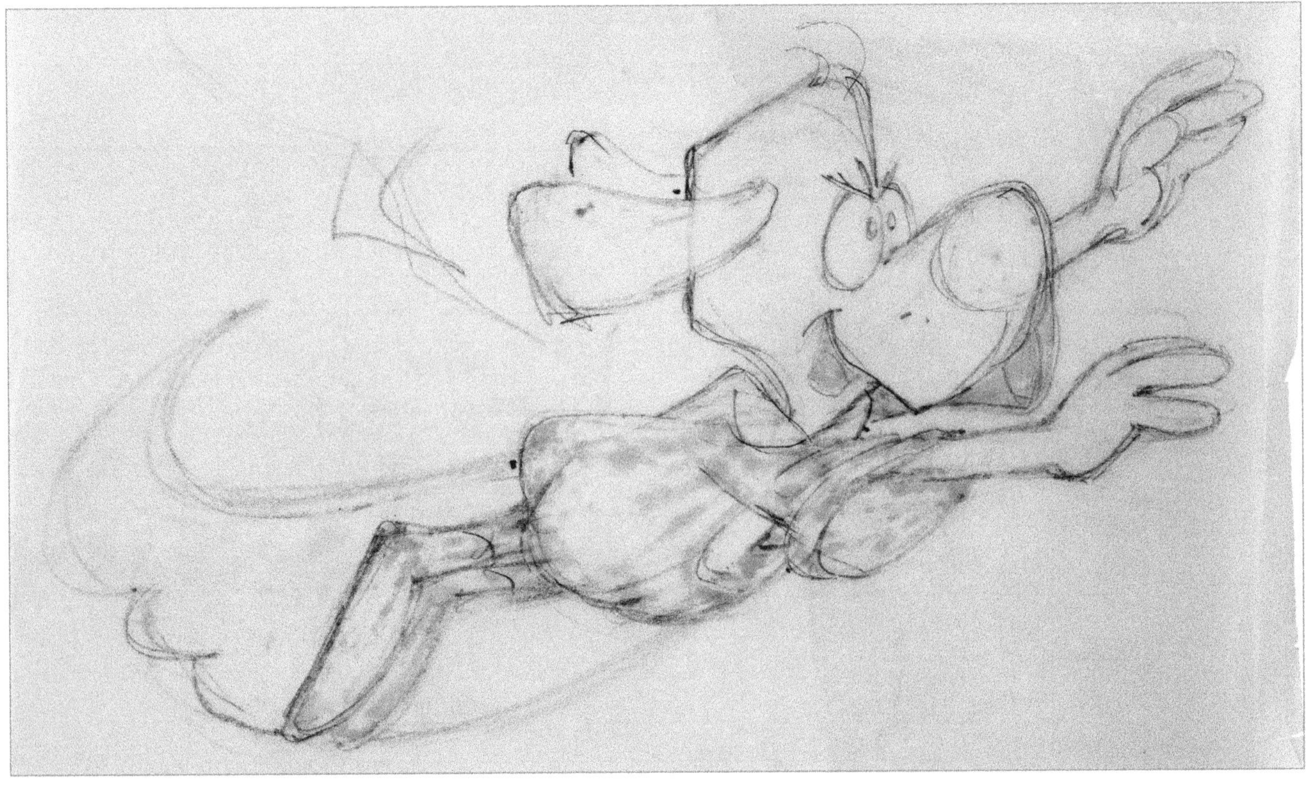

6 Comic Book Art and Other Stuff

by Mark Arnold

Many comic books of TTV shows have been produced over the years, mainly of *King Leonardo* and *The Underdog Show*. Surprisingly, no comic books were ever produced of *Tennessee Tuxedo* or any other TTV segments, but there was a comic book one-shot produced of *The Colossal Show*, a cartoon show that was sold to the network, but canceled at the last minute. It is rumored that a pilot was produced through New York's Terrytoons studios after Gamma was winding down, but in a personal conversation I had with Ralph Bakshi, he claimed no knowledge of such a pilot. It is also true that Bakshi may have left Terrytoons by the time *The Colossal Show* pilot was produced.

According to Wikipedia, "After the departure of Bakshi, the studio petered out, and finally closed in 1972. The studio's last short was an unsold TV pilot called *Sally Sargent*, about a 16-year-old girl who is a secret agent. Soon after *Sally Sargent* was completed, Viacom International ended their relationship with Fox and re-releases ceased. Terrytoons' existence soon came to an end."

Sally Sargent was made for Fred Calvert Productions in 1968. Their studio is better known for the Saturday morning animated series *Emergency +4* and *I Am the Greatest: The Adventures of Muhammad Ali* in the 1970s. It is at this same approximate time that *The Colossal Show* pilot could have also been produced, and subsequently lost.

This is not to say that *The Colossal Show* doesn't exist, as memories could be faulty or the pilot may not have been produced through Terrytoons. In any case, no pilot has turned up and the Gold Key comic book is the only public record of the show.

The following is a sampling of original art courtesy of Heritage Auctions:

BLACKTHORNE PUBLISHING, INC.
786 Blackthorne Avenue • El Cajon • California 92020 • (619) 463-9603
OUTSIDE FRONT COVER (Comic Book Format)
BOOK TITLE & ISSUE NO.
PENCILLER:
INKER:
COLORIST:
OTHER:
BINDING EDGE
BLACKTHORNE INCORPORATED PUBLISHING
NO. 1
$2.50 U.S.
$3.50 CANADA
BLACKTHORNE COMICS PRESENTS:
UNDERDOG
3-D
COMING SOON!
UNDERDOG
3-D
©1987 LEONARDO-T.T.V.
EXTEND IMAGE TO THIS OUTSIDE BLACK LINE FOR BLEED

FIRST LET ME THANK YOU ALL FOR THIS LANDSLIDE VICTORY. THEY TELL ME I'M THE FIRST MAYOR IN THE HISTORY OF THE CITY, TO BE ELECTED TO A FOURTH TERM!
BUT NOW ON TO SOME SERIOUS BUSINESS.
DURING MY FOURTH TERM AS MAYOR, I INTEND TO CONTINUE MY POLICY TO KEEP CRIME IN THE STREETS WHERE IT BELONGS.
AND TO HELP ME REALIZE MY GOAL, I HAVE APPOINTED TAP-TAP AS OUR NEW POLICE COMMIS-SIONER.
.. AND ALSO TO ACHIEVE THAT GOAL, I'M ALSO RAISING THE REWARD FOR UNDERDOG TO $2,000,000..
DEAD OR ALIVE!!
HE'S A THREAT TO OUR WAY OF LIFE.. Y'KNOW, YOU LOOK MORE THAN A LITTLE BIT LIKE HIM!!

I WONDER WHAT ALL THE FUSS IS ABOUT?
CUP-O-COFFEE
HAIR 'N' NOW
HAIR 'N' NOW
RRRRRR
?
RIFF RAFF FOR MAYOR
WHAT'S GOING ON?
MAYOR RIFF RAFF HAS BEEN RE-ELECTED FOR HIS FOURTH TERM AS MAYOR, AND HE'S ABOUT TO MAKE HIS ACCEPTANCE SPEECH.
HELLO FELLOW CITIZENS!!

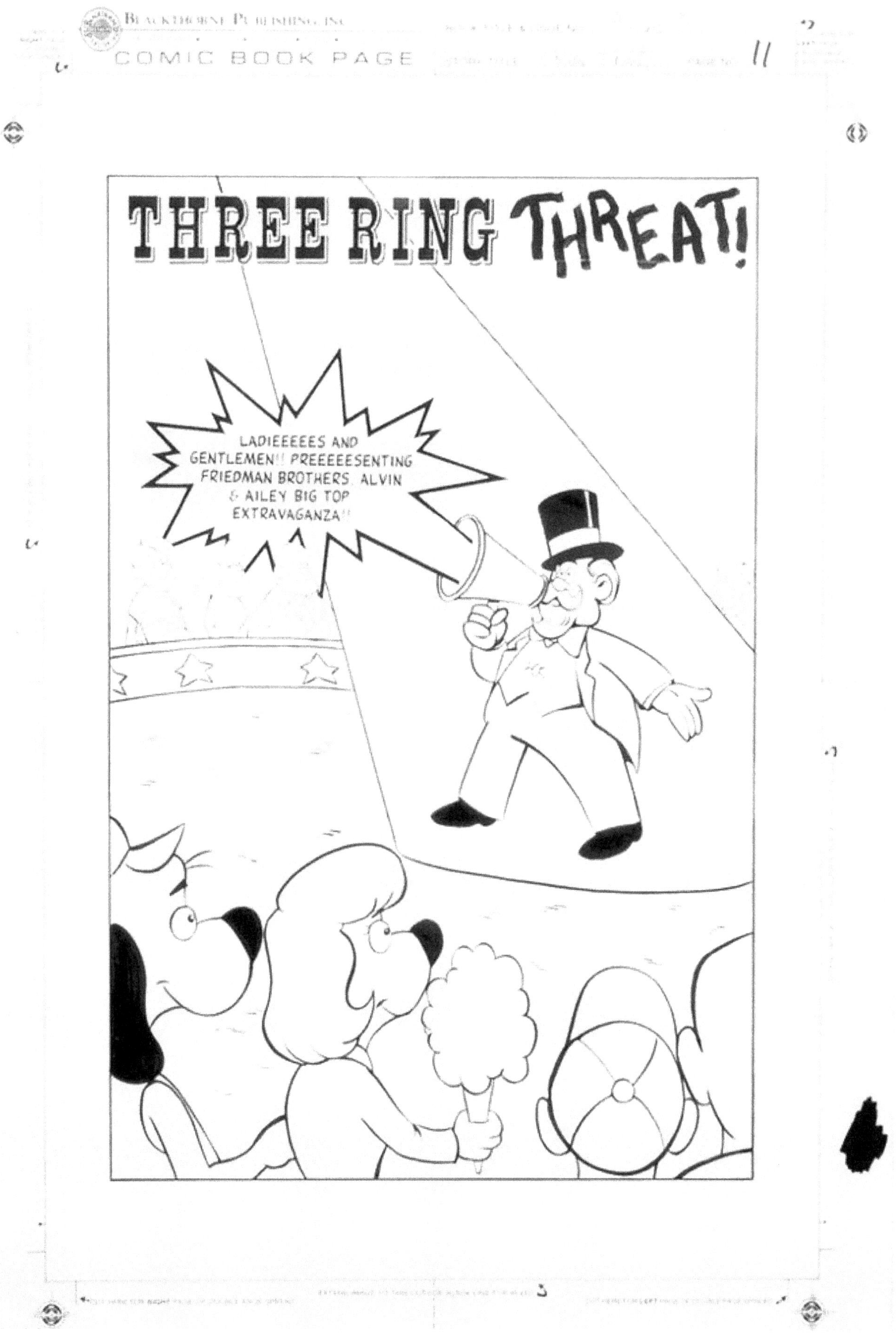

COMIC BOOK PAGE

THREE RING THREAT!

LADIEEEEES AND GENTLEMEN!! PREEEEESENTING FRIEDMAN BROTHERS, ALVIN & AILEY BIG TOP EXTRAVAGANZA!!

HAVE NO FEAR....
UNDERDOG
IS HERE!
Phone

6 3/4

BANK
TAKE TH--
YEOW!

#3 NOV.
25 TEXT
26
DO EVEN SMALL JOBS WELL!
SHINE
D-650

Underdog #3 June 6-2714
FREEZE CART

6 5/8

U
6 11/16"

9
SO THIS IS EARTH!
THERE CERTAINLY IS PLENTY OF FOOD HERE-LOOK AT ALL THESE DELICIOUS ROCKS!

CRUNCH
CAN'T YOU STOP EATING FOR ONCE! HAND ME THE STONE PHONE!

MISSION I CALLING PLANET GRANITE, MISSION I CALLING PLANET GRANITE-COME IN PLEASE!

IS THAT YOU, CRUSHER!
YES, LET ME TALK TO CAPTAIN MARBLEHEAD!

THIS IS CAPTAIN MARBLEHEAD!
WHAT ARE YOUR ORDERS, OH FEARLESS LEADER!
2

10

TAKE THE GRANITE GUN I GAVE YOU AND CAPTURE TWELVE EARTH PEOPLE TO WORK AS SLAVES IN THE ROCK MINE!
YES, MY LEADER, OVER AND OUT!

LET'S GO, CRUSHER
BEFORE WE GO TO WORK, LET'S EAT!

GOOD IDEA! CAN'T DO A GOOD JOB ON AN EMPTY STOMACH!
MUNCH! MUNCH!

HEY, GRAVEL, YOU SHOULD TRY SOME OF THIS LIMESTONE, IT'S GOOD!
IT IS GOOD - BUT NOT AS GOOD AS BACK HOME!

...AND FOR DESSERT SOME NICE WHITE MARBLE -
ZIP
3

15AD/16
THE
Underdog in MARBLE HEADS
THERE THEY ARE! FIRE!
CHAPTER III
WE'RE BEING ATTACKED!
THIS OUGHT TO BE FUN!
ZAT
1

17

LET 'EM HAVE IT!

ZAT

WELL, THAT DIDN'T TAKE LONG!
NOW, LET'S LOAD THESE BLOCKHEADS INTO THE SHIP AND HEAD BACK TO THE PLANET GRANITE...

...AND SOME DECENT FOOD!
BURP!

A SHORT TIME LATER
WE ARE BACK, OH FEARLESS LEADER, WITH THE SLAVES!
AND WE ARE RETURNING TO YOU THE MIGHTY GRANITE GUN!
S
PLANET GRANITE HEADQUARTERS

2

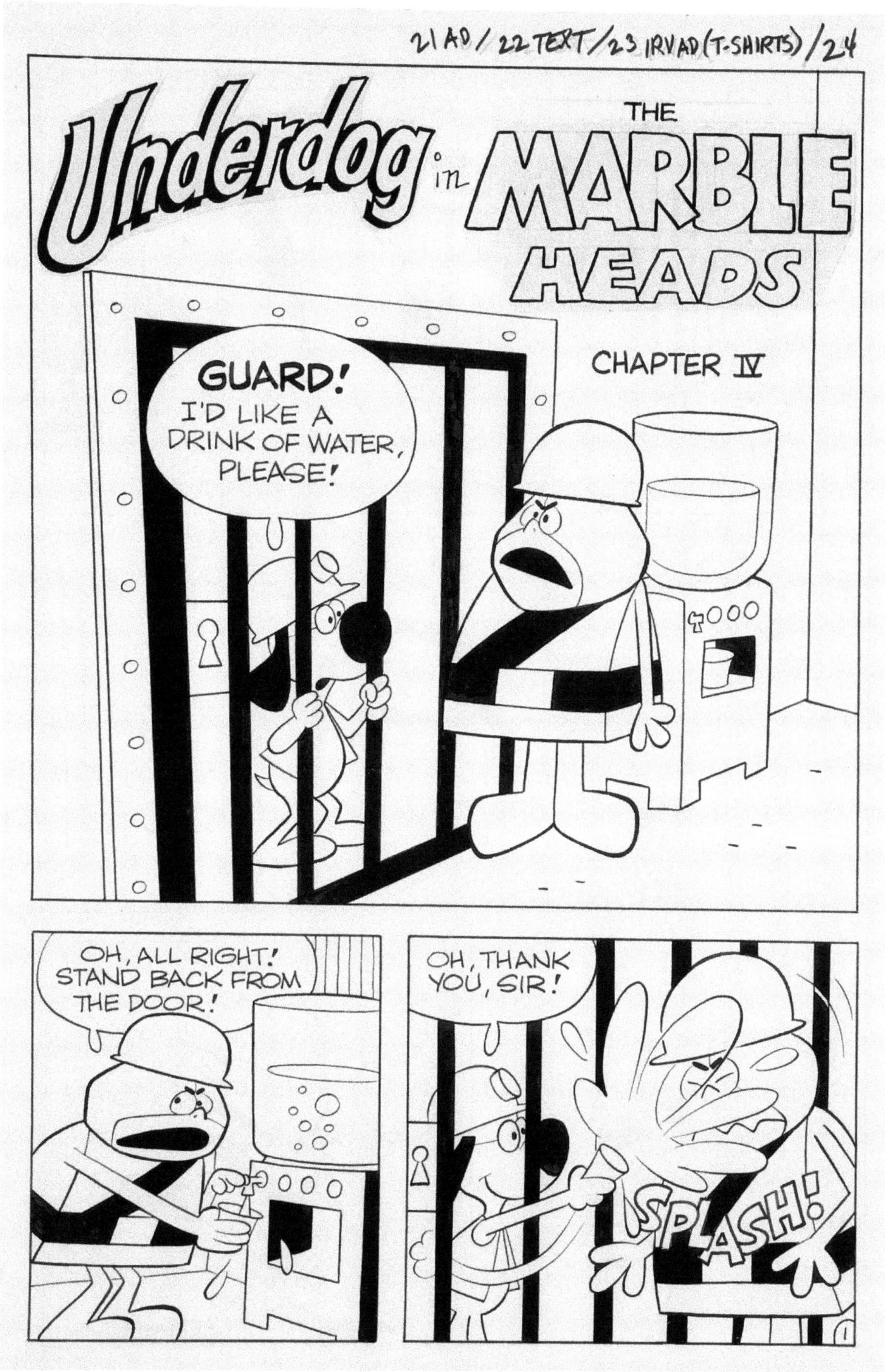

21 AD / 22 TEXT / 23 IRV AD (T-SHIRTS) / 24

Underdog in THE MARBLE HEADS

CHAPTER IV

GUARD! I'D LIKE A DRINK OF WATER, PLEASE!

25

NOW TO CAPTURE
THE GRANITE GUN!

BOING
WHAT'S GOING ON
HERE? GUARDS!
GUARDS!

RUN! RUN!

THIS WILL STOP
THEM!

2

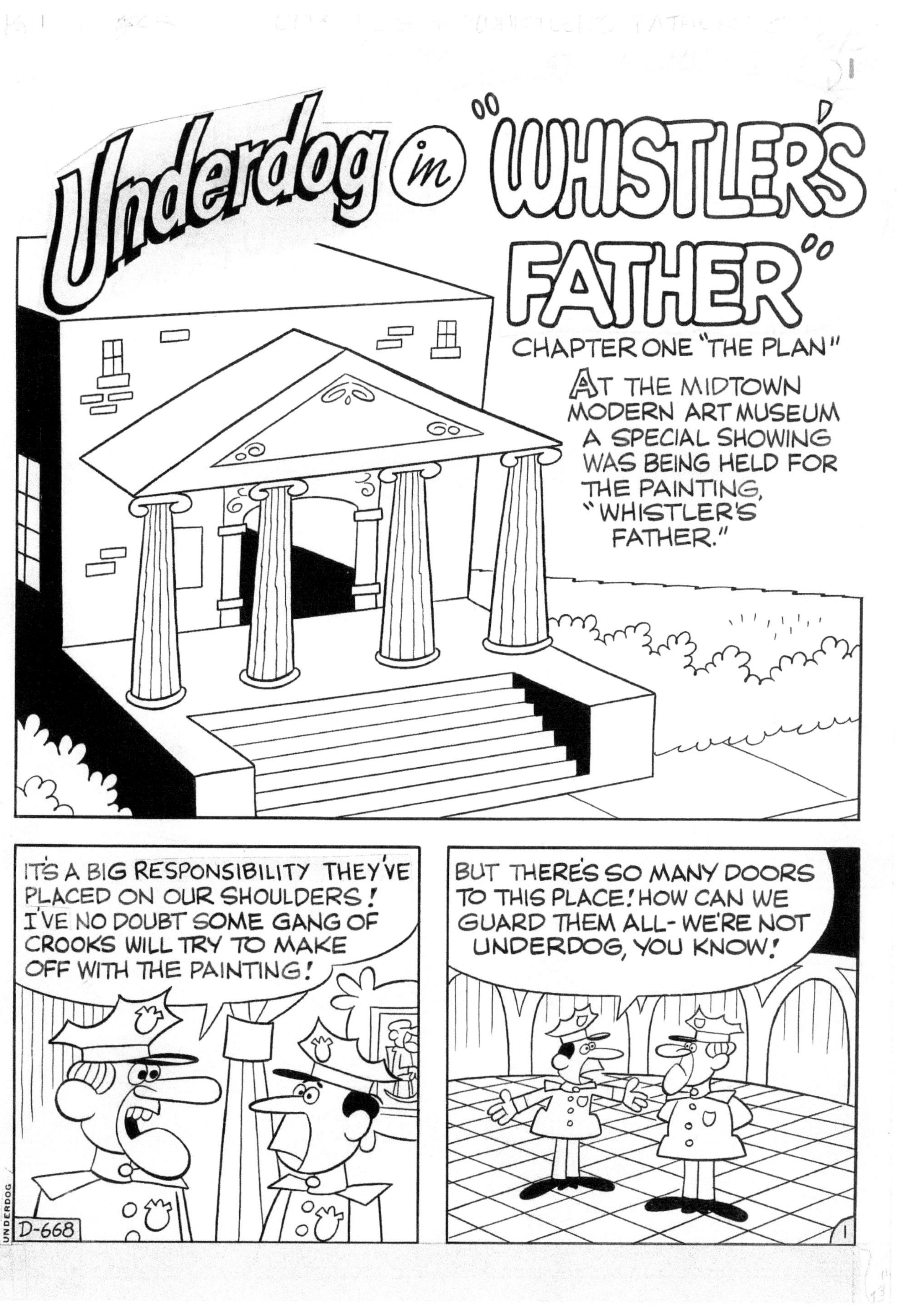

Underdog in "WHISTLER'S FATHER"

CHAPTER ONE "THE PLAN"

AT THE MIDTOWN MODERN ART MUSEUM A SPECIAL SHOWING WAS BEING HELD FOR THE PAINTING, "WHISTLER'S FATHER."

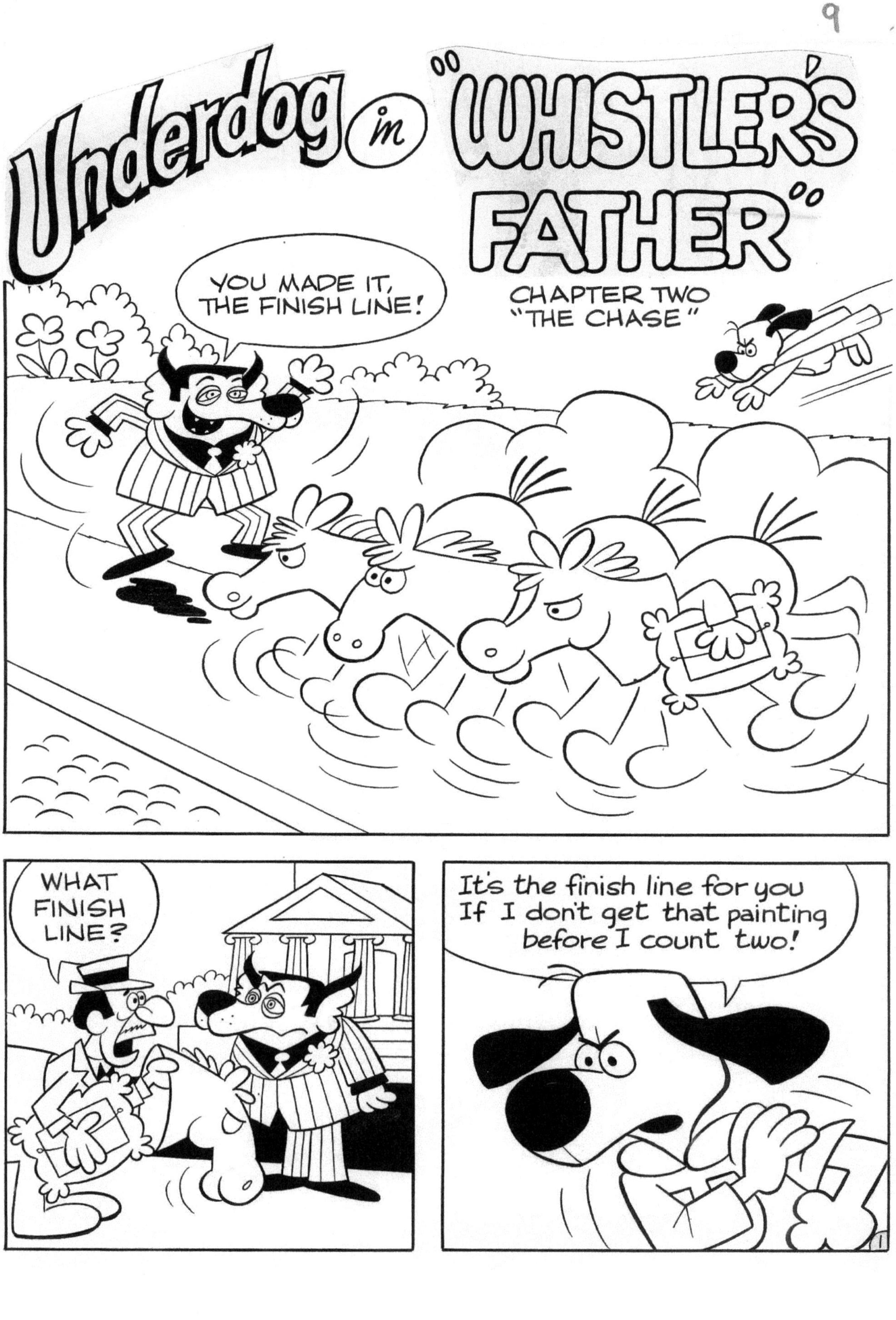

Underdog in "WHISTLER'S FATHER"

YOU MADE IT, THE FINISH LINE!

CHAPTER TWO
"THE CHASE"

CONTINUED AFTER FOLLOWING PAGE

18
Underdog in "WHISTLER'S FATHER"
CHAPTER 3 "THE DISCOVERY"
SHOE SHINE

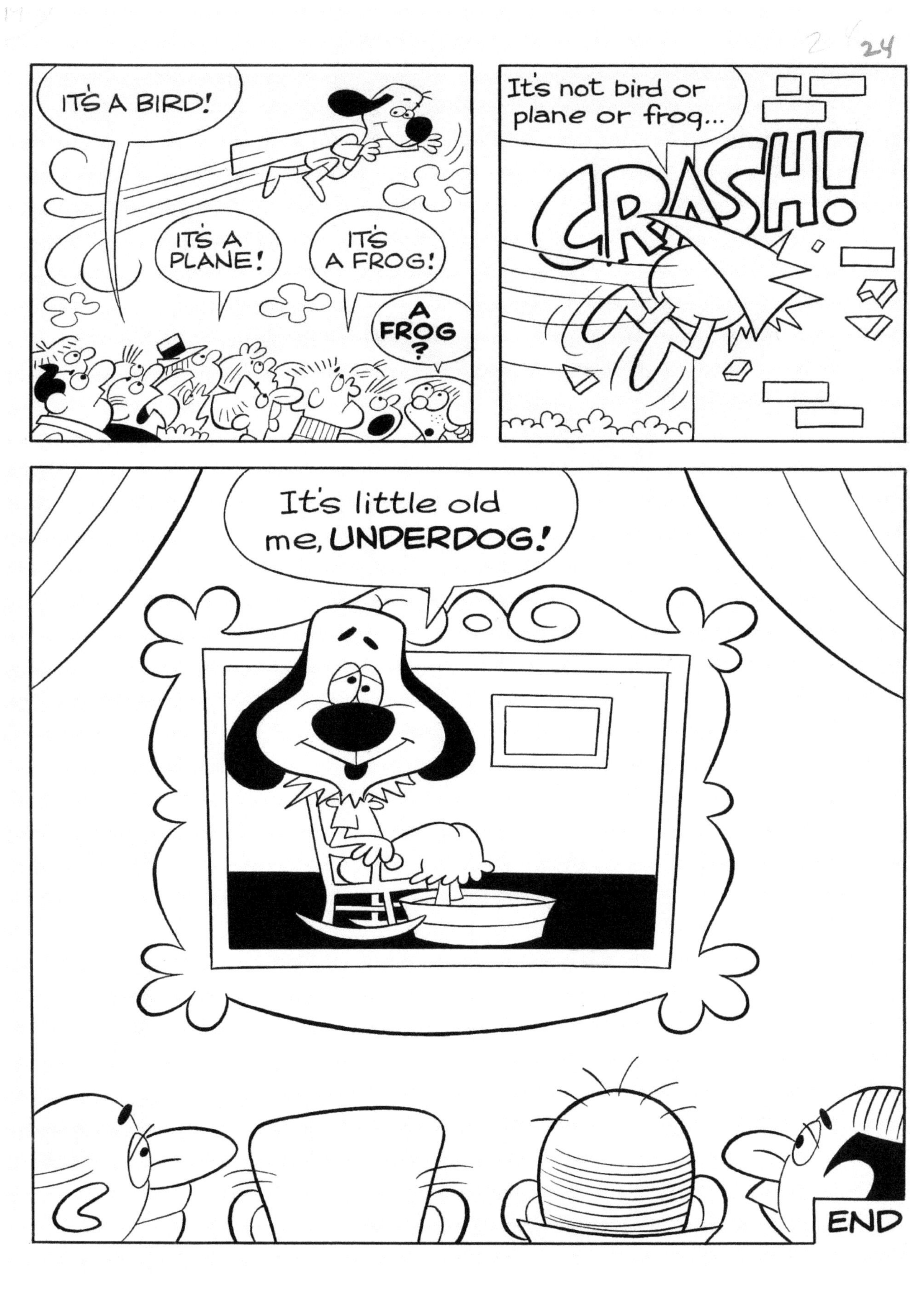

It's little old me, **UNDERDOG!**

END

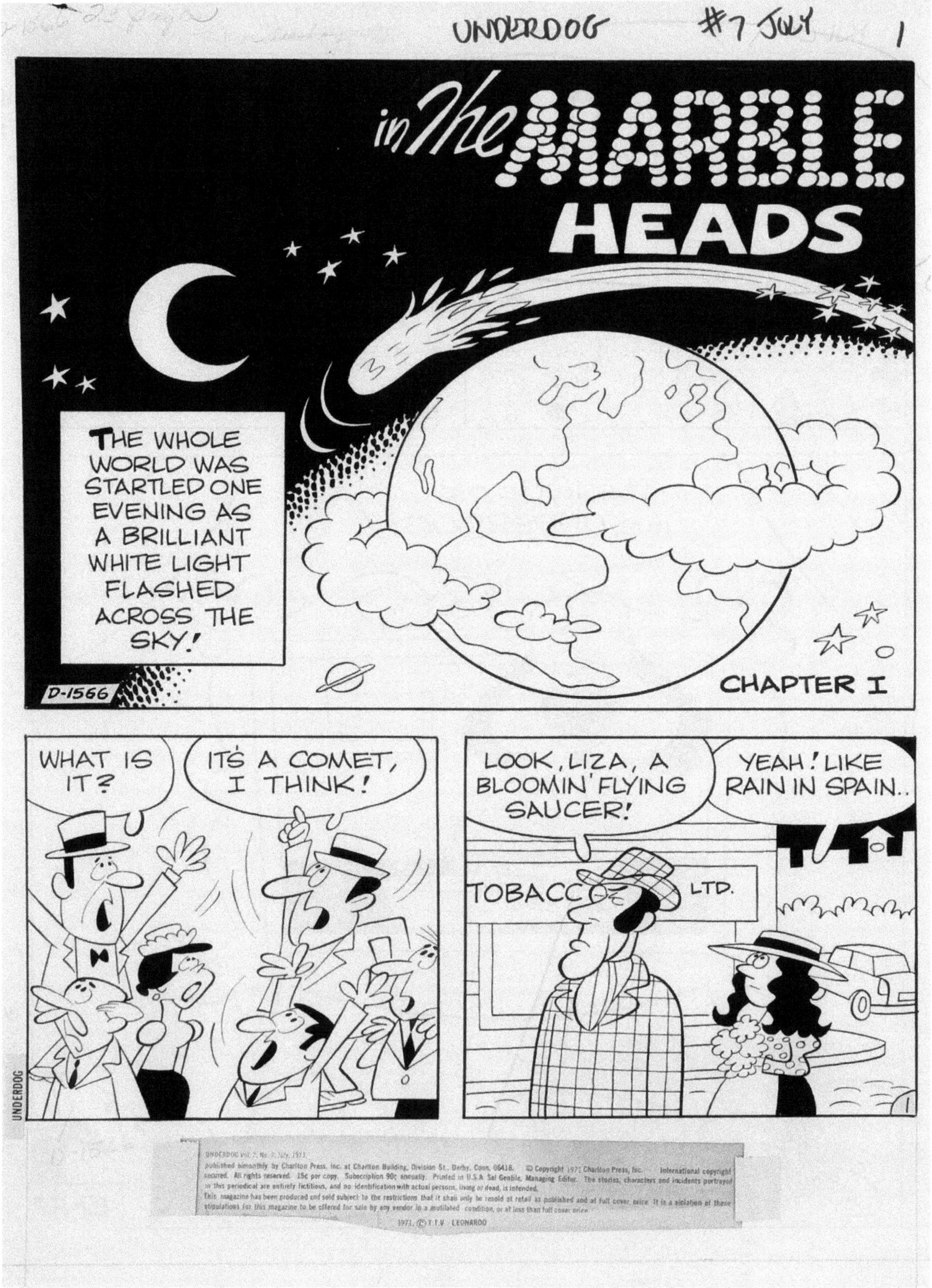

UNDERDOG #7 JULY 1

in The MARBLE HEADS

THE WHOLE WORLD WAS STARTLED ONE EVENING AS A BRILLIANT WHITE LIGHT FLASHED ACROSS THE SKY!

D-1566

CHAPTER I

UNDERDOG Vol. 2, No. 7, July, 1971,
published bimonthly by Charlton Press, Inc. at Charlton Building, Division St., Derby, Conn. 06418. 15¢ per copy. Subscription 90¢ annually. Printed in U.S.A. Sal Gentile, Managing Editor.

BOAKAK
LOOK UP IN THE GLORIOUS PEOPLE'S SKY, ANOTHER GLORIOUS PEOPLE'S SATELLITE!
YEK! YOU'VE SEEN ONE, YOU'VE SEEN THEM ALL!

HEY, JOHNNY, LOOK! NORTHERN LIGHTS!
DON'T BE STUPID - IT'S SKY WRITING!

A COMET!

A METEORITE!

A BIG FIREFLY!
A GREAT GIANT BALLOON!
ZOOOOOM
2

VANDERCOOK
UNDERDOG #8 SEPT.
CHARLTON COMICS
741-971
All NEW Stories & Art
APPROVED BY THE COMICS CODE AUTHORITY
UNDERDOG
NO.8 SEPT. CDC
15¢
Underdog
The Phoney Booths
DIRECTORY
FRANK JOHNSON

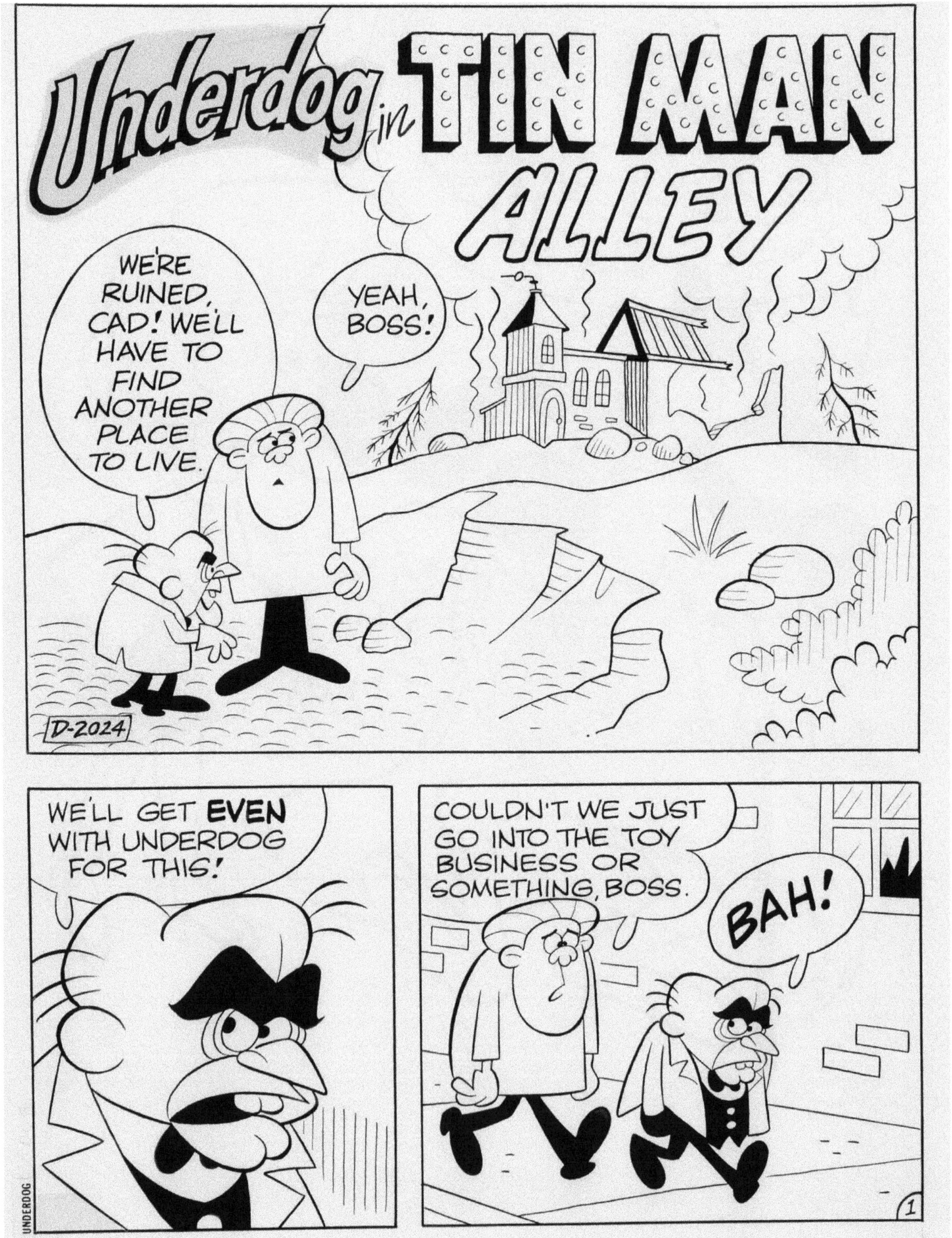

Underdog in TIN MAN ALLEY

WE'RE RUINED, CAD! WE'LL HAVE TO FIND ANOTHER PLACE TO LIVE.

YEAH, BOSS!

D-2024

UNDERDOG

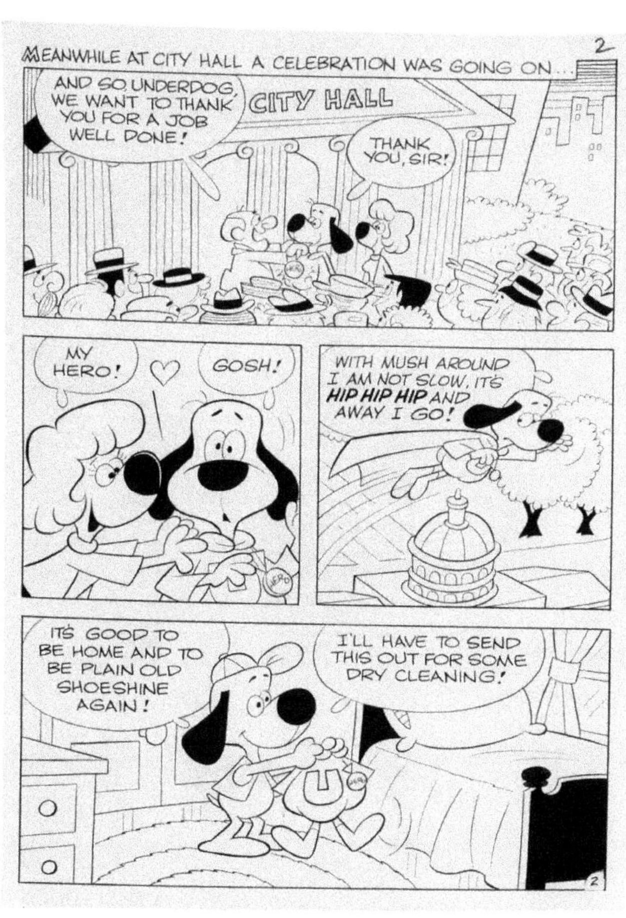
MEANWHILE AT CITY HALL A CELEBRATION WAS GOING ON...
AND SO, UNDERDOG, WE WANT TO THANK YOU FOR A JOB WELL DONE!
CITY HALL
THANK YOU, SIR!
MY HERO!
GOSH!
WITH MUSH AROUND I AM NOT SLOW. IT'S HIP HIP HIP AND AWAY I GO!
IT'S GOOD TO BE HOME AND TO BE PLAIN OLD SHOESHINE AGAIN!
I'LL HAVE TO SEND THIS OUT FOR SOME DRY CLEANING!

LATER
JUST PRESS THAT BUTTON, CAD, AND WE'RE IN BUSINESS!
ONCE AGAIN I SHALL HAVE A CHANCE TO RULE THE WORLD!
I CAN HARDLY WAIT, BOSS!
SOON, CAD, THE DOOR WILL OPEN, AND...
CLANG
CLANK
CLUNK
END CHAPTER I

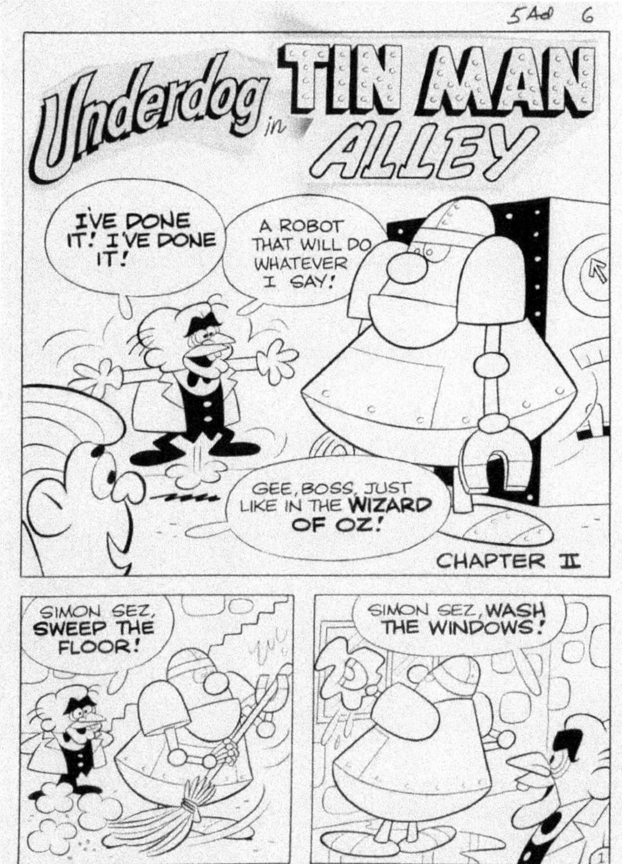
Underdog in TIN MAN ALLEY
I'VE DONE IT! I'VE DONE IT!
A ROBOT THAT WILL DO WHATEVER I SAY!
GEE, BOSS, JUST LIKE IN THE WIZARD OF OZ!
CHAPTER II
SIMON SEZ, SWEEP THE FLOOR!
SIMON SEZ, WASH THE WINDOWS!

AND THAT'S NOT ALL, CAD. WE CAN FIT RIGHT INSIDE HIM!
GREAT, BOSS!
FIRST, CAD, WE'LL TAKE OVER ALL COMMUNICATIONS!
CLUNK
CLUNK
SO, DEAR FRIENDS, THIS IS SWEET POLLY SIGNING OFF.
CRASH
TV
LET ME GO!
WE HAVE YOU NOW, SWEET POLLY!
CLUMP
CLUMP
MY ROBOT CAN IMITATE YOUR VOICE SO THAT YOUR LISTENERS WILL BELIEVE WHAT THEY HEAR!
OH, NO!

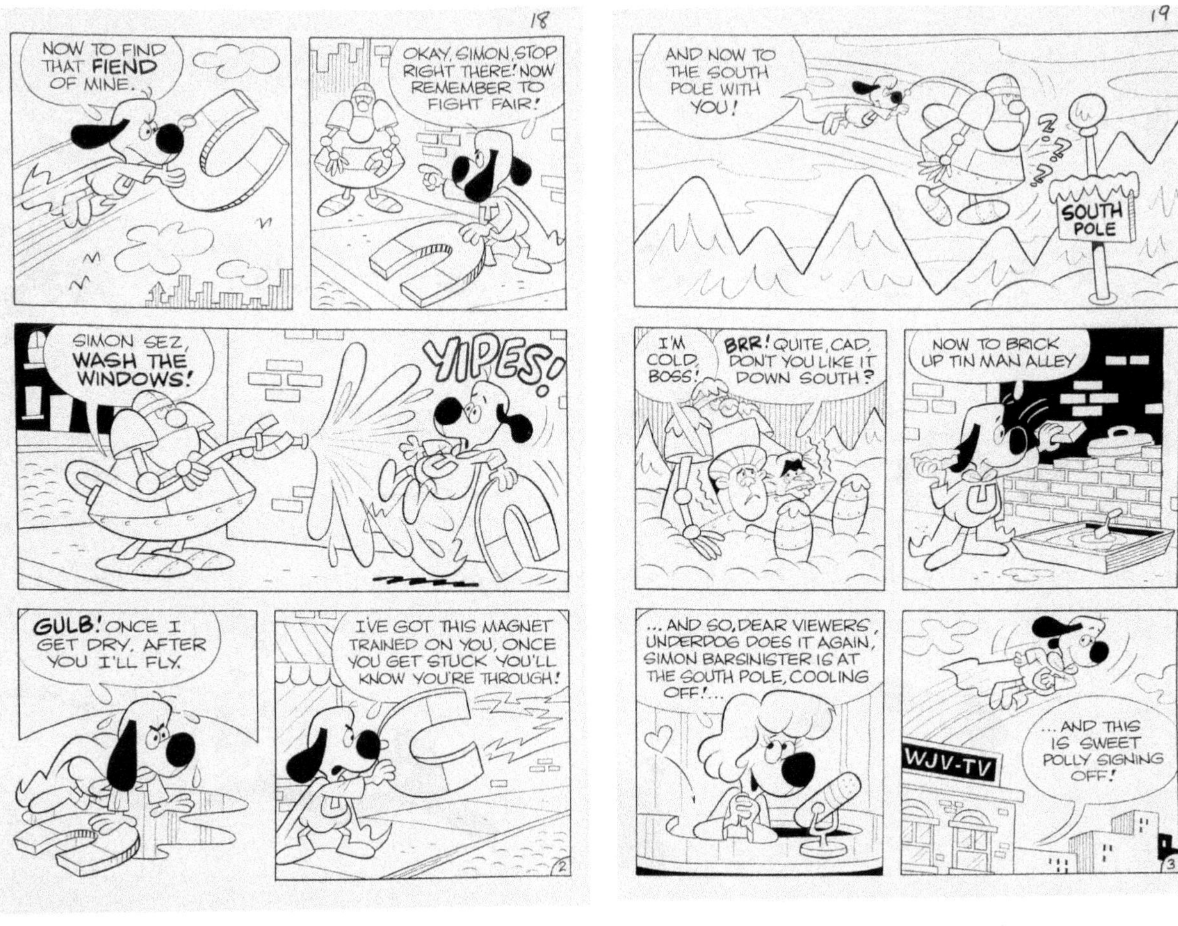
18
NOW TO FIND THAT FIEND OF MINE.
OKAY, SIMON, STOP RIGHT THERE! NOW REMEMBER TO FIGHT FAIR!
SIMON SEZ, WASH THE WINDOWS!
YIPES!
GULB! ONCE I GET DRY, AFTER YOU I'LL FLY.
I'VE GOT THIS MAGNET TRAINED ON YOU, ONCE YOU GET STUCK YOU'LL KNOW YOU'RE THROUGH!
19
AND NOW TO THE SOUTH POLE WITH YOU!
SOUTH POLE
I'M COLD, BOSS!
BRR! QUITE, CAD, DON'T YOU LIKE IT DOWN SOUTH?
NOW TO BRICK UP TIN MAN ALLEY
... AND SO, DEAR VIEWERS, UNDERDOG DOES IT AGAIN, SIMON BARSINISTER IS AT THE SOUTH POLE, COOLING OFF!...
WJV-TV
... AND THIS IS SWEET POLLY SIGNING OFF!

20
LOOK! UP IN THE SKY!
IT'S A PLANE!
IT'S A BIRD!
IT'S A FROG!
A FROG?
CRASH!
IT'S NOT PLANE, NOR BIRD, OR EVEN FROG! JUST LITTLE OLD ME, UNDERDOG!
The END

25
KIDS — COLOR THIS PAGE!

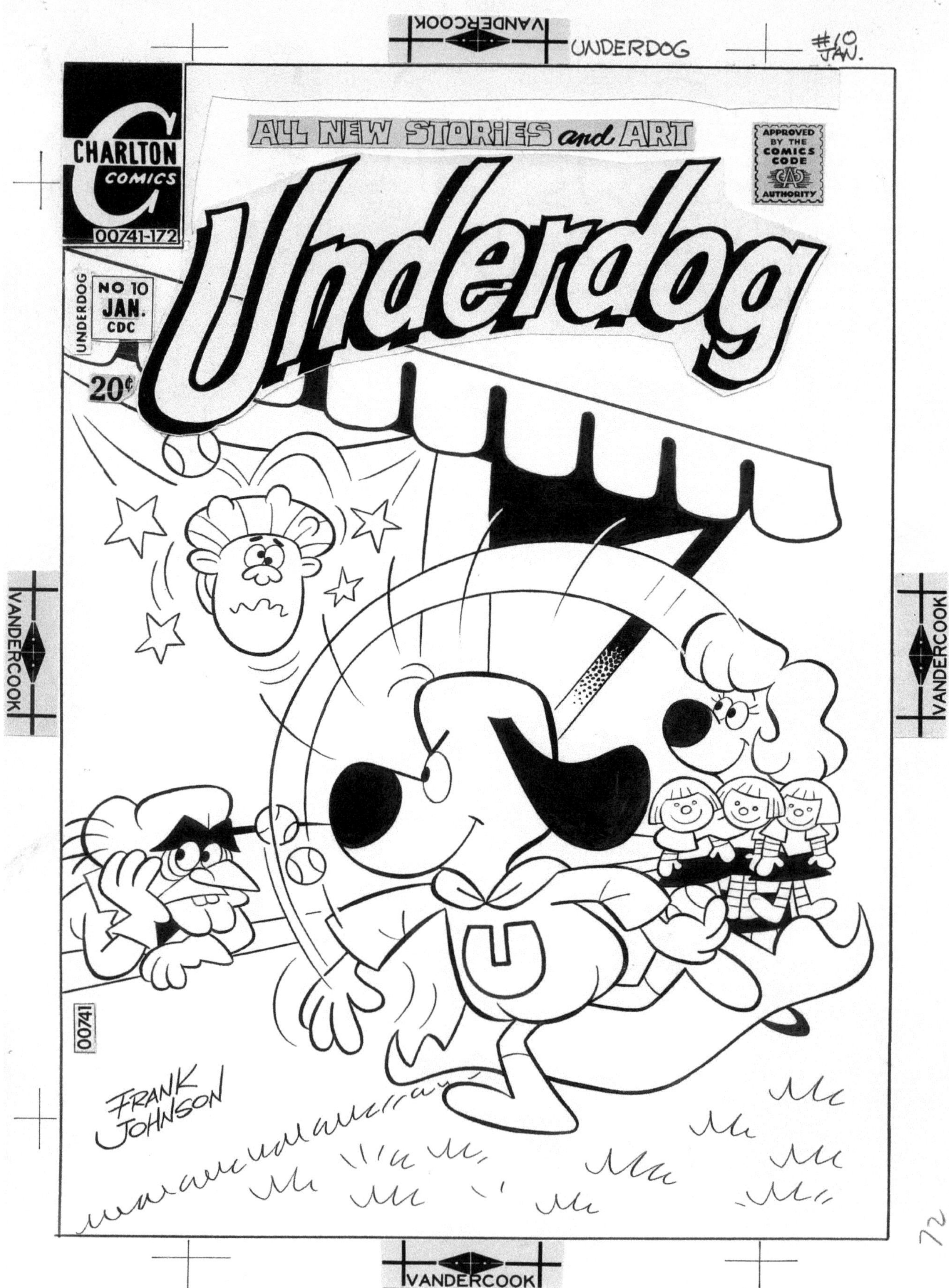
VANDERCOOK
UNDERDOG
#10 JAN.
CHARLTON COMICS
00741-172
ALL NEW STORIES and ART
APPROVED BY THE COMICS CODE AUTHORITY
Underdog
UNDERDOG
NO 10 JAN. CDC
20¢
U
00741
FRANK JOHNSON
VANDERCOOK
VANDERCOOK
VANDERCOOK
72

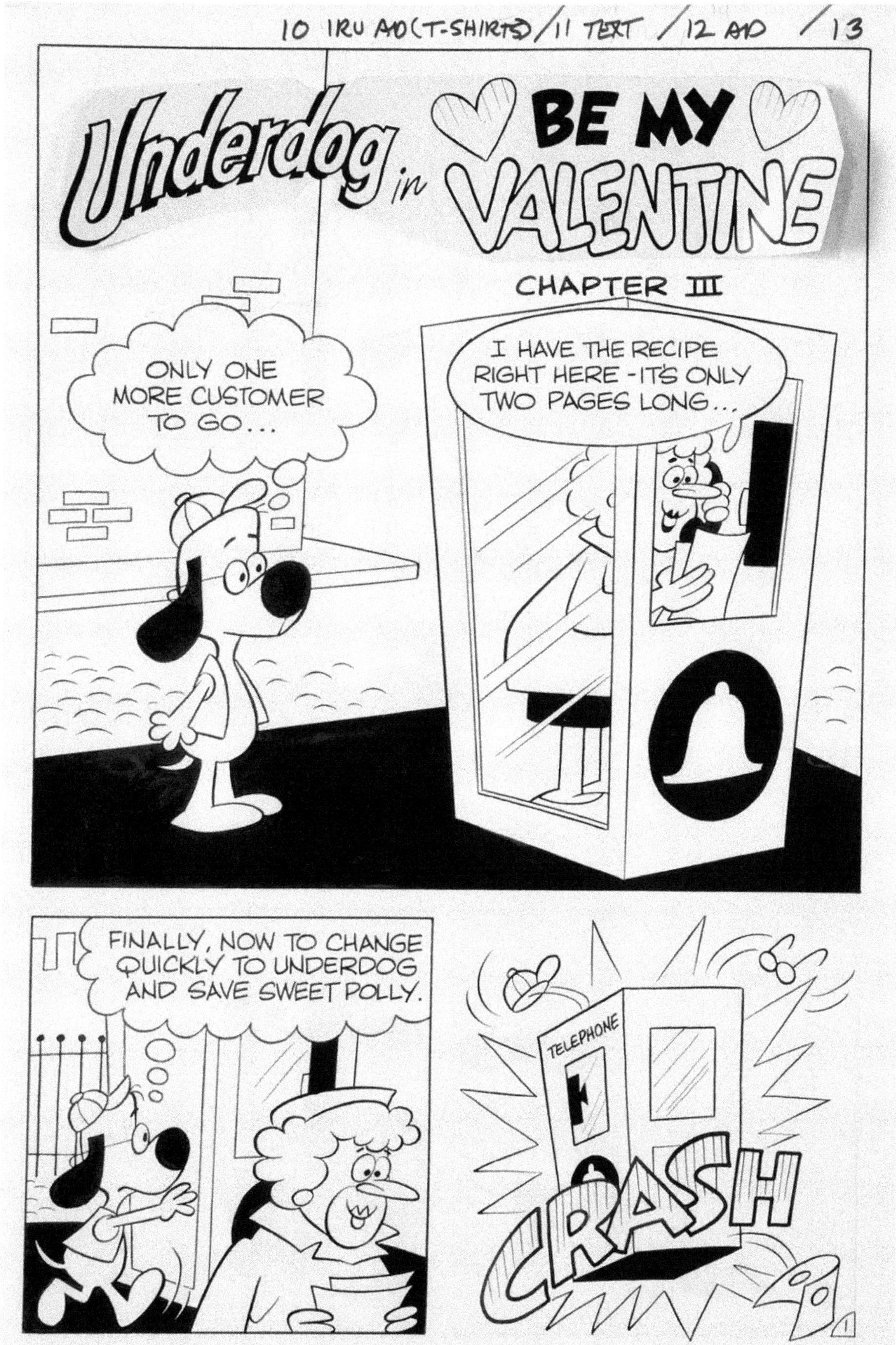

10 IRU AD (T-SHIRTS) / 11 TEXT / 12 AD / 13

Underdog in BE MY VALENTINE

CHAPTER III

ONLY ONE MORE CUSTOMER TO GO...

I HAVE THE RECIPE RIGHT HERE - IT'S ONLY TWO PAGES LONG...

27
CRASH!
OH, UNDERDOG, YOU'RE ALL RIGHT!
WE MUST HURRY TO THE OFFICIALS AT CITY HALL BEFORE SIMON MAKES VALENTINES OF THEM ALL!
IF ONLY WE AREN'T TOO LATE ALREADY!
DON'T ANYBODY MOVE! I'M HERE TO TAKE OVER CITY HALL!
YOU TRIED BEFORE SIMON BARSINISTER.
AYOR
PUT HIM IN THE MACHINE, BOYS!
CONTINUED AFTER THE NEXT PAGE

14

WHEN POLLY'S IN TROUBLE
I AM NOT SLOW...
IT'S HIP HIP HIP
AND AWAY I
GO!

THERE'S SIMON'S LAB
IN VIEW - VERY SOON
HE'LL MEET HIS DUE.
KEEP
OUT

CRASH!
THERE'S NO
NEED TO FEAR!
UNDERDOG
IS HERE!
WAIT, SWEET
POLLY, IS OVER
THERE BY THAT
DOOR!

I'M COMING,
SWEET
POLLY!

OOPS!
MISSED!
CLANG!

2

REDUCE TO 6 11/16"

same size — 6 11/16"
APRIL 78 UNDERDOG #19
90294-806
G-5492
DUE 11/25

CUCKOO
CUCKOO
UNDERDOG #20

POWER PLAY
I WONDER WHAT SIMON'S BEEN UP TO! LATELY HE HASN'T BEEN BOTHERING ME!
MAYBE I'LL JUST SNEAK A PEAK INTO HIS LAB AND SEE WHAT I CAN SEE!

I'VE DONE IT, CAD! I'VE CREATED A RAY-GUN THAT'LL GIVE ME SUPERSTRENGTH!
NOW I'LL BE ABLE TO BEAT UP THAT UNDER-DOG!

BUT FIRST I WANT TO TRY THE RAY-GUN OUT ON YOU, AND SEE IF IT WORKS!
BZZZT!
BZZZT

CAD! WHAT'S WRONG? WHY ARE YOU--
GRRRR!

?
SMRASSH!

HA HA HA! THAT'S ONE OF THE FUNNIEST THINGS I'VE EVER SEEN!...
NOT ONLY DID YOUR NEW RAY MAKE HIM SUPERSTRONG, IT ALSO MADE HIM SUPERMEAN!
AW, SHUT UP!
The END

6 3/8"

S/S GLOSSY POS

D.P. UNDERDOG - #467 - D5617 - JULY '80

MARCH OF COMICS

G-6112

THE RUBBER DUCK
OUR TALE BEGINS WITH A PRISON BREAK...
YA HA HA! I'M FREE! I'M FREE!
NO CRUMMY PRISON CAN HOLD THE ALL-MIGHTY DUCK! NOT FOR LONG ANYWAY!
AMD

WOW! A POND! THIS MUST BE MY LUCKY DAY!
IT'S BEEN MONTHS SINCE I'VE HAD ME A LITTLE SWIM!

WHA--?
SLOOP!

YICK! THIS POND IS SO POLLUTED, THE WATER HAS CHANGED INTO SOME SORT OF ICKY, STICKY GLOP!

I'M STUCK IN HERE! CAN'T GET OUT!
IF ONLY I COULD REACH THAT BRANCH OVER THERE!

NOW, I'VE GOT TO FIGURE SOME WAY TO DEFEAT THAT DUCK!
WOW! THIS CERTAINLY IS A MESS!

WAIT A MINUTE! I'VE GOT A PLAN, AND IT JUST MIGHT WORK!
CLICK!
NEXT TIME I'LL TURN THE TABLES, AND HE'LL LOOK LIKE THE JERK!

HELP, UNDERDOG, HELP!
WHEW! SOUNDS LIKE I CAME UP WITH MY PLAN JUST IN TIME!

ALREADY THAT RUBBER DUCK IS COMMITTING AN-OTHER CRIME!

BEFORE I SHOW UP AT THE BANK, I'VE GOT SOMETHING ELSE TO DO, SO I'D BETTER MOVE FAST!
THIS MAY NOT BE THAT DUCK'S FIRST CRIME, BUT I PLAN TO MAKE IT HIS LAST!

MEANWHILE...
THAT'S IT! JUST HAND OVER ALL THAT LOVELY MONEY!

GEE, I WONDER WHERE UNDERDOG IS!
I WAS HOPING HE'D SHOW UP SO I COULD MAKE A FOOL OUT OF HIM AGAIN!

LET'S NOT FORGET THE POGO-MASTER! HE HAS BEEN A REAL THORN IN UNDER-DOG'S SIDE...
I'LL PUT UNDERDOG IN HIS PLACE!

AND HOW EXACTLY TO DEFEAT THE SODA JERK OUR HERO HAS OFTEN HAD TO DECIDE...
I'LL SPRAY HIM RIGHT IN THE FACE!

BUT ALL THESE SUPERSTRONG VILLAINS WERE MERE CHILD'S PLAY...
HO-HUM!

...WHEN COMPARED TO THE FOE UNDERDOG WILL HAVE TO FIGHT TODAY!
GOOD GRIEF! I WAS ABOUT TO FALL ASLEEP, BUT NOW I'M FULLY AWAKE...
...BECAUSE SOMETHING SOMEWHERE IS REALLY MAKING MY HOUSE SHAKE!

HEY, UNDER-DOG! WHEREVER YOU ARE, COME OUT SO I CAN BEAT THE TAR OUT OF YOU!
WHA--?

IF SOME-ONE'S GOING TO CHALLENGE ME, I THINK HE OUGHT TO DO IT TO MY FACE!

AH! THERE'S THE LOUD-MOUTH WHO SHOUTED!
HE'S BIG, BUT I'LL PUT HIM IN HIS PLACE!

Go Go Gophers Storyboard

CUT · SGT WIGGLES FINGER IN
EAR – WINCES AT NOISE – PULLS
BACK A LITTLE FROM RADIO
CONT: eeeeeeee!

PULL BACK ·
SARG: I guess he means fire.

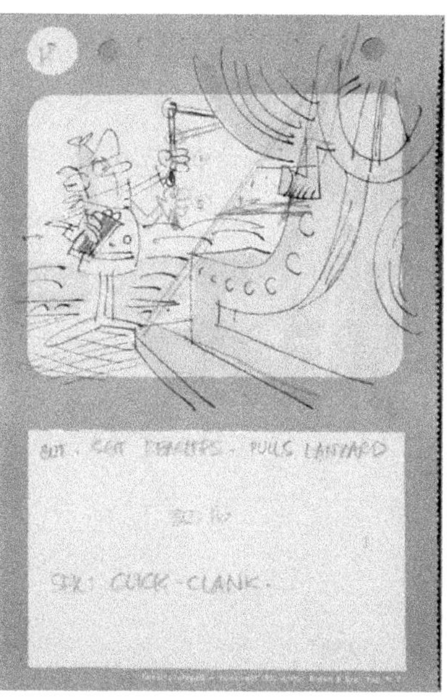
CUT · SGT PULLS LANYARD
SFX: CLICK · CLANK ·

CUT · COL LOOKS UP FOLLOWING
BALL ·
SFX: SHRILL WHINE UP TO PEAK

SAME BKG
HEAD TURN
COL · FOLLOWS BALL WITH HEAD
SFX: WHINE STARTS DOWN –

CUT TO PEACEFUL TEEPEE
SFX: WHINE DOWN ALMOST
TO END

BIG EXPLOSION IN FRONT · SC.
SHAKES HARD ·
SFX: KARRRUMP!

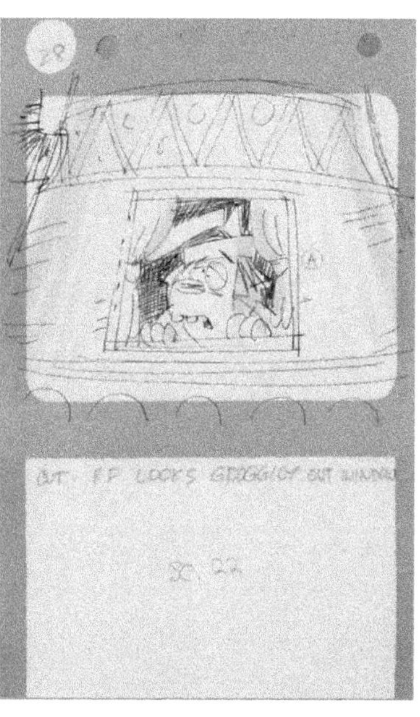
SC. 22

CUT TO CU AS FF REACTS
SC. 23

CONT:fonthrlldikgkwcannon

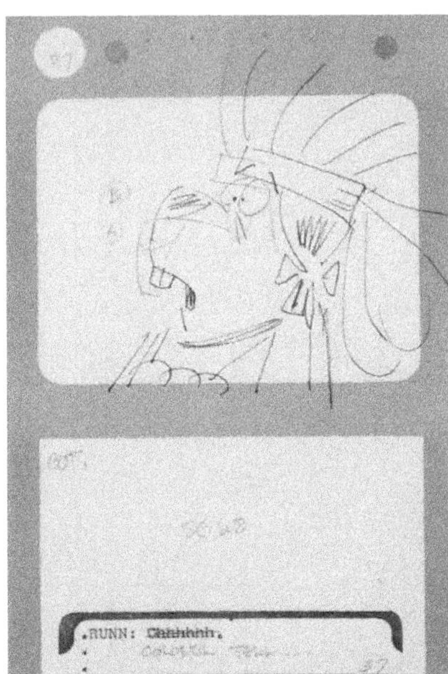
CUT.
.RUNN: [illegible].

.CONT: Colonel tell Sergeant
.where to fire cannon.

CUT
SC. 29

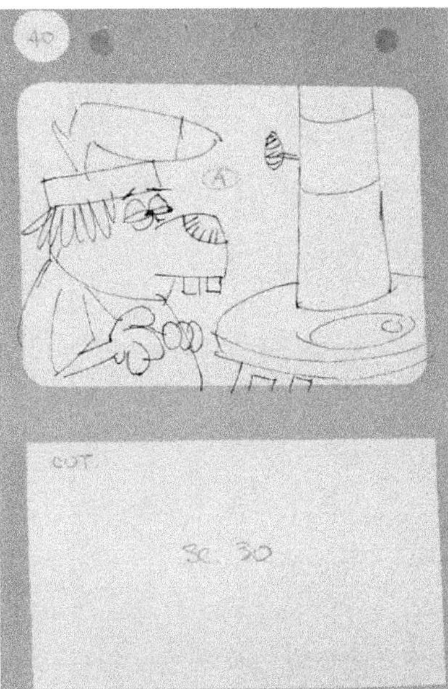
CUT.
Sc. 30

CUT.
Sc. 32

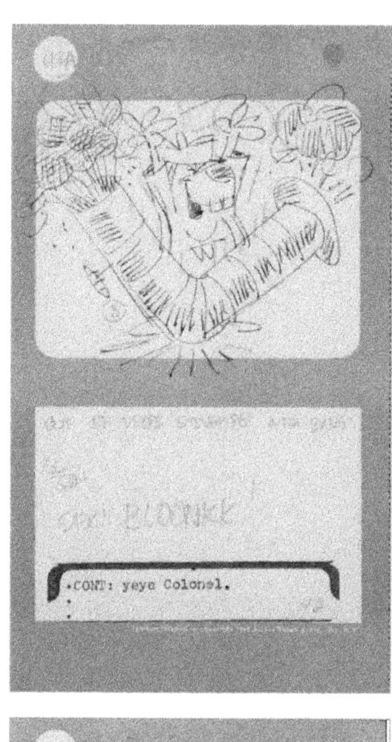
SFX: BLOONK
CONT: yeye Colonel.

OUT:
SC. 33

OUT:
RUNN: Whoopee, doopee, we

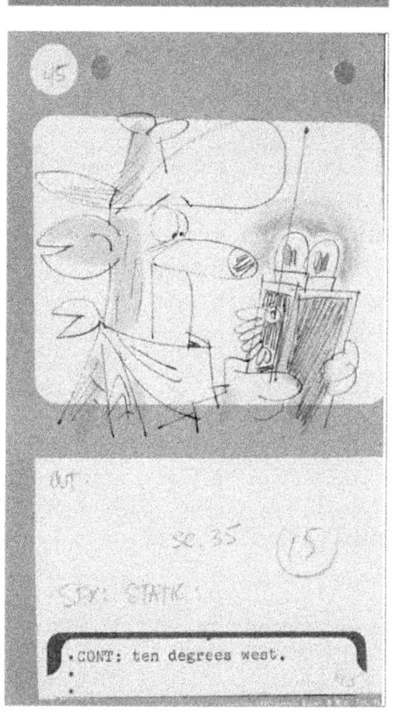
OUT:
SC. 35
15
SFX: STATIC
CONT: ten degrees west.

OUT: SGT CRANKS
11
SC. 36
SFX: CLANKING

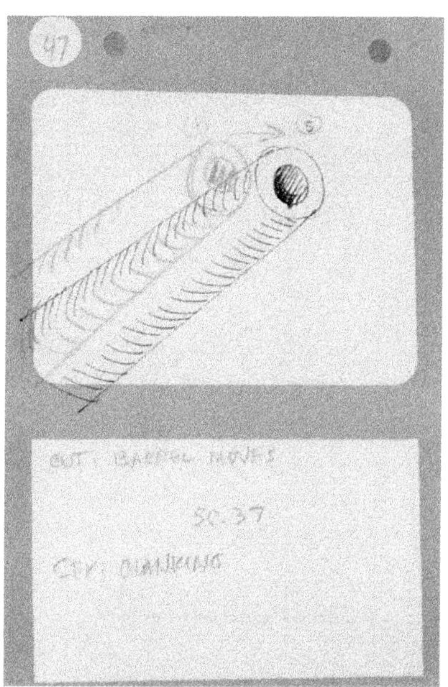
OUT: BARREL MOVES
SC. 37
SFX: CLANKING

OUT: SGT SALUTES
10
SC. 38
SARG: Ready, Colonel.

OUT:
SC 39
COL: THEN...

OUT:
COL: Then, chargeeeeeeeee

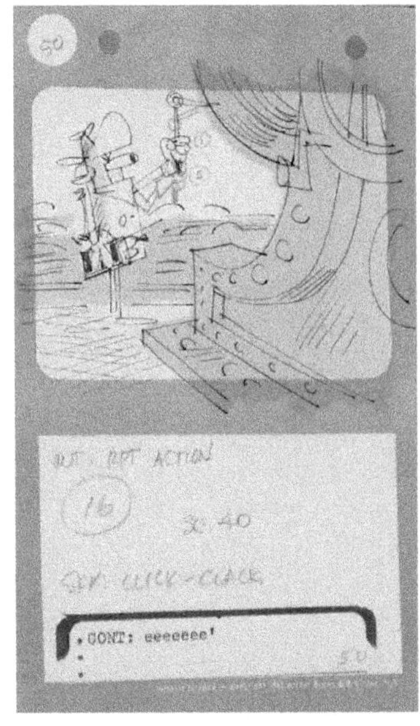
CUT: RPT ACTION
16
SC. 40
SFX: CLICK-CLACK
CONT: eeeeeee!

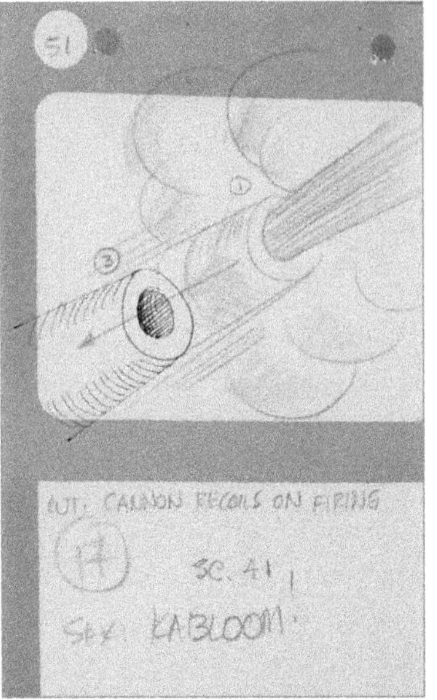
CUT: CANNON RECOILS ON FIRING
17
SC. 41
SFX: KABLOOM!

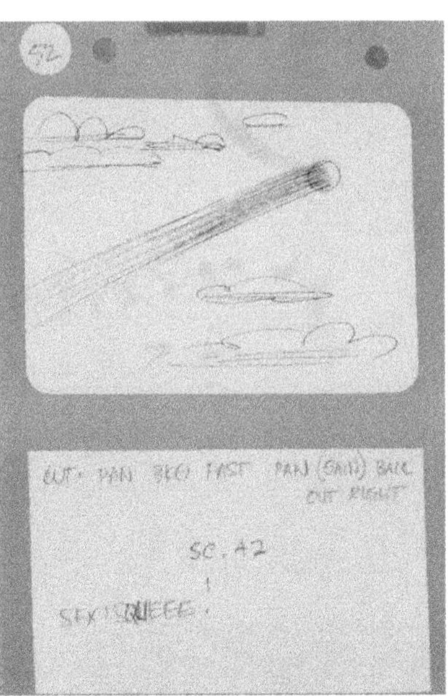
SC. 42
SFX: SQUEEE!

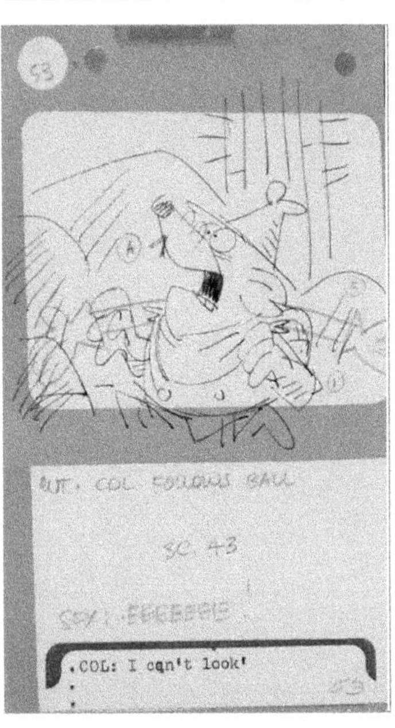
CUT: COL. FOLLOWS BALL
SC. 43
SFX: EEEEEEE!
COL: I can't look!

COL COVERS EYES
SFX: START WHINE DOWN—

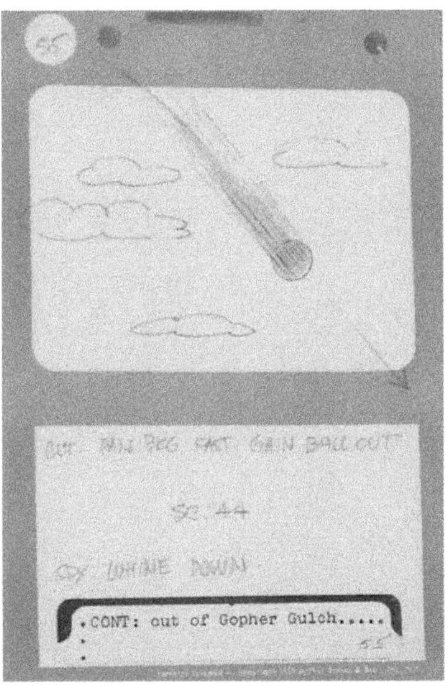
SC. 44
SFX: WHINE DOWN
CONT: out of Gopher Gulch.....

CUT: ZOOM TO CU TOP TEEPEE
SC. 45
SFX: WHINE LOUDER

HOLD TEEPEE TOP WIGGLES
SFX: WHINE LOUDER

TOP POPS BACK - GOPHERS POP UP
WITH CURVED STOVEPIPE
SFX: CONT.

59

60
GO-41
OUT: ZIP BALL THROUGH LEFT
SC. 46
SFX: PHWEEE!

61
OUT: COL UNCOVERS EYE.
SC. 47
SFX: WHISTLE LOUDER...
CONT: The cannon ball seems to

61A

62
COL TURNS
SFX: CONT
CONT: and closer and ...

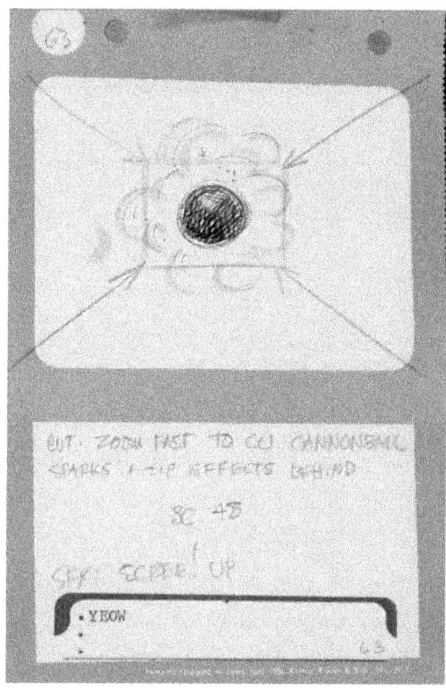
63
SC. 48
YEOW

64
OUT.
SC. 49
SFX: CONT
CONT: ywwwwwww

65
SFX: CONT

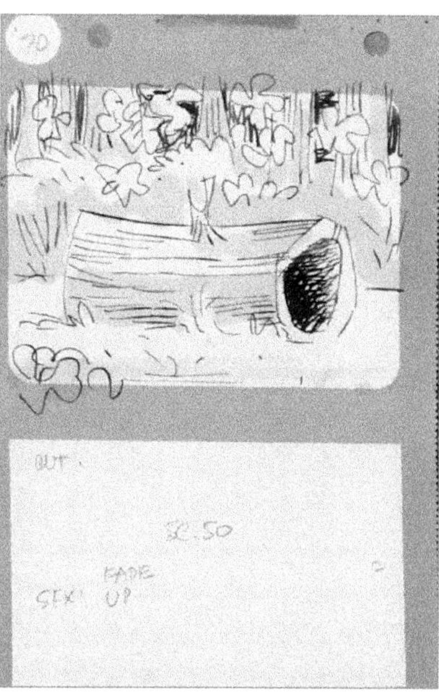
70
OUT.
SC. 50
FADE
SFX: UP

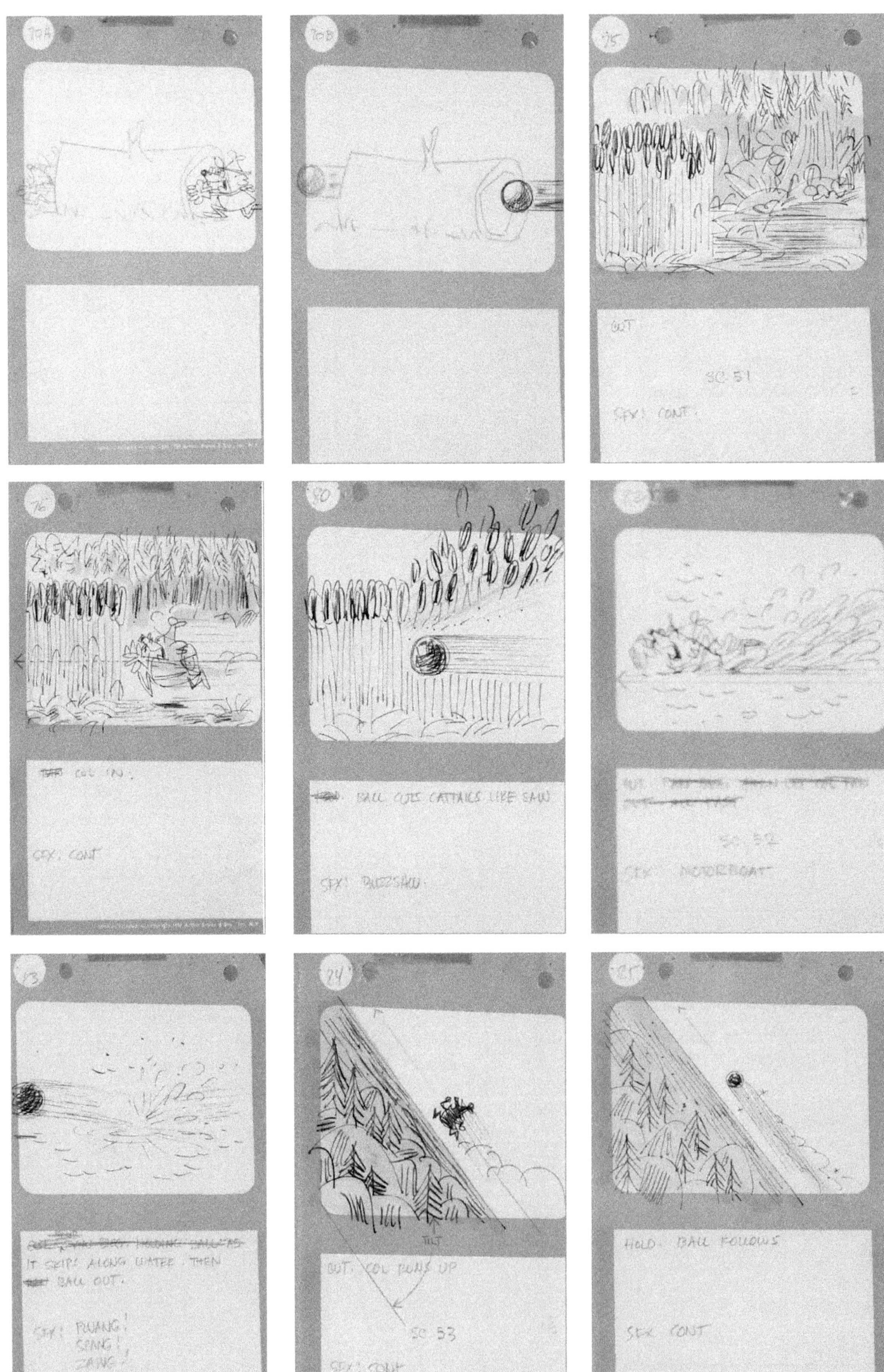
OUT
SC 51
SFX: CONT.
COL IN.
SFX: CONT
BALL CUTS CATTAILS LIKE SAW
SFX: BUZZSAW
SC 52
SFX: MOTORBOAT
IT SKIPS ALONG WATER. THEN
BALL OUT.
SFX: PWANG!
SPANG!
ZANG!
TILT
OUT. COL RUNS UP
SC 53
SFX: CONT
HOLD. BALL FOLLOWS
SFX: CONT

TILT
CUT · COL RUNS DOWN
SC. 54
SFX: CONT

BALL ZIPS DOWN
SFX: CONT

CUT · PAN BKG ·
SC. 55
SFX: CONT

HOLD BKG AT CAVE
HOLD MOMENTARILY ·
BG WILL PAN MORE TO RIGHT ·
SO COL IS INTO CAVE
SFX: CONT THEN FADE OUT

CUT · COL BEHIND ROCK PANTING HEAVILY ·
SC. 56
SFX: HEAVY PANTING.
NO OTHER NOISE

CUT · BALL ZOOMS INTO CAVE
SC. 57
SFX: GO INTO ECHO ·

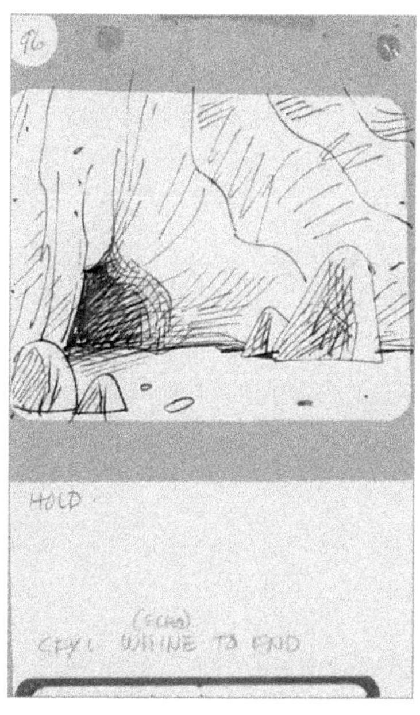
HOLD ·
(ECHO)
SFX: WHINE TO END

F.O.
SC SHAKE · EXPLOSION F.O.
SFX: KA BROOMMM ·

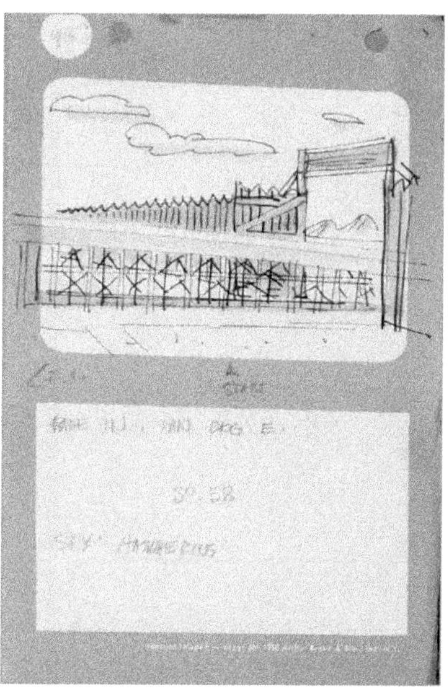
SC. 58

CONT: but it won't happen this time.

SARG: What are we building now, Colonel?

COL: A bowling trough -

CONT: one end and will be here where you will start the cannon ball

CONT: at the Gopher Indian tepee.
SARG: Wow!!!

CONT: Seems like we can't miss

COLL: (WHISPERING) All right
Sergeant, the bowling trough
is finished.

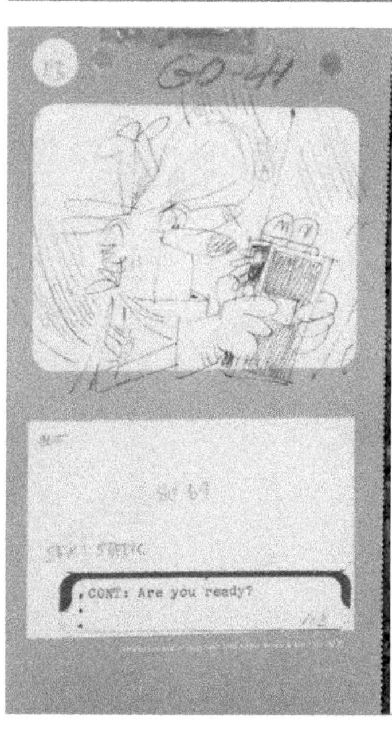
GO-41
CONT: Are you ready?

SC. 69
SARG: Ready, Colonel.

CUT. SAME AS SC. 14

COL: chargeeeeee

CUT. SAME AS SC. 50
SFX: CLICK BT-
CONT: eeeeeee

SFX: FADE IN RUMBLE

CUT: R.F. HOLDS UP HAND,
LOOKS UP, WILL IT RAIN?
SC. 75
SFX: RUMBLE UP

CUT: RF PUZZLED –
SC. 77
SFX: RUMBLE UP

RF TURNS
SFX: CONT

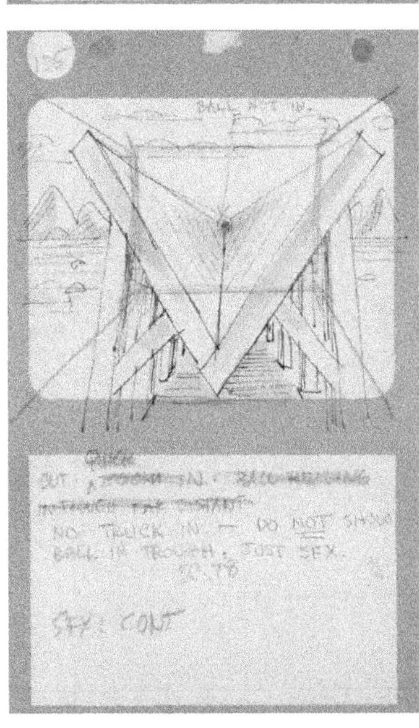
CUT: QUICK
NO TRUCK IN — DO NOT SHOW
BALL IN TROUGH, JUST SFX.
SC. 78
SFX: CONT

CUT.
SC. 79
SFX: CONT

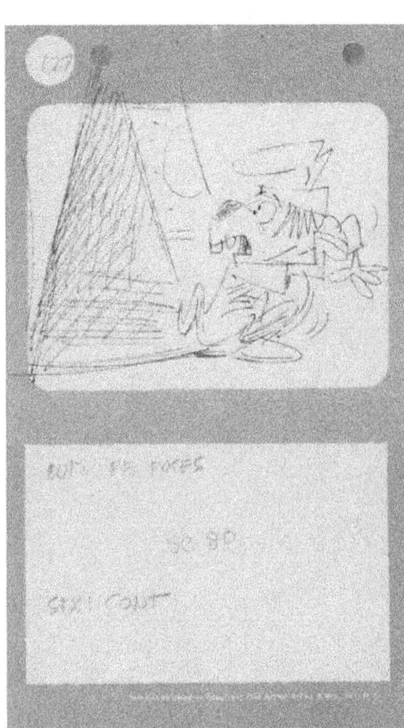
SFX: CONT

SC. 82
SFX: THUD!
CONT: kdktpybowl.

SFX: THUD!
RUNN: Uh, oh.

SC. 83

CONT: ~~Tepee~~ like tenpid.
133

SC. 84
CONT: What we do?

SFX: ZIP!

CUT. THEY ZIP OUT TO TROUGH
SFX: ZIP

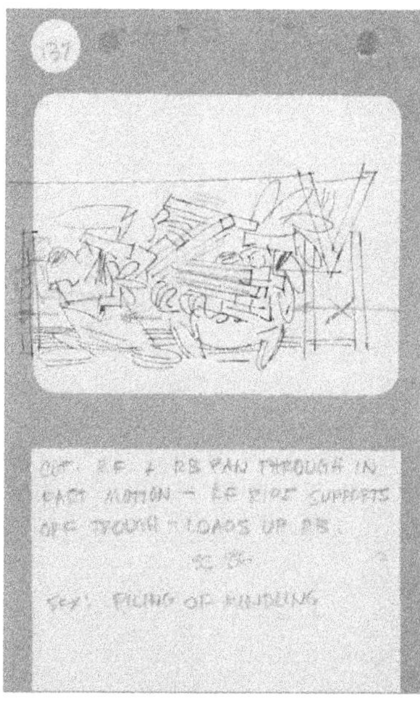
CUT: RF & RB PAN THROUGH IN FAST MOTION – RF RIPS SUPPORTS OFF TROUGH – LOADS UP RB.
SFX: PILING OF KINDLING

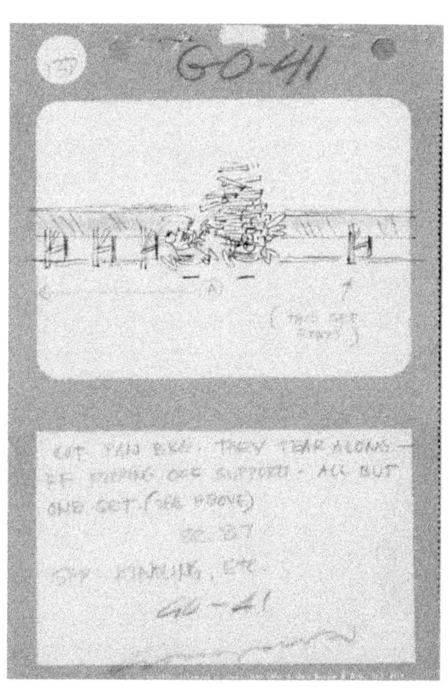
GO-41
SC. 87

RB BRAKES
SFX: BRAKES

SFX: RUMBLE
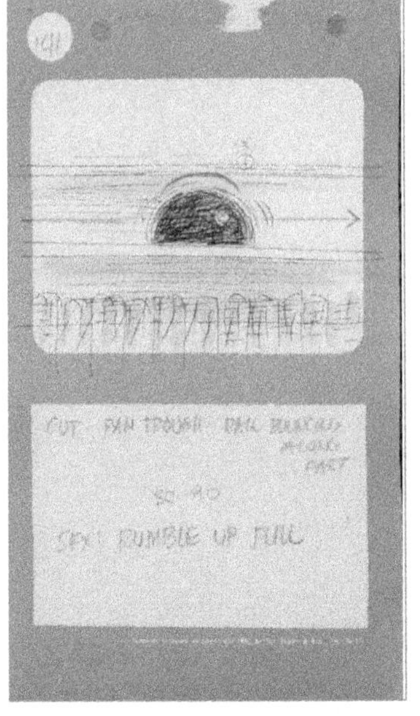
SFX: RUMBLE UP FULL

BALL PASSES– THEY TURN
SFX: BALL UP THEN DOWN
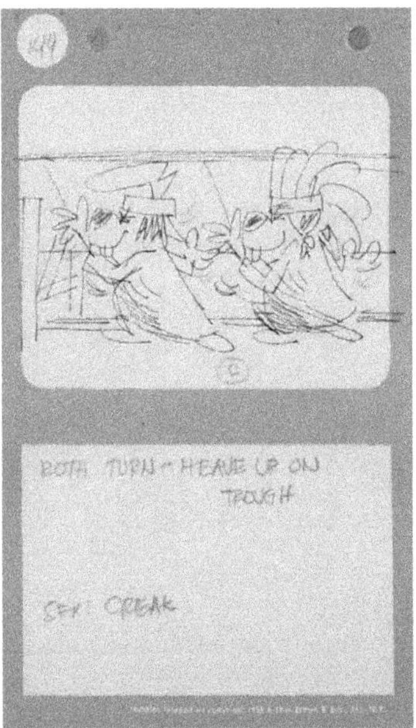
BOTH TURN– HEAVE UP ON TROUGH
SFX: CREAK

COL: I can't bear to watch it.
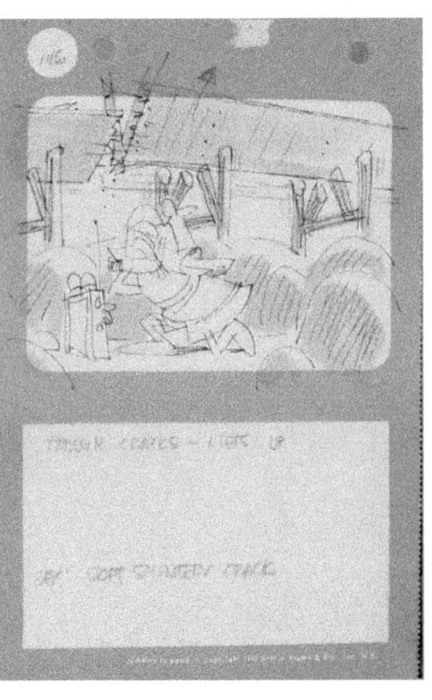

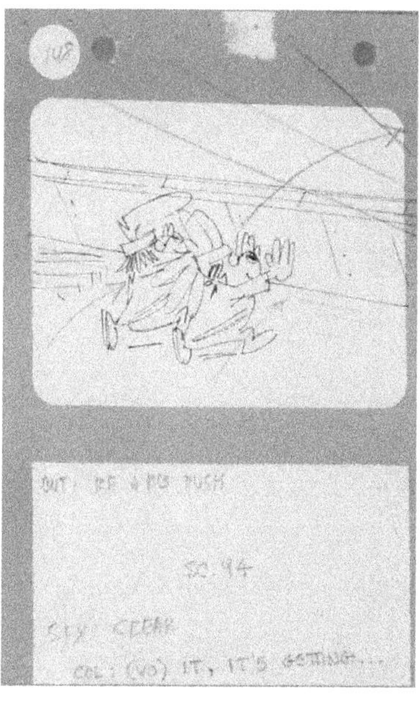
148
SC. 94
SFX: CREAK
COL: (VO) IT, IT'S GETTING...

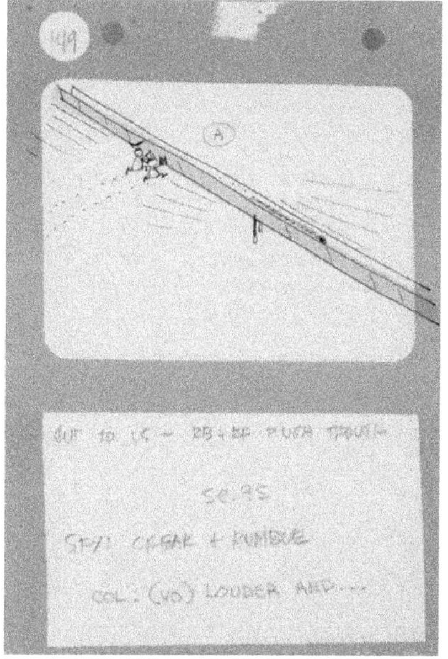
149
SC. 95
SFX: CREAK & RUMBLE
COL: (VO) LOUDER AND...

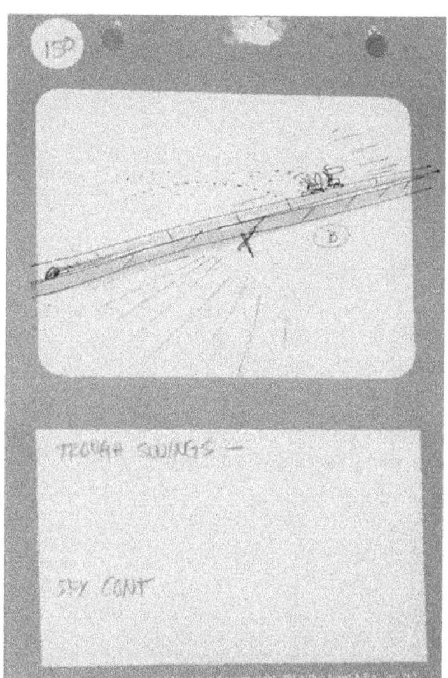
150
TROUGH SWINGS —
SFX CONT

151
CUT: END SWINGS & STOPS BEHIND COL.
SC. 96
SFX: RUMBLE
COL: LOUDER...

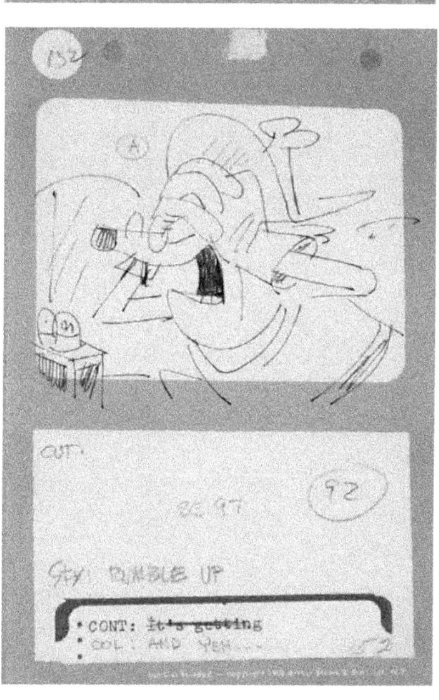
152
CUT.
SC. 97
SFX: RUMBLE UP
CONT: It's getting
COL: AND YEH...

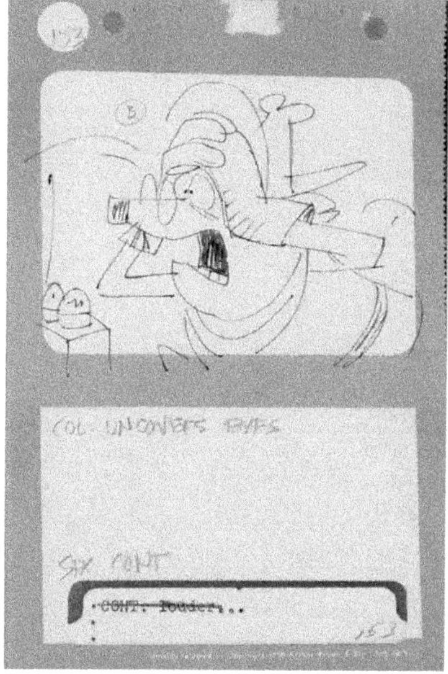
153
COL: UNCOVERS EYES
SFX CONT
CONT: louder...

154
CUT: TROUGH QUIVERS
SC. 98
SFX: CONT
CONT: and louder....

155
COL TURNS.
SFX CONT
CONT: and

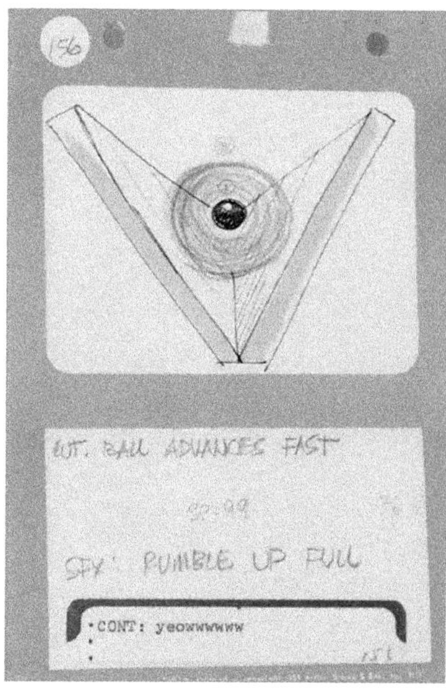
156
CUT. BALL ADVANCES FAST
SC. 99
SFX: RUMBLE UP FULL
CONT: yeowwwwwww

CUT. COL RUNS IN PLACE
SC.100
SFX CONT
RPT
SC.102
SAME AS SC.51
S. B. 75
RPT
SC.103
SAME AS SC.52
S. B. 82
RPT
SC.104
SAME AS SC.53
S. B. 84
RPT.
SC.105
SAME AS SC.54
S. B. 86
RPT
SC.106
SAME AS SC.55
S. B. 91
RPT
CUT: COL NOW CROUCHED BEHIND ROCK
SC.107
SFX: PANTING
GO-41
F.I.
F.I. ON BUSH. TOP RUSTLES.
SC.119
SFX: BOOP-BOOP + RUSTLING

COL. WALKS FROM BEHIND BUSH
(HAT WAS TOP OF BUSH)
SFX: BOOP BOOP

PAN. TEEPEE BKG IN. COL.
HOOKS HOMER ON
SFX: CONT BOOPS
CONT: I'm putting the himing d

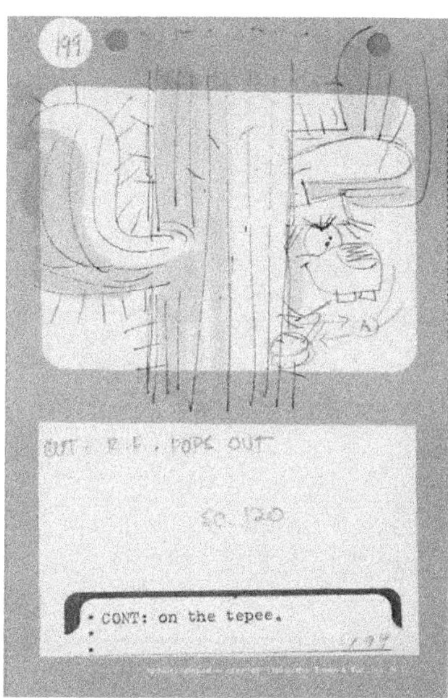
OUT. R.F. POPS OUT
SC. 120
CONT: on the tepee.

OUT. COL. DRAWING BACK
SC. 121
CONT: I'm

COL. TURNS. DOES NOT SEE R.F.
CONT: creeping

OUT R.F. GRABS HOMER
SC. 122
ENCENDER Y APAGAR APARATO
CADA OCHO CUADROS.

ENCENDER Y APAGAR APARATO
CADA 8 CUADROS
SC. 123

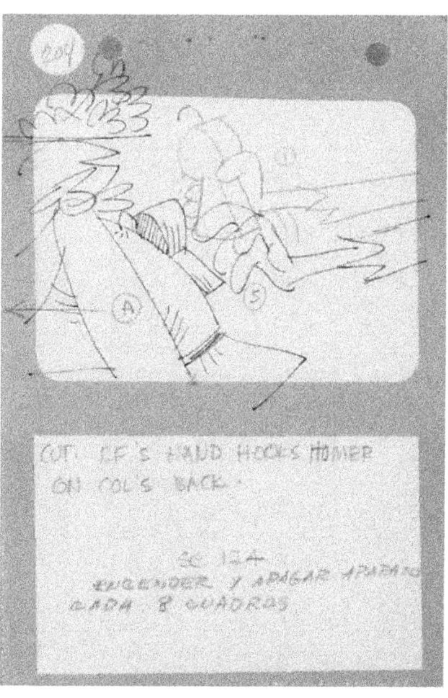
OUT. RF'S HAND HOOKS HOMER
ON COL'S BACK.
SC. 124
ENCENDER Y APAGAR APARATO
CADA 8 CUADROS

OUT. COL RUNS INTO LITTLE
AREA AMONG BOULDERS
SC. 125
ENCENDER Y APAGAR APARATO
CADA OCHO CUADROS.
CONT:

206
MOVE
CONT: chargeeeeeeeee'

207
CUT – RPT
SC. 126
SFX: RPT.

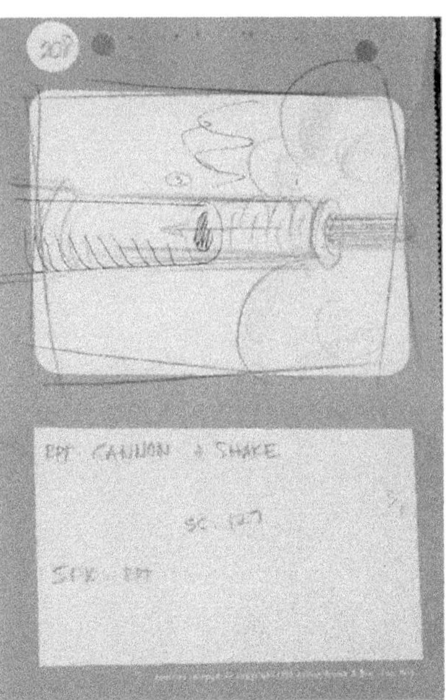
208
RPT CANNON & SHAKE
SC. 127
SFX: RPT

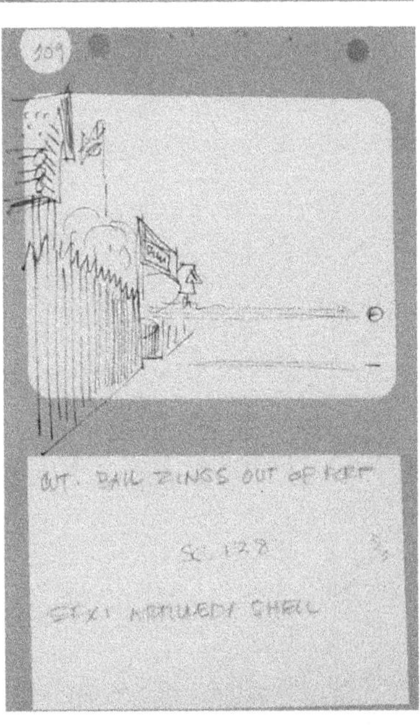
209
CUT: BALL ZINGS OUT OF FORT
SC. 128
SFX: ARTILLERY SHELL

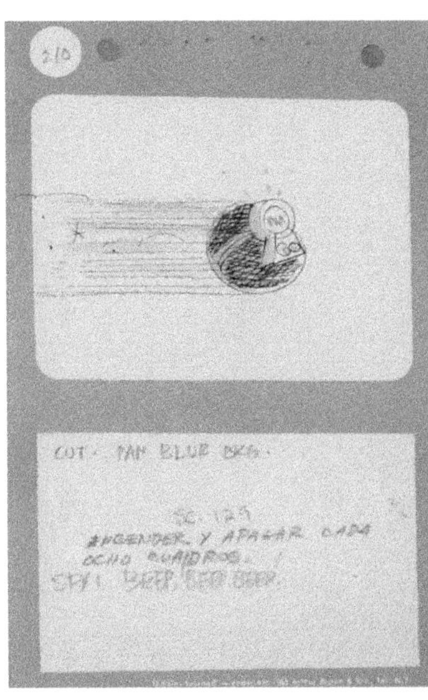
210
CUT: PAN BLUR BKG.
SC. 129
ENCENDER Y APAGAR CADA
OCHO CUADROS.
SFX: BEEP BEEP BEEP.

211
CUT
SC. 130
SFX: SHELL MOVE UP

212
HOLD: BALL ZIPS IN
APAGAR Y ENCENDER
CADA 8 CUADROS.

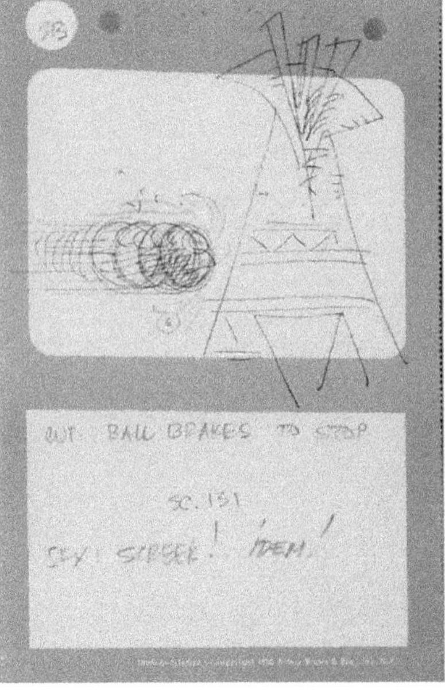
213
CUT: BALL BRAKES TO STOP
SC. 131
SFX: SCREEE! ¡IDEM!

214
CUT. BALL TURNS — HOMER
FACES WEST
SC. 132 ¡IDEM!
SFX: BEEP BEEP

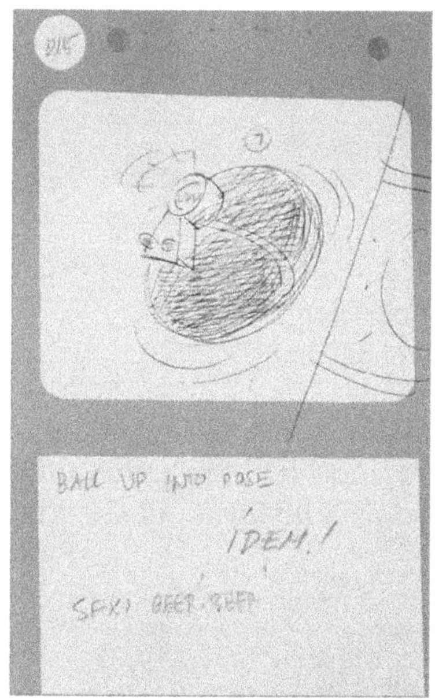
BALL UP INTO POSE
IDEM!
SFX: BEEP BEEP

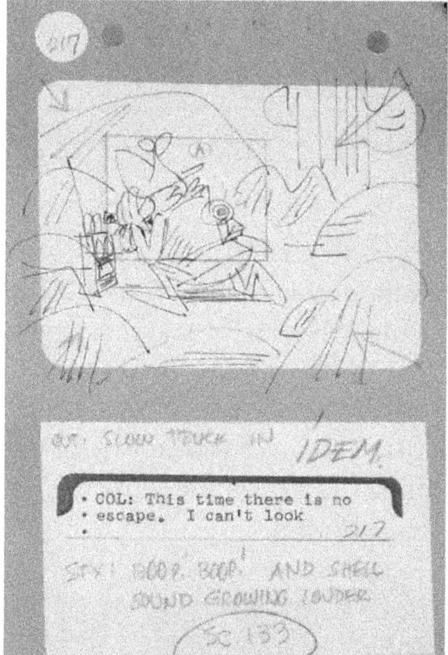
IDEM.
COL: This time there is no escape. I can't look
SFX: BOOP BOOP AND SHELL SOUND GROWING LOUDER
SC 133

IDEM.
SFX: CONT
CONT: It's getting louder,,, and louder...

CUT
APAGAR Y ENCEN
DER CADA 6
SC. 134 CUADROS

COL TURNS
IDEM.
SFX: UP
CONT: and

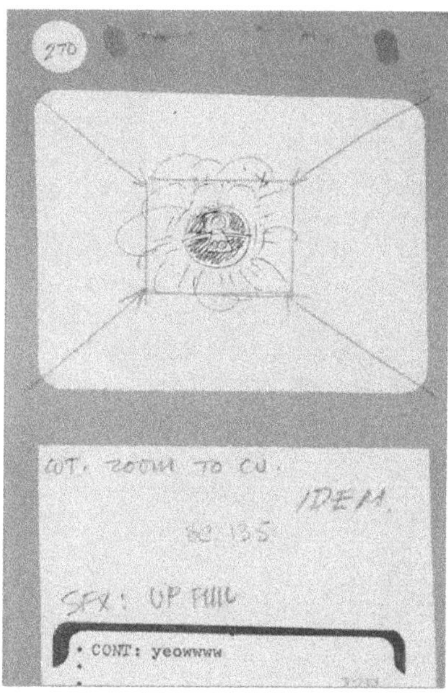
CUT: ZOOM TO CU.
IDEM.
SC. 135
SFX: UP FULL
CONT: yeowwww

SC. 150
SARG: Maybe'

FREE! ACTION GAME FOR YOUR CARTOON CARNIVAL
COLLECT ALL EIGHT and HAVE A CARNIVAL OF FUN, EVERY DAY
GAME RULES
Place "Bent Feather" about 1 foot from booth; load arrow, aim and shoot at bullseye. Each player takes 5 shots. Player with the most bullseyes wins.
CUT ON ALL RED DOTTED LINES
FOLD ON ALL BLUE DOTTED LINES
"BENT FEATHER"
GO, GO GOPHER ARROW SHOOT!

7 The Macy's Thanksgiving Day Parade Underdog Balloon

by Bill Smith

Image/photo credit for this chapter: The Bill Smith Collection
On particular pictures that I have taken myself - Photo: Bill Smith

I am excited about your book and the inclusion of the Macy's balloon! I have been called upon by Macy's, Goodyear and NBC for archival materials and historical factoids and am recognized as a historian of the Macy's Parade and the balloons.

I own my own balloon company, Smith Special Productions / Balloonworks, which has been in the business of designing and creating large figure balloons that have appeared in parades and special events since 1987. While my balloons do not appear in the Macy's Parade, I am fortunate enough to do seasonal work for Macy's with their balloon program and the parade each year. My job is to coordinate the movement of the balloons to deflation after they pass through the NBC television zone on West 34th Street. I have been to the parade since 1975, and have participated and worked on it since 2002. I have watched every parade on NBC from 1963 until 1974. Macy's Parade is a part of my life.

I had the good fortune to know many of the employees of The Goodyear Tire and Rubber Company and In my personal collection, I have many many treasured photographs and drawings and blueprints that were given to me. I have one of the largest single archives of Macy's parade materials and memorabilia outside of Macy's themselves.

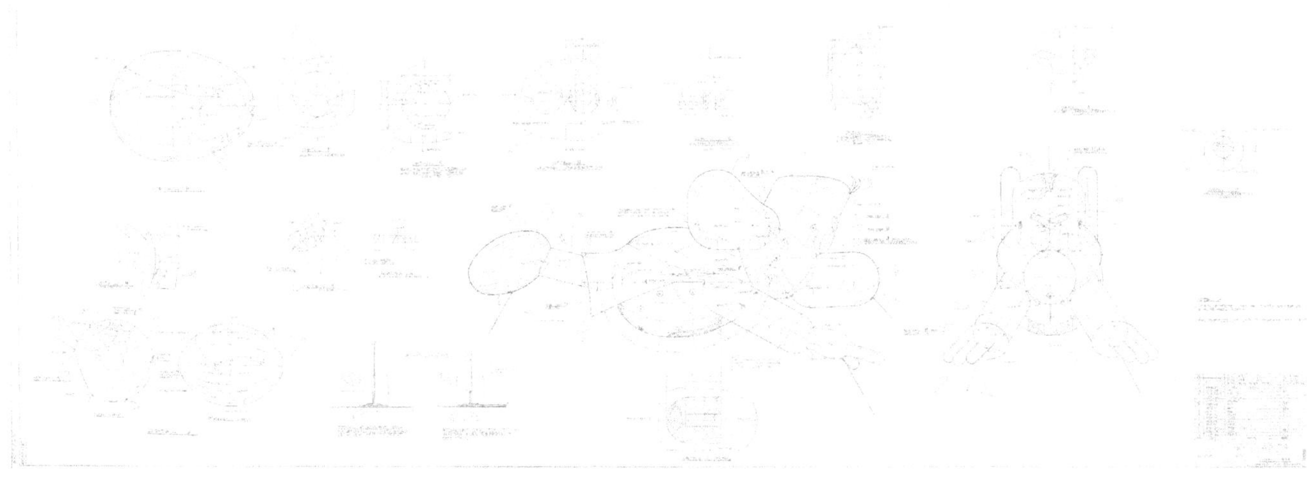

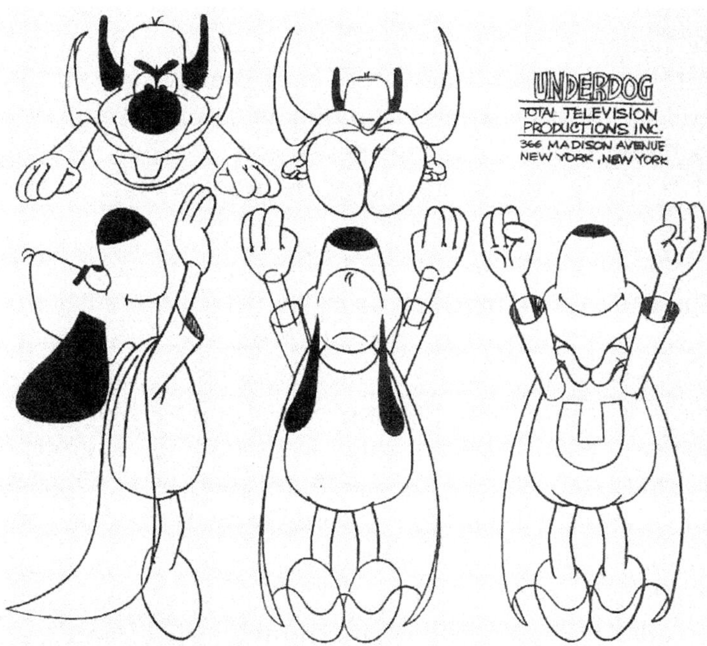

This is the actual blueprint / mechanical drawing for Macy's Underdog balloon from 1965. This blueprint is the actual Goodyear Tire and Rubber Company drawings from which the balloon was created. As you will see, it is highly detailed and quite informative.

Next is the Joe Harris balloon model sheet which was given to Macy's, then passed along to Goodyear to create the mechanical drawings from. If you study closely, you will see that Goodyear's engineer stayed as close to Harris' art as possible, and the balloon form of the pose is composed of geometric shapes joined together to create one visual "envelope." Considering the technology available in 1965, I'd say the balloon is pretty incredible.

The following information pertains to the Macy's Underdog balloon that was designed and created in 1965.

The project originally began as NBC television (who held Broadcast rights to the Macy's Parade) was also the network which broadcast the animated series *The Underdog Show*. High on Macy's list of potential licensed characters was Underdog.

In the spring of 1965, conversations began with NBC and TTV (Total TeleVision) about the prospect of Underdog becoming a balloon. Upon negotiating a deal, TTV artist Joe Harris submitted a series of drawings and a model sheet of the pose that would lend itself well from an aerodynamic standpoint, while capturing the spirit of the animated cartoon character, the flying pose.

Macy's sent the artwork and some color renderings of the character over to Goodyear at the end of June 1965. The mechanical drawings were done and approved on July 25, 1965. Goodyear Engineer Sid Smith added the final touches and on July 29, 1965, the balloon began its production at The Goodyear Tire and Rubber Company's Rockmart, Georgia facility. Two and a half months later - the finished canine superhero was packed in a large wooden crate and trucked to Akron, Ohio and the waiting hands of Goodyear and project engineer William "Bill" Ludwick and Goodyear's Frank Jenkins, who directed the balloons down the parade route for 30 years prior and was retiring after the 1965 parade.

Underdog, completed and ready for his first helium test flight at the Goodyear Wingfoot Lake blimp hangar in Akron, Ohio was held on Monday, October 11, 1965. It was a sunny yet windy morning and Underdog was inflated inside the very same hanger which was home to the Goodyear Blimps. A private inflation with all parties present and Goodyear's photographers and film crew on the scene, Underdog awakened from the hanger and like a dog emerging from a colossal doghouse, Underdog sailed out into the sunshine for his "test flight" and 31 strong volunteers, many the production crew and Goodyear employees.

A vast amount of footage was shot in color and from this extensive footage, approximately one minute was edited for a film that would be distributed by The Goodyear Tire and Rubber Company to NBC and other media sources and Macy's for pre-parade publicity. Filmed at Goodyear's Wingfoot Lake property, a group of children are playing ring-around-a-rosy when suddenly Underdog appears from behind a huge log structure. The scene fades to a group of children standing inside the blimp hanger as workers inflate the huge balloon - once fully inflated, 31 handlers "walk the dog" out of the huge doorway of the hanger into the sunshine.

Underdog (the balloon) does some "push-ups" and covers a Volkswagen with one of his huge hands. The balloon flies around the airfield and then returns to the hanger where he is deflated and packaged for his big trip to New York for the his big day - as Underdog will become the 85th balloon constructed by Goodyear for the 39th Annual Macy's Thanksgiving Day Parade on November 25, 1965.

Underdog made his debut in the parade joined by other Goodyear balloons of Sinclair Oil Companies Dino The Dinosaur, Borden's Elsie The Cow, Bullwinkle, Donald Duck, Linus The Lionhearted and Popeye The Sailor Man and The Happy Dragon. Eight balloons in all.

It may interest you to know that the engineers who worked on the Macy's balloons were in fact aerospace engineers. The same dynamics were involved in creating good old Underdog!

Next is a series of images of Underdog in his "test flight" in Akron, Ohio. The two shots of the balloon tethered to sandbags were taken inside of Goodyear's Wingfoot Lake blimp hangar. The other three images were taken on the airfield outside of the hangar. As you can see, it was a breezy day. The balloon was filled with a helium/air mixture for this occasion, with enough lift for flight to "show off" the balloon and get photos and film footage.

The Underdog balloon was built at The Goodyear Tire and Rubber Company in Rockmart, Georgia in 1965. The balloon was trucked to Akron, Ohio for this test flight. Upon completion, he was repacked and trucked to NYC Thanksgiving week - 1965 for his very first Macy's Thanksgiving Day Parade appearance.

The photographs were publicity photos courtesy The Goodyear Tire and Rubber Company, and were used by Macy's and Goodyear and NBC for PR purposes. These images were given to me by a friend at Goodyear when I was in my teens.

Coming next - parade images! Here are some assorted Macy's Underdog balloon related visuals.

biggest
store
TURNS

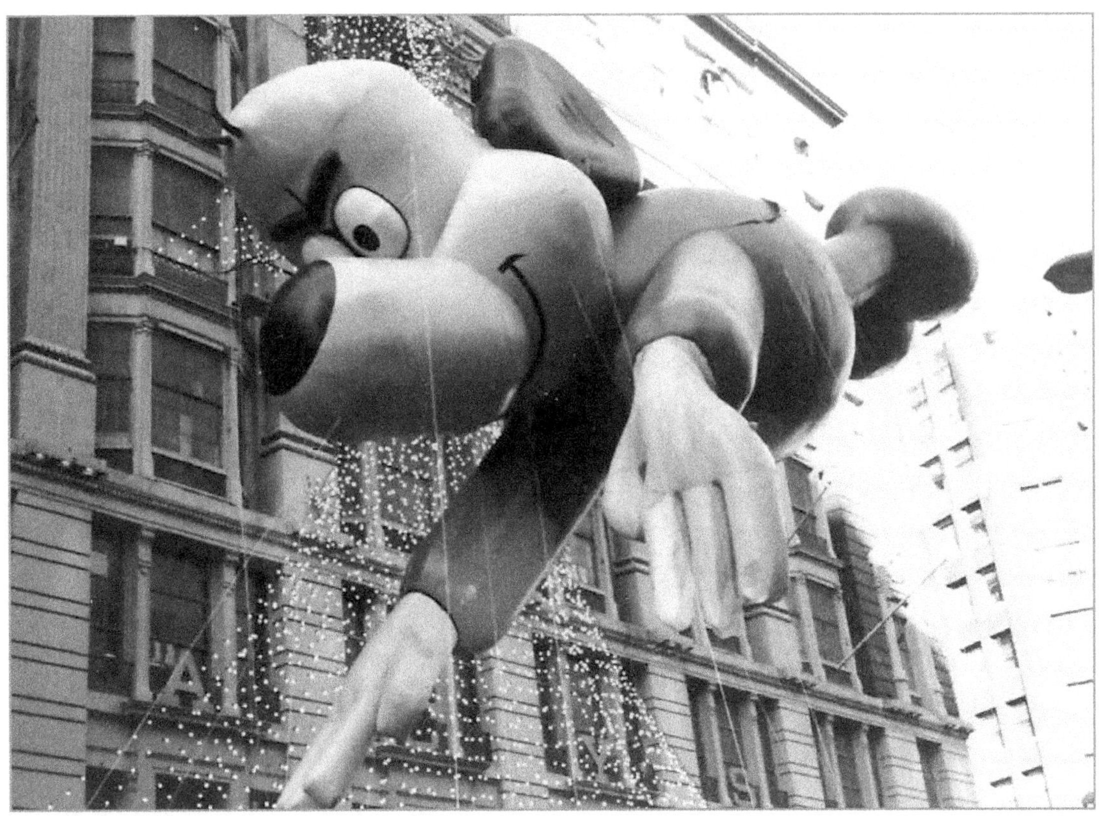

The promotional 45 RPM record that was produced to commemorate the balloon in the parade in 1965. There was a special dust jacket that was printed, and that copy of the record was included in Macy's Parade 1965 Press Kit which was distributed to news media, radio stations, television and talk shows and children's shows. As you can see, there was also a cover that featured the title of the cartoon that aired on NBC immediately following the Macy's Parade telecast.

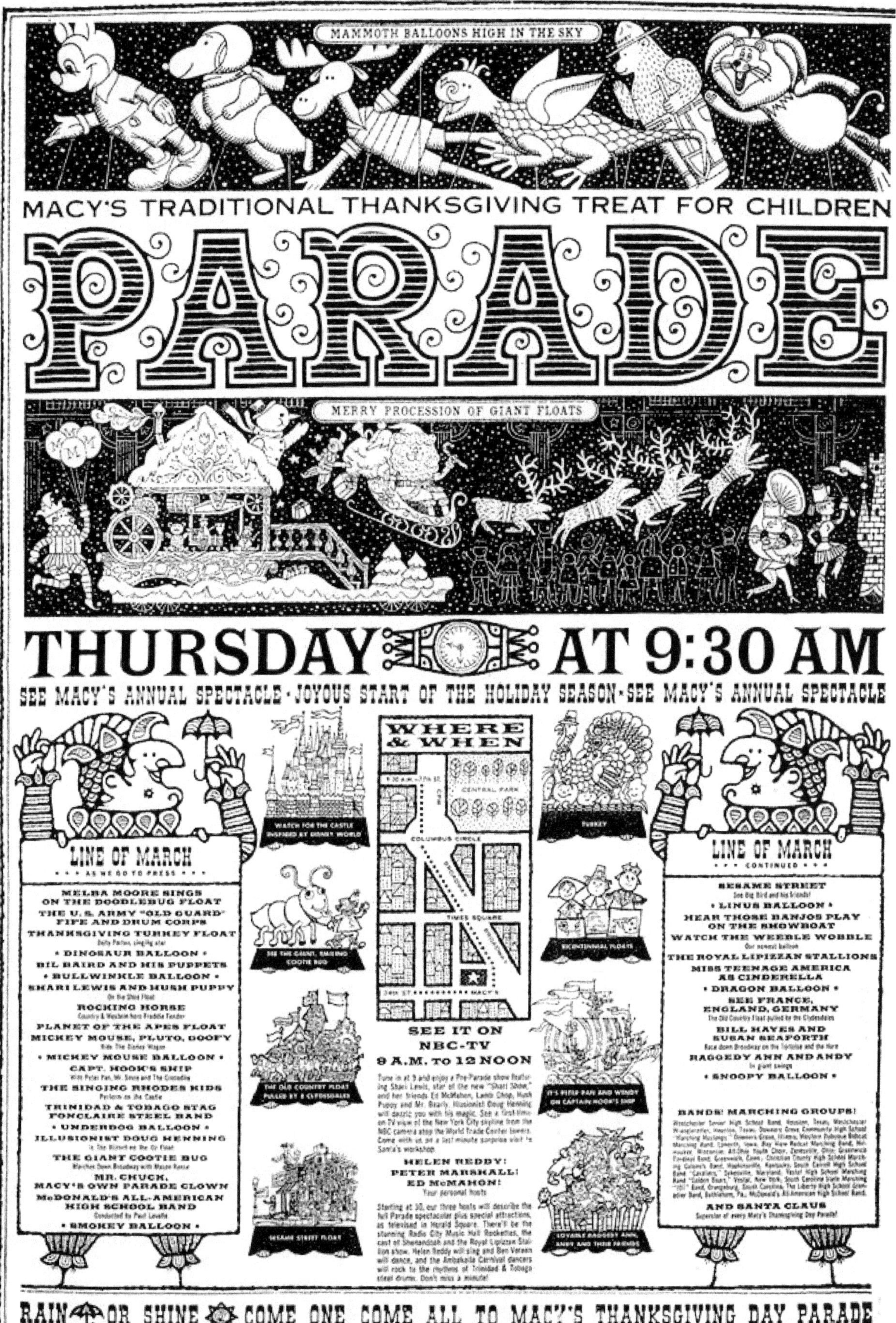
MAMMOTH BALLOONS HIGH IN THE SKY
MACY'S TRADITIONAL THANKSGIVING TREAT FOR CHILDREN
PARADE
MERRY PROCESSION OF GIANT FLOATS
THURSDAY AT 9:30 AM
SEE MACY'S ANNUAL SPECTACLE · JOYOUS START OF THE HOLIDAY SEASON · SEE MACY'S ANNUAL SPECTACLE
LINE OF MARCH
AS WE GO TO PRESS
MELBA MOORE SINGS ON THE DOODLEBUG FLOAT
THE U.S. ARMY "OLD GUARD" FIFE AND DRUM CORPS
THANKSGIVING TURKEY FLOAT
• DINOSAUR BALLOON •
BIL BAIRD AND HIS PUPPETS
• BULLWINKLE BALLOON •
SHARI LEWIS AND HUSH PUPPY
ROCKING HORSE
PLANET OF THE APES FLOAT
MICKEY MOUSE, PLUTO, GOOFY
• MICKEY MOUSE BALLOON •
CAPT. HOOK'S SHIP
THE SINGING RHODES KIDS
TRINIDAD & TOBAGO STAG FONCLAIRE STEEL BAND
• UNDERDOG BALLOON •
ILLUSIONIST DOUG HENNING
THE GIANT COOTIE BUG
MR. CHUCK, MACY'S OWN PARADE CLOWN
McDONALD'S ALL-AMERICAN HIGH SCHOOL BAND
• SMOKEY BALLOON •
WATCH FOR THE CASTLE INSPIRED BY DISNEY WORLD
SEE THE GIANT, SMILING COOTIE BUG
THE OLD COUNTRY FLOAT PULLED BY 8 CLYDESDALES
SESAME STREET FLOAT
WHERE & WHEN
CENTRAL PARK
COLUMBUS CIRCLE
TIMES SQUARE
34th ST
MACY'S
SEE IT ON NBC-TV
9 A.M. TO 12 NOON
HELEN REDDY!
PETER MARSHALL!
ED McMAHON!
Your personal hosts
TURKEY
BICENTENNIAL FLOATS
IT'S PETER PAN AND WENDY ON CAPTAIN HOOK'S SHIP
LOVABLE RAGGEDY ANN, ANDY AND THEIR FRIENDS
LINE OF MARCH
CONTINUED
SESAME STREET
• LINUS BALLOON •
HEAR THOSE BANJOS PLAY ON THE SHOWBOAT
WATCH THE WEEBLE WOBBLE
THE ROYAL LIPIZZAN STALLIONS
MISS TEENAGE AMERICA AS CINDERELLA
• DRAGON BALLOON •
SEE FRANCE, ENGLAND, GERMANY
BILL HAYES AND SUSAN SEAFORTH
RAGGEDY ANN AND ANDY
• SNOOPY BALLOON •
BANDS! MARCHING GROUPS!
AND SANTA CLAUS
RAIN OR SHINE COME ONE, COME ALL TO MACY'S THANKSGIVING DAY PARADE

Underdog "the balloon" was featured on a number of magazines including *TV Magazine* and *The New Yorker*.

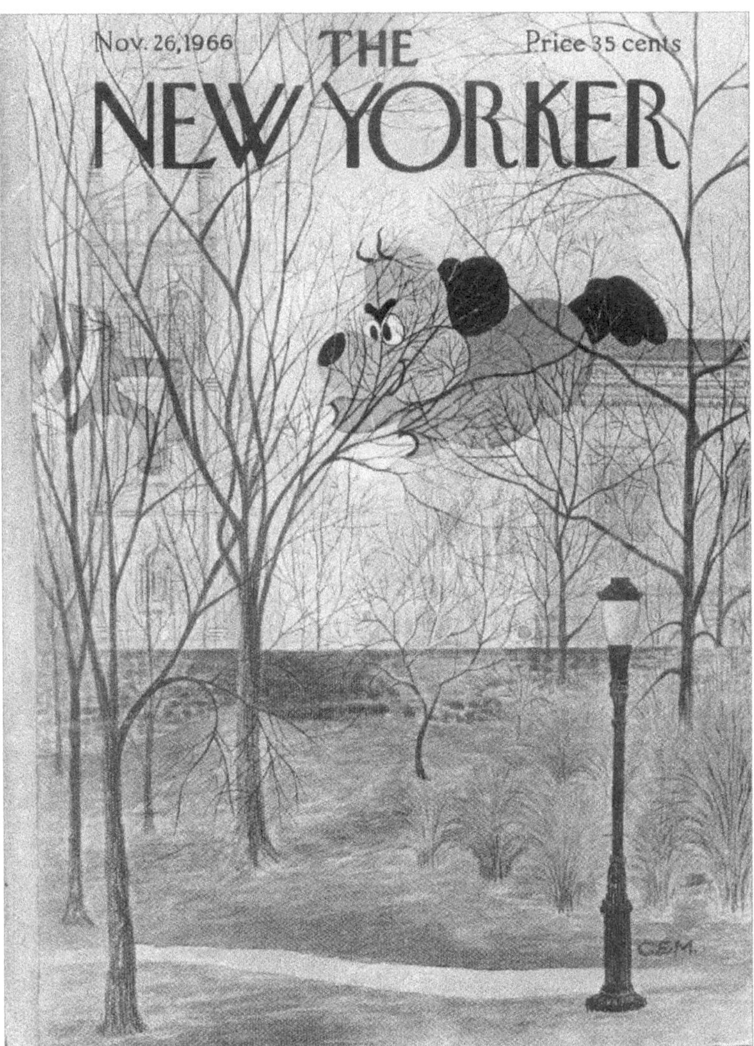

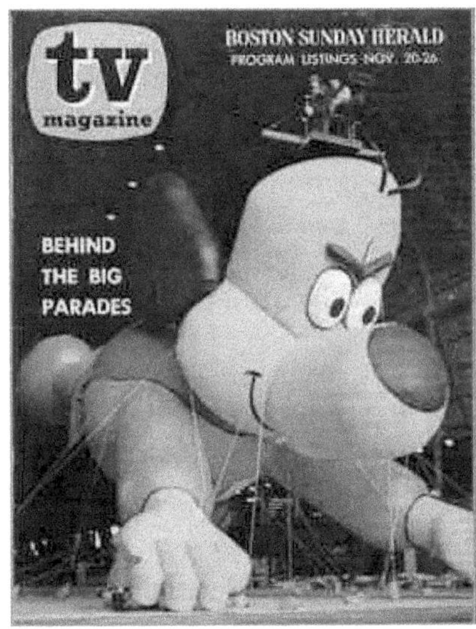

You will also see the special illustration of Underdog as a balloon in the Macy's parade that Joe Harris did. I came across this on the internet and captured it. It's so great as it features Underdog himself holding down his own balloon with his cartoon baddies joining him.

Two Goodyear images (in color) of the head of Underdog that were taken in 1967 in the Rockmart Gym, Rockmart, Georgia, along with a few other Macy balloon favorites for publicity. While the heads were up - paint touch ups were done!

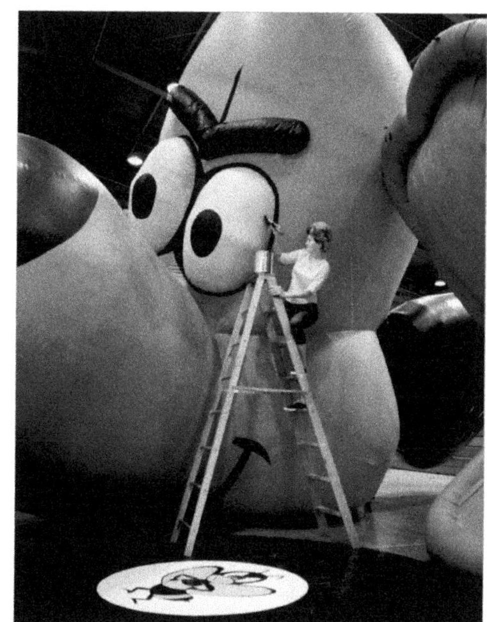

Underdog, the balloon's vital statistics are:

Length: 63 feet, 6 inches long

Width: 34 feet, 9 inches wide

Height: 35 feet tall

Weight (Deflated): 320 pounds

Helium Volume: 9,600 Cubic Feet

Total Lift: 619 pounds

Free Lift: 299 pounds

Handling Lines: 31

Sandbags: 150 to tether during helium inflation

Inflate: on stomach

Parade appearances: 1965, 1966, 1967, 1968, 1969, 1970, 1972, 1973, 1974, 1975 (crashed in Times Square - pulled from parade), 1976, 1977, 1978, 1979, 1980, 1981, 1982, 1983, 1984. Retired.

The material used to create the Underdog balloon was 530 square feet of nylon fabric that weighed 4.04 ounces per square yard. Covering this material inside and out was a synthetic rubber substance called neoprene. A heavy coat on the inside gives the balloon "body" and extra strength at the seams. It also acts as a sealer to prevent loss of helium gas when the balloon is inflated. Applied to the outside in combination with a rubber-based paint in various colors, it provides a tough skin which minimizes abrasions if the balloon rubbed up against a building or flag pole or tree.

When Underdog was painted for the first time, a rubber-based white primer paint was applied, followed by two coats of the various colors needed for Underdog. The paint adds a lot of weight when first applied, but it evaporates to one-seventh of its original poundage after air-curing.

To debut the balloon in its first appearance, a special *Underdog Show* float was built. Representing the very first balloon-float combo, the float depicted the lab of bad guy Simon Bar Sinister and his sidekick Cad. Having captured Underdog's girlfriend Polly and holding her captive atop a towering cliff, Simon threatens to "shrink" Polly, but his dastardly plans backfire when his shrink ray goes into reverse, and as Underdog approaches to rescue Sweet Polly, Simon's shrink-ray enlarges Underdog to his mammoth proportions and flying overhead (directly behind the float) comes Underdog!

A special soundtrack is recorded for this performance and the special costumed characters act for the NBC television cameras, as we hear Underdog (Wally Cox) shouting, "There's no need to fear - Underdog is here!", and he saves the day and Sweet Polly! A huge banner which proceeds the float is carried along by girls wearing underdog style costumes and long capes and on the banner "There's No Need To Fear - Underdog Is Here!"

The Macy's Underdog balloon also made a cameo appearance in the motion picture *Broadway Danny Rose* (1984) with Woody Allen and Mia Farrow. Orion Pictures.

Underdog is one of the best loved Macy's balloons and people still request that Underdog return to the parade. All that exists of the original balloon is the huge letter white letter "U" on red fabric and this is framed and hangs in Macy's Annual Events offices in a huge frame. The material began to decompose over the years and the seams were so weak that the balloon would not hold helium and could not be flown safely.

On a side-note - a story told by Joe Harris was that one year in the early 80s, Harris was invited to a party of friends who lived on West 77th Street the night before Thanksgiving. He happened to look out the window and noticed on the street below that the balloons were being inflated for the Macy's Parade. Ironically, directly below his POV was Underdog! It was the very first time that he saw the balloon in person. He excused himself from the gathering to go downstairs to introduce himself to the Goodyear team who were overseeing the inflation of the balloons, and took some pictures. The Macy's and Goodyear crew invited Harris to walk in the parade the next morning with Underdog and he did! Years later, he also met with Macy's parade officials and there were discussions about bringing Underdog back to the parade.

Factoid: The first balloon built by Goodyear for Macy's was Felix The Cat in 1927. The final Macy's balloon Goodyear built was Superman in 1980. In 1981, Goodyear contracted Kemp Balloons, Inc. in Glen Burnie, Maryland to take care of the Macy's Balloons and to refurbish them and make new ones. This arrangement ran from 1981 to 1983. In 1981, Kemp Balloons totally refurbished the Underdog balloon for Macy's. The balloon program moved in house at Macy's Studio in 1984. It remains there today.

8 The Beagles

by Mark Arnold

The big mistake I made in my previous TTV book is saying that *The Beatles* cartoon show, not *The Beagles*, aired on CBS. This is absolutely wrong as the John, Paul, George and Ringo *Beatles* show aired on ABC!

Joe Harris passed away in 2017, but his daughter and son-in-law still have access to The Beagles interpositives, which I would still love to get released onto DVD, but the issue is and always has been the little amount of *Beagles* episodes there actually were, and the relative disinterest in the series. It is a shame that since this is a limited-animation TV cartoon made during the 1960s, no one cares. If it were a silent film from the 1920s and on nitrate film, there would be tons of interest to restore and release this archival material. The sad part is that we may have to wait until the 22nd century before anyone else cares, and by that time it may be too late. Perhaps a Kickstarter is waiting in the wings here.

Updated episode listing:

The Beagles (18 shows, 36 episodes)

The Beagles show from 1966-1967 consisted of two Beagles segments, a Klondike Kat segment, and a fourth segment that presumably consisted of any number of repeat TTV or Jay Ward segments, plus a small segment that was presumably a repeat Commander McBragg, Bullwinkle's Corner or Mr. Know-it-All, or an all-new Sing-a-Long Family. All segments were repeated during the 1967-1968 season.

First Season: 9/10/66-1/7/67, CBS (36 episodes, 2 per show)

The Beagles #1 Ghosts, Ghouls and Fools Part 1 (9/10/66)
The Beagles #2 Ghosts, Ghouls and Fools Part 2 (9/10/66)
The Beagles #3 Dizzy Dishwashers Part 1 (9/17/66)
The Beagles #4 Dizzy Dishwashers Part 2 (9/17/66)
The Beagles #5 Dizzy Dishwashers Part 3 (9/24/66)
The Beagles #6 Dizzy Dishwashers Part 4 (9/24/66)
The Beagles #7 Drip, Drip, Drips Part 1 (10/1/66)
The Beagles #8 Drip, Drip, Drips Part 2 (10/1/66)
The Beagles #9 Drip, Drip, Drips Part 3 (10/8/66)
The Beagles #10 Drip, Drip, Drips Part 4 (10/8/66)
The Beagles #11 Tubby Troubles Part 1 (10/15/66)
The Beagles #12 Tubby Troubles Part 2 (10/15/66)

The Beagles #13 Tubby Troubles Part 3 (10/22/66)

The Beagles #14 Tubby Troubles Part 4 (10/22/66)

The Beagles #15 I'm Gonna Capture You Part 1 (10/29/66)

The Beagles #16 I'm Gonna Capture You Part 2 (10/29/66)

The Beagles #17 I'm Gonna Capture You Part 3 (11/5/66)

The Beagles #18 I'm Gonna Capture You Part 4 (11/5/66)

The Beagles #19 Foreign Legion Flops Part 1 (11/12/66)

The Beagles #20 Foreign Legion Flops Part 2 (11/12/66)

The Beagles #21 Foreign Legion Flops Part 3 (11/19/66)

The Beagles #22 Foreign Legion Flops Part 4 (11/19/66)

The Beagles #23 The Braves Part 1 (11/26/66)

The Beagles #24 The Braves Part 2 (11/26/66)

The Beagles #25 The Braves Part 3 (12/3/66)

The Beagles #26 The Braves Part 4 (12/3/66)

The Beagles #27 The Man in the Moon Part 1 (12/10/66)

The Beagles #28 The Man in the Moon Part 2 (12/10/66)

The Beagles #29 The Man in the Moon Part 3 (12/17/66)

The Beagles #30 The Man in the Moon Part 4 (12/17/66)

The Beagles #31 Captain of the Ship Part 1 (12/24/66)

The Beagles #32 Captain of the Ship Part 2 (12/24/66)

The Beagles #33 Captain of the Ship Part 3 (12/31/66)

The Beagles #34 Captain of the Ship Part 4 (12/31/66)

The Beagles #35 I Feel Like Humpty Dumpty Part 1 (1/7/67)

The Beagles #36 I Feel Like Humpty Dumpty Part 2 (1/7/67)

"The Sing-a-Long Family" (3 episodes)

These episodes first aired in 1966 as part of The Beagles and later on the syndicated Underdog Show.

The Sing-a-Long Family #1 Picnic

The Sing-a-Long Family #2 Skating

The Sing-a-Long Family #3 Fair

TTV'S WHO WHO:

Don Adams (voice artist):

Frank Andrina (animator):

Roman Arambula (animator):

Jackson Beck (voice artist):

Sandy Becker (voice artist):

Buck Biggers (writer, creator):

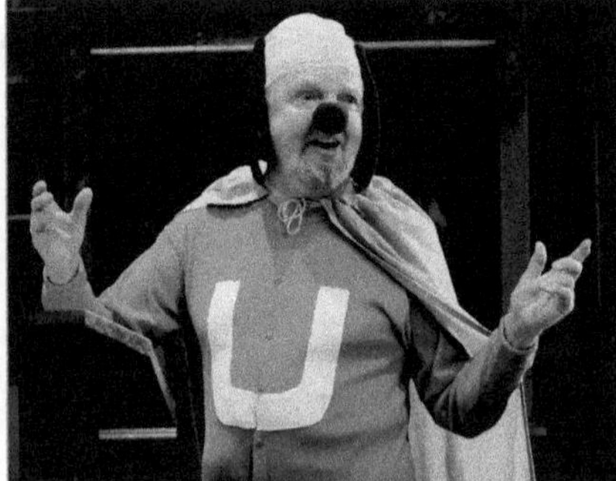

Ellie Bogardus (animator):

Bradley Bolke (voice artist):

Wally Cox (voice artist):

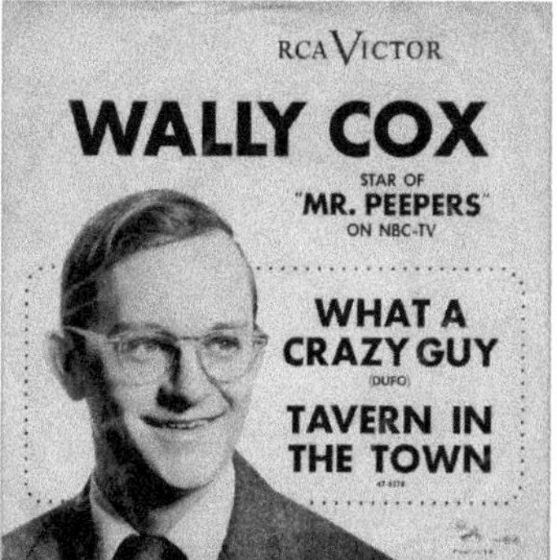

Kenny Delmar (voice artist):

AH REFUSE TO RIDE IN A SHERMAN TANK

AH'M FROM TH' SOUTH — DIXIE, THAT IS

AH ONLY KISS BABIES WITH GREY EYES

ALWAYS USE SOUTHERN PINE TOOTHPICKS

Herb Duncan (voice artist):

Sal Faillace (animation director):

Charles Fox (music):

Herschel Burke Gilbert (music):

Norm Gottfredson (animator):

Lu Guarnier (animation director):

Lee Blair and Lu Guarnier, *Graphic studio, N.Y., 1946.*
Picture courtesy of Lu Guarnier.

Doing research for a series of films for the U.S. Information Service
(In front), Don Towsley and Phil Kellison (Poppin' Fresh Doughboy), traveling westerly, covering the Orient, meet up with Max Furland and Lu Guarnier, traveling easterly, covering the Middle East, at the Grand Hotel, Calcutta, during a wonderful four month round-the-world trip for Lee Blair's Film Graphic Studio, 1951.
Picture courtesy of Lu Guarnier.

Ronald Hanmer (music):

Joe Harris (character designer):

Charlotte Huffine (animator):

George S. Irving (voice artist):

Norma MacMillan (voice artist):

Carlos Manriquez (animator):

Mort Marshall (voice artist):

Chuck McCann (voice artist):

Frank Milano (voice artist):

Lee Mishkin (animation director):

Marty Murphy (animator):

Sam Nicholson (animation director):

Van Phillips (music):

Gerry Ray (storyboards):

Kurt Rehfeld (music):

Dun Roman (animator):

Phil Roman (animator):

Norman Rose (voice artist):

Winston Sharples (music):

Harvey Siegel (production):

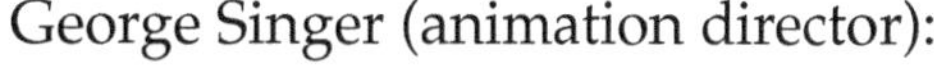

George Singer (animation director):

Ben Stern (sound):

Larry Storch (voice artist):

Chet Stover (writer, creator):

Allen Swift (voice artist):

Ernie Terrazas (animation director):

Sammy Timberg (music):

Ernest Tomlinson (music):

Stuart Upson (DFS ad agency):

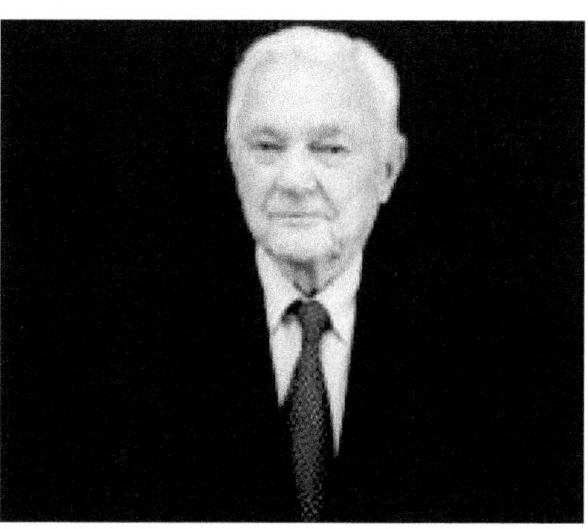

Fred Von Bernewitz (film editor):

Ben Washam (animator):

David Weidman (animator):

Victor Young (music):

Rudy Zamora (animator):

Lucille Ball and Superman (inspiration for Underdog):

9 Victoria's Scrapbook

by Victoria Biggers

DADDY IS BORN

Daddy came into the world in 1927, the first child born in Avondale Estates, Georgia, in the Atlanta area.

Even from the start, he was a born advertising man. His Uncle Lloyd proudly related how, as a baby in his highchair, Dad wouldn't simply whine and cry for food as other toddlers would. Instead, when he was ready for his breakfast, he would raise his spoon, smile happily, and shout the then popular 1920s advertising slogan: "Bring on the Cream of Wheat!" (Although being so little he could only say the word "bing" instead of "bring").

Years later, after attending North Georgia Military College and Emory University, Dad decided to head North to New York City, where his cousin "Hatch" (Norman Hatcher) was living at the time. Hatch was a superb Miami architect who had studied under Frank Lloyd Wright.

While in the city, Hatch and Dad shared an apartment and even formed a two-man band, called "The Long and Short of It". At six foot four inches tall, Hatch towered over my father.

My grandfather had been a musician as well, playing the banjo in "The Georgia Serenaders", the first band to play on radio down South and the band that opened for crooner Sophie Tucker at the prestigious Blue Room in New Orleans' Roosevelt Hotel.

Grandpa Biggers with banjo.

At one time Grandpa later told me, they were booked into almost every Loew's Theatre in the country, but when Daddy came along, he decided to slow down.

Daddy must have inherited from my grandfather that same performing ambition because he became a fabulous saxophone, clarinet and guitar player as well an expert pianist, which helped Dad to compose those wonderful theme songs he did for: *King Leonardo, Tooter Turtle, The Beagles, Go Go Gophers, Klondike Kat, Tennessee Tuxedo,* and of course, *Underdog….*

JOB HUNTING

Daddy at DFS.

When Daddy arrived in New York City - a young man just out of college in Georgia - he was naturally anxious to find work. One early Friday afternoon, exhausted from a long morning of job hunting - he suddenly came across a group of men lined up near Madison Avenue. A sign said: "Job interviews today". As Dad got in the very back of the line, he noticed something curious: Every man being interviewed was being asked a specific question Daddy couldn't hear and each time the man would answer: "no", and then immediately exit the line.

"What in the world are they being asked?". Dad thought. Finally, getting closer to the front of the line, he heard the prospective employer asking each man if they had any experience with furs, and he was getting a resounding "no" each time.

Desperate for work and tired of pounding the pavement, Dad knew there was only one thing to do. The minute he got to the front of the line, he smiled and, with a firm nod of his head answered "yes", to the question. Naturally, being the only person who had answered in the affirmative, Dad was hired on the spot as an "expert" in distinguishing different types of fur for a well-known coat manufacturing company.

Of course, the fact was that Dad knew as much about furs as he did about building a rocket - but do you think that bothered him? Not one bit. The minute he finished his interview, he dashed a few blocks over to Fifth Avenue and 42nd St., anxious to start his first job in the Big Apple. There, he spent the rest of that Friday afternoon and all day Saturday in the New York Public Library, reading voraciously every book in the collection that pertained to the fur industry.

On Monday morning he started work and - amazingly - with no prior experience in the field - managed to stay in the company until he landed his first job in advertising. This was one of Dad's favorite stories. He would always add that, once in a while, he wasn't quite sure what kind of fur he was looking at. At those rare times he would inevitably glance up at his boss, shake his head and say, "sometimes the furs look so much alike that you just can't tell."

MITCH MILLER'S CHRISTMAS PARTY

Mitch Miller.

If it weren't for the great record producer Mitch Miller, my brother and I would never have been born. Why? Because my parents met at his Christmas party in 1949.

At the time, my father was an account trainee at DFS and my mother worked at Columbia Records as secretary to both Mitch Miller and bandleader Percy Faith. Percy is known today as having ushered in the "easy listening" era.

According to my parents, it was a wonderful party (Mitch really knew how to give them) with lots of entertainment, music, singing and laughter. But then something happened. Mom and Dad suddenly spotted each other across the room and - in an instant - it seemed that everyone else inside the four walls had faded away. Without a pause, they both began to inch their way over to each other through the boisterous, noisy crowd and instantly got into a quiet yet scintillating conversation.

"When I set eyes on your mother at that party," Dad told me years later, shaking his head and thinking back, "she was so beautiful that the whole world seemed to stop. It was as if I couldn't hear the music or people talking in the room anymore. There was only her." And my mother felt the same way about Dad.

"It was love at first sight," Mom agreed. "I knew instantly, just by the ambition your father had, that he was going to be a tremendous success one day. It was just electrifying speaking to him. Not only that, he was handsome, too! How could I resist him?"

On that same note, it was easy to see why Dad fell in love with my mother. With her raven black hair, flawless complexion and stunning looks she was so beautiful that people would actually turn their heads to glance at her when she passed by, even on the busy streets of Manhattan.

After meeting my mother, Dad knew immediately that he had met his match intellectually; something that was very important to him. When my brother and I were growing up, in fact, my parents always maintained a well stocked library in our house that included the classics as well as books on psychology, archeology, science, philosophy and history. They both believed that life was a constant learning experience.

Mom and Dad.

After the party, Dad asked Mom to go out for a late night supper at a nearby restaurant.

"I'll never forget what happened the next day," my mother once told me. "I confided to Mitch that I had met your father at the party and he was so thrilled. Right after work, I walked into the elevator at Bonwit Teller's department store on Fifth Avenue. All of sudden I just knew that the two of us were going to be married. I was so happy that, right in the elevator, I waved my arms in the air and yelled out loud, "Hooray!"

She was right. A year and a half later, they were married at St. Joan of Arc Church in Jackson Heights, New York.

And Mitch Miller was always proud of the fact that, in some small way, he had contributed to making it all happen!

ON TO DFS

It looked like Dad might be staying in the fur business forever, but a ride on a bus in midtown Manhattan changed all that when he met a young man in advertising.

Dad went to DFS (Dancer Fitzgerald Sample) and started out in the mailroom. To many people, the mailroom was the lowest rung on the ladder in the advertising industry, but Daddy used it to his best advantage.

Reading virtually every piece of discarded mail he could get his hands on, Dad soon learned the machinations of how the great advertising firms on Madison Avenue worked.

In a very short time, he had moved on to directing radio commercials, looking so young, in fact, that once, when a well-known seasoned actor had just gotten a piece of direction from Dad, the man put up his hand and politely but firmly said, "Son, I was in this business before you were born and I think I know how to read a line."

Mom and Dad.

"You're quite right," Dad said, not missing a beat, "but our client on this project wants the copy to be read a certain way, and that way only. Could we try one more take to see how it sounds?"

"Well put," the famous actor remarked, "Let's do it!"

From there, my father went on to direct TV commercials, pioneering the use of the hidden camera. One of these ads, Dad told me, showed a group of supermarket shoppers getting enraged at an announcer who was trying to take away their local brand of flour in order to replace it with a new one. One woman, in fact, got so upset that she tried to hit the announcer over the head with her own sack of flour! According to my father, that commercial became such a tremendous success down South that it ran for years. Leave it to Dad!

A TIP FROM MIX DANCER

Daddy always liked to tell a story about an incident that changed his life. One day, not too many years after he started working at DFS, he heard a knock on the door beside his desk. It was Mix Dancer.

"Buck, could I see you for a minute?", Mix said, his head peeking through the doorway. Immediately, Dad put down the stack of paperwork he had in his hand and stood up.

"Please come in," he said, quickly pulling up a chair for his boss.

"Thank you," Mix replied. He sat down and made small talk for a minute or two. There was a pause and then Mix cleared his throat and began to speak again.

"Buck," he said, "I want to talk to you about something." Dad inched forward in his chair in anticipation of what his boss had to say.

"I'm all ears," Dad said, "What's on your mind?"

"Well, Buck, I'm a little concerned. I've noticed that for the past couple of weeks, you've looked tired. That's not like you. Is everything all right at home?"

"You're right," Dad answered, nodding, "I am a little tired. But to tell you the truth, I've been staying very late at the office to finish the projects I'm working on. I guess it's caught up with me."

Mix shook his head. "Buck, I know you're a hard worker. But what you do after 5pm is your own business. You're not required to be here. Now, I'm going to tell you a secret that's going to make your life a little easier."

Mix put his index finger in the air for emphasis. "I arrive at this company every morning 30 minutes ahead of everyone else. It's been the key to my success. I'm always in my office at 8:30 am before the phones start ringing, and I get more accomplished in that half hour than in the entire 9 to 5 work day. If you try this routine, I think it's going to help."

Daddy thanked his boss for taking the time to speak to him. The next day and the next, as my father began arriving at DFS at 8:30 am instead of 9, he quickly noticed with astonishment that he was getting so much more work completed during the day that he was able to leave the office closer to 5PM. Mix Dancer had been right!

From then on, even in the biting cold winters of Manhattan, when blizzard conditions would force buses and taxis to be at a standstill, Daddy would always leave early for the office - even wrapping newspapers around his boots for extra warmth when temperatures got into the single digits - to make sure he got to his desk at least one half hour before 9am.

And, like his boss Mix Dancer, Daddy was always proud to say that this simple change was in a large part responsible for the success he enjoyed later in life - first when he got promoted to the position of Account Manager for General Mills at DFS - then when he and his business partners formed TTV - and finally when he became Vice President in charge of Advertising and Promotion at NBC.

See what a small bit of advice can do?

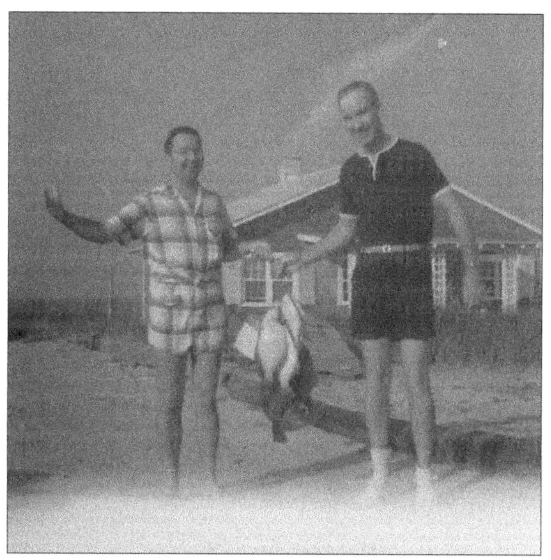

Dad and Tread Covington.

NEW IDEAS

Trying his hand in all aspects of advertising before he became a Vice President at DFS, Dad came up with several new ideas, many of which involved food. Being an Atlanta boy, for example, Dad was especially proud that his own recipe for "coca cola pound cake" went into the *Betty Crocker Cookbook* at General Mills. And it's still there!

One time though, when Daddy tried to interest an advertising executive in one of his potential new products, he was quickly turned down.

"I know you have a lot of enthusiasm for this idea of yours," the executive told Dad, "but mothers today want to save money on family meals and that means making bigger servings that go a long way, not smaller ones. I'm sorry, but I don't think putting dehydrated soup into single serving packets is going to sell right now."

Not going to sell? It seems an impossible thought today! "But in all fairness," Dad told me, years later, "the man was probably right. My idea was - very simply - ahead of its time."

The rest is history. Soup in single serving packets finally came on the market when Lipton introduced Cup-a-Soup many years later in 1972. By that time, of course, consumer tastes had changed and the product became an instant success.

Oh well. As Dad said, sometimes wonderful ideas are indeed way ahead of their time. Because of this, people can miss taking advantage of a golden opportunity that may be staring them right in the face. Famed comedian Milton Berle, for example, always regretted turning down the very profitable opportunity to invest in the teleprompter, when it was first introduced to the television industry in the 1950s. At the time Berle thought that there was little future in the gadget - that traditional cue cards were a better choice.

In the same way, in the early 1970s, Dad turned down the very lucrative chance to purchase the rights to dozens of classic films and television shows for the home viewing market - which was then just about to be introduced to the public. It would have cost him only a small sum of money at the time, but the idea just didn't interest Dad.

"I'll never make a dime out of it," Dad told my mother and I. "Who in the world would want to clutter their shelves with those huge cassette boxes?"

At that time, of course, Dad had no way of knowing that one day "those huge cassette boxes" were going to be replaced by DVDs, computer downloads and video streaming. If only we could all see into the future!

THE FINE PRINT

One of the most interesting people Dad worked with in the advertising business was a gentleman named Gordon Johnson, one of the top executives at DFS and General Mills. One day, Dad told me, Gordon said: "If they can put the minimum daily dose of vitamins in a pill - why can't they do it in a cereal?" And in 1961 General Mills introduced "Total Cereal" to the market!

In addition to his skills in the advertising field, Dad told me, Gordon had an interesting hobby: fine print. That's right. Gordon had a unique talent for being able to memorize the fine print on absolutely everything: matchbooks, laundry slips, candy wrappers, cigarette packs, movie stubs, hotel receipts, etc.

Now the average person might have thought that Gordon's prodigious "fine print" collection would never come in handy. Wrong! One time, my father told me, it was responsible for saving a very important company meeting. According to Dad, it happened like this:

Dad and Gordon were on the way to the airport to fly to Minneapolis, where they were meeting important heads of General Mills at the corporate headquarters. Suddenly, the cab they were in hit traffic. And more traffic. It seemed as if there was no way they were going to get the plane on time for their important meeting.

Finally, they arrived at the New York airport and, with only minutes to spare, Gordon and Dad raced to the airline ticket booth, happy that they were about to board the plane at last, or so they thought. Just as they arrived at the desk, breathless, they were stopped short by the ticket agent.

"Sorry," he said, "It's too late to get on the flight. You'll have to take a later plane." My father just stared at him, his mouth open in shock.

"But we can't do that," Dad protested, putting down his suitcase, "We'll never make our meeting!"

"Sorry," the agent said, "I can't help you." He turned to wait on another customer.

"Just a minute," Gordon said, suddenly stepping forward, "Read this."

Gordon took out his boarding pass and turned it over, placing it right in front of the ticket agent's face so he could read … you guessed it….. The "fine print."

To the ticket agent's surprise, the contract on the back of the boarding pass specifically listed the exact number of minutes before take-off that passengers were still allowed to board the plane, and Dad and Gordon had arrived within that time frame.

"You're right," gasped the agent, "but for a problem like this, you're going to have to see the manager."

The young man rang a buzzer and, after a few minutes, an airport manager entered the room. Gordon re-told his story, showing the manager the back of the boarding pass, as he had done with the ticket agent. The manager was astounded.

"I can't believe it," he said. "I've never seen this contract. Even so, I don't think we can let you on the flight now because it would be an inconvenience to other passengers so close to take off."

Dad and Gordon looked at each other, exasperated.

"I'm going to have to call my head office," the manager said. He picked up the phone as Gordon turned to my father.

"Buck," he said, motioning down the hallway, "while he's on the phone, you'd better start moving closer to the plane in case we have to get on quickly."

In a flash, suitcase in hand, Dad started walking briskly down the aisle toward the runway. Then he got an idea. My father not only moved closer to the plane, as Gordon had suggested - he went one step further: He continued walking right onto the runway and then - still gripping the suitcase - planted his two feet firmly right in front of the plane. "If this doesn't stop them from taking off without us," Dad said to himself, "Nothing will."

He looked up at the clock on the wall on the inside of the terminal. The minutes were ticking by. Dad squinted as he tried to look through the window at the figures of Gordon and the manager. Their hands were moving in the air as they talked to each other. Now, it looked like the manager was picking up the telephone again to speak to another co-worker. On and on it went. It seemed like it was hopeless. Surely, Dad thought, they were never going to make their meeting now.

And then - like a miracle - Dad saw the manager suddenly point to the ticket agent and then gesture to the runway with a sweeping motion of his hand. The next instant - Gordon and Dad were being ushered onto the plane.

Whenever he told this story, Dad would always shake his head at the last part. "By the time we got on that plane," Dad would say, "we were so far behind schedule that not one passenger on board would even look at us. But by God," he'd say, proudly, nodding his head and smiling, "we made that meeting. Thanks to Gordon."

It just goes to show you: Always read the fine print!

SAY "GOODNIGHT" CHUMLEY

When I was growing up, my contact with the talented actors who voiced the Total TeleVision cartoon characters was limited. Several times a year, Don Adams (voice of Tennessee Tuxedo) would call to ask my father a question or two about a script and if I answered the phone, there would be a pleasant exchange of greetings before I handed the receiver to my Dad.

Other than that, I didn't get a chance to interact with wonderful voice actors like Jackson Beck (King Leonardo, Biggy Rat) and Alan Swift (Simon Bar Sinister) until I met them years later at Nostalgia conventions, or - in the case with Larry Storch (Phineas J. Whoopee) - at several of the yearly conventions for NBC when my Dad was Vice President in charge of Advertising and Promotion. Larry was a smiling, energetic presence at these events and always made sure he asked questions about me whenever we spoke. What a thoughtful, gracious man!

My dear friend Will Jordan (famed for his wonderful "really big shew" impersonation of Ed Sullivan), called Larry "the world's greatest mimic". "Larry could," Will always told me with great relish, "imitate precisely any voice and any accent to perfection."

Will was so right. Whenever I'm watching a *Tennessee Tuxedo* episode, for example, I never fail to close my eyes for a moment when Mr. Whoopee's character appears on screen, just to hear the precision and clarity of Larry's wonderful voice. He not only sounds like, but seems to embody the very soul of the actor the character was based on: Frank Morgan! Yes, Larry has his own remarkable way of bringing to vivid life any character he portrays.

Somewhere in storage, in fact, I have a reel-to-reel tape from the 1960s of Larry reading lines from a *Tennessee Tuxedo* script in his Tiger Tornado voice. Based on boxer Muhammad Ali (who was still Cassius Clay at the time), the characterization is filled with the tremendous vitality and humor that Larry gives to all his on-screen personalities.

Oddly enough, Allan Melvin, another well-known actor at the time (I always remember him from the *Gomer Pyle* TV show and as the voice of Magilla Gorilla), does his own version of Tiger Tornado on this tape, too. Although Larry ended up with the part, of course, Alan's personal technique for voicing the character is also excellent, but a little slower-paced. Is this an audition tape? I haven't a clue. But what a treasure!

Of the many voice actors I've interacted with throughout the years, though, there is one who always remained very special to me: Bradley Bolke, voice of Chumley the Walrus on *Tennessee Tuxedo*. What a rare talent!

One time, when the two of us were walking in New York City, I asked Bradley how much rehearsal time the actors needed when they would sit down at a Total TeleVision recording session .

"None," Bradley told me. "Usually, we'd walk in and Larry Storch would wave 'hello' and chat for a minute, then we'd all go right into the script. When you're professionals and as good as we all were - you don't need any rehearsal time."

The son of Kenny Delmar agreed. Kenny did many, many, voices for Total TeleVision; the most famous, of course, being the voice of The Hunter. But as for the amount of rehearsal time the veteran actor needed when he got into the studio?

"Zero," Ken Delmar, Jr., recently told me. "My father never even rehearsed his voices at home. When Tread Covington would come over for dinner at our house, it was just to relax. They never talked about work they were going to do in the studio. Dad was well-known in the business for being able to sit down in a recording session and immediately go into several voices almost simultaneously. He was able to play so many characters at once, in fact, that one time he even arrested himself!"

"It also helped," Bradley told me during our walk that day, "to have wonderful people like Tread Covington and Ben Stern in the recording studio."

Ben Stern, father of TV and Radio superstar Howard Stern, has always been considered one of the most talented recording engineers in the business. "When you have a professional like Ben in the studio, any actor is put immediately at ease so he can do his work," Bradley confided to me.

My father was a big fan of Ben Stern, too. "There was absolutely no one like him,"

Tennessee Tuxedo cels.

Daddy said. "Not only was he a tremendous presence in the studio, but in addition to his expertise as a director, producer and editor, he also had a terrific sense of humor. I'll never forget the day we marked a tape in order to do an edit." Daddy closed his eyes and laughed, remembering, "And suddenly the mark just seemed to vanish. Finally, after marking the tape over and over again, we realized that a chemical - maybe cleaning fluid - had somehow gotten onto the tape and caused all the marks we kept making to 'disappear'. Ben and I laughed a lot that day. God, was he a lot of fun!"

As for Bradley Bolke, he and I always stayed close friends. We spoke on the phone every few weeks, in fact, and always, at the end of each and every phone call, he would end the conversation in the same wonderful way.

"Please Bradley," I'd beg, "Say goodnight to me as Chumley."

"Duuuhhhh, all right," Bradley would say. "Duhhhh, ... Goodnight, Victoria!"

I'd suddenly become a little girl again, watching a *Tennessee Tuxedo* episode.

"Goodnight, Chumley!", I'd answer back.

DINNER WITH CHET

Ambience had a great deal to do with being able to " create "for Dad, whether it was the relaxed atmosphere of the 1812 house - where he met Chet once a week - or the serene, quiet setting of our Cape Cod home on the sparkling waters of Nantucket Sound. Truly a writer's paradise!

Interestingly, the large estate had been built in the 1940s for a doctor - one half had originally been the living quarters and the other half the office - and the two sides were connected by an enclosed breezeway. Best of all, it had two large kitchens, a spare shower outside for washing off the salt water after a swim and wild roses that grew in pink and white clusters all over the fence in the summer. Beautiful!

Outside, a generator was attached to the house in case the power went out and, in the main kitchen, there was a fabulous red brick indoor grille built right into the wall with a black mesh screen. That was one of Dad's favorite places. Why? Because he was a fabulous cook and his specialty was grilling steaks. Delmonico steaks.

Whenever Chet Stover was staying with us for the weekend, Dad loved to talk to him as he painted the steaks with his special sauce using a small wire brush, turning them over and over again as they sizzled over the burning coals. But one thing that Dad couldn't get used to: Chet hated hot food. Yes, that's right. Dad was always particular to make sure the steaks were piping hot. But, during the dinner conversation, usually chatting with my mother, Chet would keep talking and gesturing until, finally, his steak would get stone cold. Then he would cheerfully pick up his knife and fork and begin to eat.

"Chet, you're letting your steak get cold again!", Dad would scold, pointing his finger at Chet's dinner plate. Chet would simply smile and wave, munching happily on his cold steak.

Chet had an interesting background. He had been the head of Creative Services when he and Dad were at DFS and had invented the famous Cheerios Kid for General Mills.

According to Dad, he had once been a children's book illustrator and seemed to know exactly how a child's mind works.

On another of Chet's visits, for example, we all went out to a French restaurant around the corner from our house and Chet kept me occupied by performing card trick after card trick as we waited for our dinner. He was a fabulous magician!

Later, when we all got back home, Chet suddenly turned to me and said: "Vicki, your Mom and Dad tell me you have over 100 dolls sitting on shelves in your room. Tell me, do they walk around at night?"

His words suddenly fascinated me because Chet wasn't joking, like an adult normally would. Instead, he was dead serious, looking at me as if he were interested in the answer. There was a long pause.

"Gosh, I don't know," I finally said, staring at him in astonishment.

"Well," he said, "I'll tell you how you can find out." He looked at me very seriously. "At night, before you go to sleep, make sure you sprinkle the floor in your room with flour."

"Flour?", I said, puzzled, knotting my eyebrows together.

"That's right," he continued, nodding his head. "If you see footprints in the flour the next morning, that means the dolls have been walking around."

Two weeks later, a wrapped package arrived for me via Dad from Chet. I couldn't wait to open it. Inside was a lovely doll: a beautiful Spanish dancer in a flowing skirt, posed with her arms in the air. I knew it was Chet's wonderful way of telling me how much our conversation had meant to him. How grand!

I've made sure I've kept that doll in my room, ever since I was a little girl, no matter where I've moved to. One of these days, I'm going to throw a handful of flour on the floor before I retire for the evening, just to see what happens....

Thank you, Chet!

THE BIG DRIP

One day, when I was about seven, Dad had just come from the projection room, at our home on the Cape where we used to show reel to reel films of *Tennessee Tuxedo*, *Underdog* and *Go Go Gophers*. (I still have the films in the original grey metal cans). I remember watching Dad thread the film through the movie projector and then seeing the 5-4-3-2-1 count flash on the white wall of the projection room in front of my brother and I. It was always so wonderful because you knew you were about to see something exciting.

Now, Dad sat down on the couch next to me in the living room and remained quiet for a moment, deep in thought.

"What is it, Daddy?", I said, turning to him. I knew something was wrong.

"Victoria," he said, shaking his head, "for some reason I've hit a snag - I'm writing the script this week for *Tennessee Tuxedo* (he alternated each week - one week Chet would write it and then Daddy) - and I can't come up with any new ideas. If you can think of any kind of a profession Tennessee and Chumley can be in - anything new - I'll double your allowance this week."

That sounded great to me! As I thought, Daddy thought. His eyes seemed to be looking at something far away as he searched for an answer. Just then an idea suddenly popped into my head.

"Wait a minute, Daddy!", I exclaimed, "How about making them plumbers?" Suddenly, my father's eyes widened and a smile brightened his face.

"Plumbers!", he said. As I mentioned before, all he needed was that one word to get the creative wheels turning in his head.

Daddy stood up and began moving his hands in circles as he thought, as if he could see a whole scene in front of his eyes. "Of course!", he laughed, "and then the kitchen faucet would explode and - whoosh!", he moved his hands up higher, as if they were suddenly two fountains of gushing water. "Tennessee would be floating in the air yelling, "Chumley! Yeeoow!" He started laughing louder as he walked around the room gesturing wildly, "and Chumley could fix the pipes and get all tangled up in them. Fantastic!" Still smiling, he nodded his head, picking up the yellow legal pad lying on the table next to the sofa.

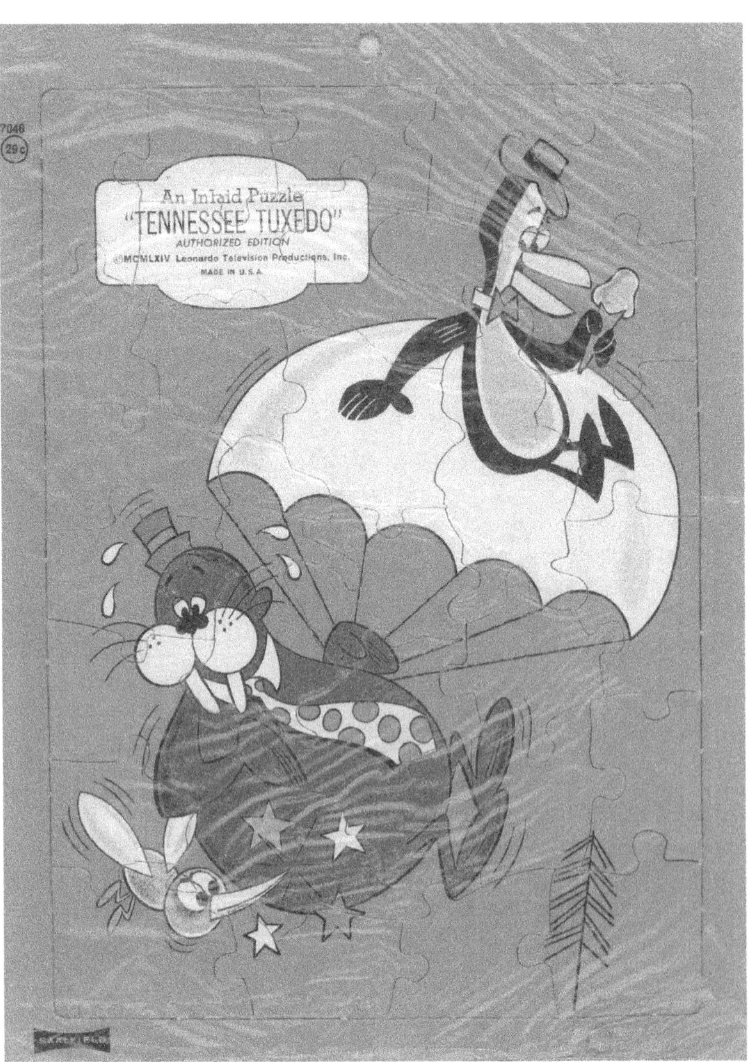

"Great job, Sugar Lump!", he said, taking his Flair pen from the pocket of his red sweater and pointing it at me. He quickly scribbled a note on the legal pad, "That's all I needed!", and with that he dashed off to his desk to write *Tennessee Tuxedo's* "The Big Drip", episode #5, season 3.

Years later, whenever Daddy and I would see that particular episode in a *Tennessee Tuxedo* DVD collection, we'd always turn to each other and Dad would say, "Well, here's our show."

Then we'd laugh and enjoy watching the whole thing all over again!

TRIVIA: At the beginning of "The Big Drip" episode, look for a shot of a classified section of a newspaper with an ad that reads: "Chet-Watts Plumbing".

A MYSTERIOUS SHADOW

My dad was never a morning person. That's the way most writers are, I guess. I read once that Daniel Defoe always did his best writing at 3 am. Well, Daddy usually didn't work on his scripts that late, but way after bedtime, to be sure.

That's why it was such a change of pace to my father when, in 1961, we moved from our apartment in Hartsdale, New York, where many people stayed up very late, to Cape Cod, Massachusetts. In those days, the Cape was practically deserted after Labor Day when the tourists went home. The small population of year-round residents that remained for the winter were mostly retirees that went to bed early.

The first winter we moved to the Cape, in fact, my father was busy at work one evening on a series of cartoon scripts when he was suddenly interrupted by a knock on the door. He quickly sprang up from his typewriter to listen again. Maybe he had imagined it.

Knock! Knock!

This time he pushed back his desk chair and ran to the front door, peering out through the side window. He saw the white glow of a flashlight and a mysterious shadow.

"Who's there?", my father asked.

"Police department!", came a voice. Dad quickly swung open the door. Sure enough, there was a policeman in uniform standing in front of him, waving a flashlight.

"What seems to be the trouble Officer?", Dad asked, "Is anything wrong?"

"I'm sorry to disturb you", said the policeman. "But I just wanted to check on you to make sure you were all right."

"All right?", Dad said.

"Yes", answered the policeman, "I saw a light in your window."

"Oh", Dad chuckled, "Well, you see, I'm a writer, and I sometimes work at night writing cartoon scripts. That's what I'm doing right now."

"I understand", said the policeman, "But even so, it's very late, Sir. We usually don't see lights on at this time."

It suddenly dawned on my father that he had become so absorbed in his writing that he hadn't even realized it was now the wee hours of the morning.

"Good Lord! I've been so busy typing that I must have lost track of the hour", my dad said, "What time is it?"

The policeman looked at his watch.

"9:45 pm", he answered.

TIMING A SCRIPT

I was always fascinated as a child with watching Dad time scripts. As a matter of fact, I still have one of his favorite stopwatches. "It is very important," he said, "when you are timing a script to say each word out

Percy Faith

Dear Grace;

I guess it's time I replied to at least one of your notes, eh? I'm a lousy letter writer but here goes.;

I never heard of but finally saw the Beagles..did you say it is yours?..but the tunes are all rock and roll and I'm hardly the boy for that!..are you a song-plugger now?!..

Take care, Grace and keep well..after that, SUCCESS!

Perc

loud because we think much faster than we speak. So if you just time it in your head, instead of actually saying the words, the script time will be completely thrown off."

Daddy would start his stopwatch by clicking the little button on top and then begin reading his script - whispering each word and enunciating each syllable clearly. Then he would push the button on top of the watch to stop it again as soon as he finished reading the script. He would even make sure he would voice all the sound effects out loud, to get the timing exactly right.

Sometimes I'd hear him saying familiar names like: "Yakety Yak". Then he'd take out his felt pen (he would only write with felt pens - red or black) and scribble on a yellow legal pad the timing for that week's script.

He was amazing to watch! What a perfectionist!

"I CAN'T"

I was listening to Daddy at the kitchen table as he picked up a basket of miniature, foil-wrapped chocolate eggs we had left over from Easter. He was busy helping me with my Elementary school level math homework.

To illustrate the point my father was trying to make, he began moving the eggs in circles and asking me what the total amount of money would be if I purchased so many of the eggs at such and such a price and then divided that price by this and that many eggs, etc.

"Don't worry, Victoria," Dad said, after trying to explain it to me for the fifth time. "Let's just go over it again." He reached down to pick up one of the eggs.

"I can't do it, Daddy. Can't you see I'm no good with math?"

"Sugar," my father said, shaking his head, "You kept saying the same thing when I wanted you to learn how to ride a bicycle. Remember?"

I remembered that fall afternoon very well. It seemed so long ago. There we were, Dad and I, the only two people down on the beach in front of our house on Cape Cod. He had surprised me with a brand new bicycle the week before but I had already given up on trying to ride it. I had attempted several times, of course, but just couldn't seem to keep my balance.

I watched him hold onto the shiny white bicycle as we stood there in the parking lot.

"You're getting too old for your three-wheeler," he told me. "Just get in the seat and I'll hold onto the bicycle and push you along. At least you'll get an idea of how it feels to ride it."

"I can't do it!", I said, shaking my head. "I'm afraid I'll fall over again!"

Dad looked me right in the eye. "Victoria, I won't let you fall," he said.

I finally agreed to get in the seat and we began to slowly move along on the black-topped parking lot in front of the sandy beach, with Dad holding onto the bicycle in back of me.

I had to admit, it was fun riding along this way. As Daddy started pushing me a tiny bit faster, I got more confidence. The sound of the waves crashing on the shore and the sight of the seagulls as they flew in circles in the blue sky above me was exhilarating. We started to pick up more speed.

"Don't let go, Daddy!", I screamed into the salty air. "Don't let go or I'll fall again!" I turned quickly to look at him.

My father was a dot.

Now, as I sat at the table with Dad, he smiled and pressed my hand reassuringly. "See? You thought you couldn't ride a bicycle and you could. You never have enough confidence in yourself."

Daddy reached for the math book in front of him and turned to a different chapter. "Let's try another lesson", he suggested.

I stood up and pushed the chair away from the table.

"I can't do it!", I said. "Daddy, - please - I just can't do it!" Tears welled up in my eyes as I ran from the kitchen toward the other part of the house and into my own room. I threw myself down on the bed, crying softly.

About ten minutes later I heard a noise. It sounded like a crunching sound. Was I dreaming? I sat up and strained to listen. There it was again! Swinging my legs toward the side of the bed, I quickly put my two feet on the floor and jumped up. As I ran to the window I saw dirt flying up into the air. I couldn't believe my eyes!

There was my father, shovel in hand, digging a hole in the backyard! What in the world was he trying to do?

I dashed outside and stood there in front of Daddy as he continued digging the hole without a word. Then - suddenly - he put down the shovel and picked up a wooden plank. On one side of it, written in huge, black letters, was the word: "CAN'T".

Daddy held up the sign so I could see it clearly.

"Take a good look at this," he said. Then he picked up the board and tossed it into the hole.

Dad and Victoria.

"Now we're going to bury this word," Daddy said. He quickly shoveled dirt back over the hole and patted it down with the shovel. My father looked up at me. "And never, ever forget this moment."

Forget that moment! How could I? As the years went by the memory of it drove me to accomplish many things I had previously thought were impossible. By my first year of High School, for example, I had already taught myself Algebra One at home and gone right into Algebra Two with a straight "A" average. Not bad for a little girl who insisted she couldn't do math! Dad was so proud of me when I became a member of the National Honor Society and graduated at the top of my class. It was all because of the confidence he had in me.

One afternoon, decades later, Daddy and I were enjoying a cup of coffee together when he suddenly smiled and said: "Do you think there are any splinters left of that board I buried in the backyard?"

I laughed and said: "Daddy, you bet!"

LIZZIE AND THE UNDERDOG SCRIPT

My Aunt Lizzie, who was really my mother's Aunt, had come into the world in 1888, the year of the Blizzard in New York City. People born in that year, it was rumored, possessed remarkable health and vigor, having been able to survive one of the most terrible winters on record. It must be true, because - at almost 80 years of age - Aunt Lizzie was a whirlwind of energy and would spend an entire vacation at our house doing what she loved to do best: clean. My grandmother, meanwhile, had been born a few years later in 1892. Her specialty was home-cooking.

So it happened on one of Nana and Aunt Lizzie's spring visits, that my father was sleeping late one Saturday. Dad was a very hard worker and, as a rule, this was the only day of the week that he would allow himself to "sleep in". Suddenly, he was awakened by what sounded like a thumping noise from the kitchen. He jolted awake and felt something pressing on the mattress. It was my mother, crawling back into bed.

"Grace, what time is it?", my father said groggily.

"7:30", my mother said, "Lizzie came over to get the mop out of the broom closet to clean your office in the other part of the house. I told her we just cleaned it last week. But it's the only thing that makes her happy."

"Oh", Daddy said, and he turned over and went back to sleep.

Suddenly, he bolted straight up, his eyes wide with panic. Clean his office? He knew what that meant! Last Christmas, Aunt Lizzie had accidentally thrown out a paper bag filled with Watts' Beatle cards and the November before that she had misplaced a photograph album of prized pictures my mother had kept from her childhood. And wasn't it only a month ago that she had come very close to throwing out one of my birthday cards with $50.00 of birthday money in it? Now, Dad thought it was going to be his turn next.

"Oh, my God!", he said, "Last night I finished the two *Underdog* scripts for my meeting with Chet on Monday. They're sitting on my typewriter!" With that, he leaned over and picked up the receiver to the phone on the table beside the bed.

Now, I've mentioned before how much Dad loved new gadgets. Our phones were no exception. In fact, they rivaled any equipment the best advertising companies on Madison Avenue had. Our phones, like offices at the time, had a red button you could push to put any call on "hold". Then, as the line would "blink", you could press a button for the intercom system at the same time to alert someone in the other part of the house that they had a phone call. When someone like Don Adams would phone my Dad, for example, we would put the call on hold and buzz my father on the intercom, yelling, "0331!" (Those were the last four digits of Daddy's business line).

Now, Dad began furiously pressing down on the buzzer of the intercom system with his index finger as he shouted into the phone: "Lizzie! Lizzie!"

Let me tell you something. My Dad was not good in the morning. At that time of day, in fact, his voice was several octaves lower than its normal register. He sounded like a bad imitation of Boris Karloff doing his "Frankenstein" voice.

"Liiizzie!"

No answer.

What my father didn't know was that Aunt Lizzie, standing in my father's office, had absolutely no clue that she was listening to an intercom system. Nana and Aunt Lizzie's mother had arrived at Ellis Island from County Cork, Ireland, in the 1800s and, believe me, they had heard from her lips many an Irish ghost story. So as she stood there, listening, she thought she was hearing a mysterious voice directly from the spirit world.

Dad slammed down the receiver. "Why won't she answer?", he said to Mom. He quickly threw on his robe and tied the belt as he stepped into his bedroom slippers and flew out of the room.

Just as Dad had gotten halfway across the breezeway, he thought he saw what looked like a sudden flash of light. Yes, it was Aunt Lizzie. Dad later said he had never seen an 80-year-old woman who could run that fast.

He turned around again and followed her back into the main house, where he had just come from. She was sitting on the living room couch trembling, looking as white as a sheet.

"They were calling me," Aunt Liz mumbled, looking up at my father and shaking her head. "But I didn't answer. You're not supposed to answer them...." She clutched at the net covering her snow-white head of hair.

Me - Aunt Lizzie - Dad!!

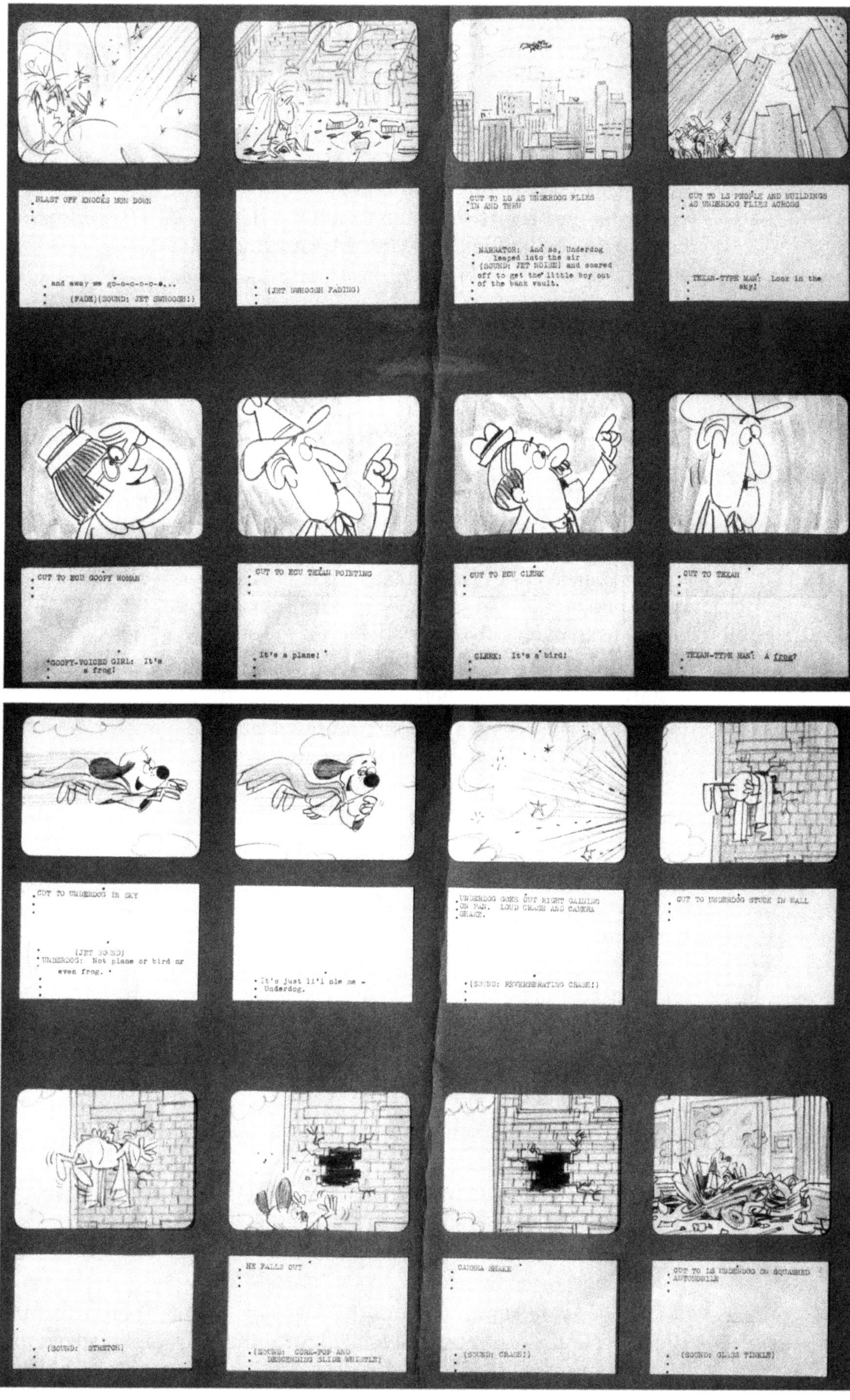
BLAST OFF KNOCKS MAN DOWN
and away we go-o-o-o-o-o-e...
(FADE)(SOUND: JET SWHOOSH!)
(JET SWHOOSH FADING)
CUT TO LS AS UNDERDOG FLIES IN AND THRU
NARRATOR: And so, Underdog leaped into the air (SOUND: JET NOISE) and soared off to get the little boy out of the bank vault.
CUT TO LS PEOPLE AND BUILDINGS AS UNDERDOG FLIES ACROSS
TEXAN-TYPE MAN: Look in the sky!
CUT TO ECU GOOPY WOMAN
GOOPY-VOICED GIRL: It's a frog!
CUT TO ECU TEXAN POINTING
It's a plane!
CUT TO ECU CLERK
CLERK: It's a bird!
CUT TO TEXAN
TEXAN-TYPE MAN: A frog?
CUT TO UNDERDOG IN SKY
(JET SOUND)
UNDERDOG: Not plane or bird or even frog.
It's just li'l ole me - Underdog.
UNDERDOG GOES OUT RIGHT GAINING ON PAN. LOUD CRASH AND CAMERA SHAKE.
(SOUND: REVERBERATING CRASH!)
CUT TO UNDERDOG STUCK IN WALL
(SOUND: STRETCH)
HE FALLS OUT
(SOUND: CORK-POP AND DESCENDING SLIDE WHISTLE)
CAMERA SHAKE
(SOUND: CRASH!)
CUT TO LS UNDERDOG ON SQUASHED AUTOMOBILE
(SOUND: GLASS TINKLE)

"Calm down, Liz," my father said, putting one hand in the air. "The voice you heard was only me. Now, did you see any papers on my typewriter?"

"Yes," she said, still trying to catch her breath, "and I started to pick them up just as a buzzer went off."....

Dad turned to run into his office in the other part of the house. He suddenly wondered if he was going to find all his hard work torn to shreds in the wastebasket. But the moment he got to the office, he glanced at the typewriter and breathed a sigh of relief. Thank God! The scripts were still there, just as he had left them. Daddy quickly counted the pages and found everything in order. "Terrific!", he said.

After a moment, he peeked over at the phone and looked at the buzzer on the intercom system. He nodded his head, smiling. "Saved by the bell!", he said to himself.

A BIRTHDAY GIFT FROM DAD

There were special touches my parents gave to my birthday celebrations that always made them unique: spectacular wrapped packages, fragrant arrangements of pink carnations and hand-decorated cakes. Looking back, there was one particular birthday that surpassed all others: one that I think of over and over again. It had to do with a very special present from my father. One that was not even gift-wrapped. Here's the story:

On one of my early-teen birthdays, I was in the kitchen, ready for all of us to start the festivities, when I suddenly heard my father shout, "Victoria!"

I peeked out the kitchen door and saw Daddy waving for me to sit beside him on the living room couch, facing the television set.

"Let me get something to drink first, Daddy," I said, turning to walk over to the large crystal bowl holding the fruit punch and sherbet my mother had just put out.

"No, don't do that," Daddy said, pointing to a glass sitting on a coaster on the coffee table. "We already have yours." He waved me over again, this time more impatiently.

"Hurry up, Vicki!", Mom chimed in, suddenly getting up from her seat and ushering me over to the couch. I quickly sat down beside my father.

"What's all the rush?", I demanded. "We don't have anywhere to go!"

"Shhh!", Daddy answered. "Look at the TV!"

I turned to glance at my father.

"No," he said, shaking his head for emphasis. "Don't look at me. Look at the TV!"

He pointed to the television screen again, wildly gesturing as if he were hammering a nail into the air with his index finger.

Mom sat back down in her chair again, her eyes now focused firmly on the TV set.

I didn't understand what all the fuss was about. There was nothing on the screen but a commercial. I looked up at the clock and realized that it was almost time for Dick Clark's *American Bandstand* to come on, which all of us made sure we never missed every week.

But why was everyone getting so excited? I glanced at my brother and he, too, had his eyes glued to the set. I sat there, silently, a puzzled look on my face - watching commercial after commercial.

Then suddenly - I couldn't believe my eyes! There, on the TV screen, was a drawing of pink and blue balloons surrounded by floating confetti and - right in the middle of the picture were the words: "Happy Birthday, Victoria Lee Biggers". At the same time, an announcer's voice was saying, "Happy birthday, Victoria Lee Biggers from the whole world. Keep us happy, as you are!"

The 10-second spot ended with the sound of a crowd cheering and then the picture went right into the opening for *American Bandstand*.

It couldn't be possible! My father had actually purchased ten seconds of commercial air time in order to send me a birthday message on television!

I turned to my father, my mouth open in astonishment. He was smiling from ear to ear.

"They weren't sure they could do it," said Dad with a wink, "but I had the idea and I knew I could make it work."

What an idea it was! Just minutes after the spot aired, friends and family began calling, letting us know they had just seen my name on the screen. Daddy planned it that way, of course. When he purchased the 10-second spot he made sure it was shown just before the opening of *American Bandstand*, in order to get the largest audience possible watching when my name appeared on the screen. He must have paid a mint for it!

My "Birthday Gift from Dad" birthday.

The best part was that Dad made sure a cassette tape was made of the spot, so I could listen to it later. He also presented me with the beautiful glass slide that was used for the artwork, with my name and the balloons on it.

I've often wondered about something: Daddy, through his television contacts, became friendly with Dick Clark and had lunch with him on several occasions. (At one of these lunches, in fact, Daddy asked him what the secret was to his youthful appearance and he replied with a smile: "No cosmetic surgery, Buck. It's my outlook. I just enjoy life.") Could Dick Clark have had a hand in suggesting that the spot come on just before *American Bandstand*? I'll never know. But I still have the slide and treasure it. Every so often I take it out of the tiny gold box Daddy gave it to me in just to remember a very, very special birthday.

GO GO GOPHERS

Nothing made Dad happier than finding just the right piece of music he needed to finish a song for one of his cartoon shows. I remember the day I was sprawled out on the living room rug, as a child, facing the TV set with chin in hand. I had just switched the channel and was busy looking at a popular Tootsie Roll commercial. On screen, a little boy was sitting in a darkened movie theatre watching a matinee performance of an exciting Western, as he munched hungrily on a Tootsie roll candy bar.

In the next second, an old-fashioned silent movie flashed on the screen with the hero and heroine clenched in an embrace. "The Tootsie Roll is lasting through the love scene," an announcer's voice was saying. A new image of a group of cowboys on horseback now appeared, amid the crackling sound of six-shooter guns and a trumpet playing the cavalry charge. "It's lasting through the chase scene," the announcer's voice continued. "It's even lasting through the…."

All of a sudden I saw my father racing from the kitchen into the living room faster than lightning.

"That's it!", he shouted, glancing at the TV set. He threw his hand up and waved his red flair pen in the air as if he had just won the lottery. "I finally got the bridge to the song!" Dad laughed jubilantly, pleased with himself, and ran back into the kitchen again.

"What are you working on, Daddy?", I yelled as I saw him disappear around the corner. "The theme song for *Go Go Gophers*!", he shouted back.

I was puzzled. I knew my father had been busy writing the scripts for this new Total TeleVision cartoon series, but what in the world could Dad have heard in the Tootsie Roll commercial to help him finish the show's theme song? It didn't take me long to find out.

In a few minutes, Dad had completed the song and he was so thrilled with the result that he sat right down at our black ebony piano in the living room to play it for me. As his fingers reached down to touch the piano keys, his foot kept time to the music and he swayed back and forth singing: "Go Go Gophers, watch 'em go, go, go. Go Go Gophers, watch 'em go, go, go."

Then, suddenly, there it was! Dad sang the next words - the bridge of the song - to the tune of the cavalry charge we had just heard in the TV commercial: "Here comes the colonel with his sergeant! Both are a roarin' and a chargin'!"

I clapped wildly as he finished the song with: "Go Go Gophers, watch 'em go, go, go. Go Go Gophers, watch 'em go, go, go!"

"That's terrific, Daddy!", I said with a giggle. I ran over to give my father a hug. Ever since that day, the *Go Go Gophers* theme has remained one of my favorites of the many tunes my father composed for a TTV cartoon series. Whenever I listen to it, I'm always reminded about the power of coincidence. Just think: if I hadn't happened to switch the TV dial in the living room at the same moment Dad was working on the bridge to the *Go Go Gophers* theme song, the cavalry charge would never have made it into the finished product. Life is so strange, isn't it?

GO GO GOPHERS
A TOTAL TELEVISION PRODUCTION

TITLE CARD: "Go Go Gophers"

(MUSICAL INTRO :05)

OPEN ON SKY FILLED WITH SEVERAL MOONS. RUGGED WESTERN LANDSCAPE BELOW.

NARR: (OVER INDIAN DRUMS) Many moons ago, somewhere west of Horace Greely, lay the Gulch of the Gopher Indians.

PAN DOWN TO GULCH FILLED WITH TEE-PEES. SMOKE FROM TOPS PUFFS INTO AIR. NO PEOPLE.

Many teepees filled the Gulch, for the Gophers were a great tribe ...

CUT TO LS MAN & WIFE IN WAGON JOGGING ACROSS PLAINS.

Unfortunately, Gopher Gulch stood right in the path of paleface progress.

OTHER VEHICLES, HORSES, PEOPLE OVERTAKE AND JOIN FIRST WAGON.

TRAIN ALSO JOINS. ALL HEAD IN SAME DIRECTION.

(SOUND: THUNDER OF TRAIN)

CUT TO E.L.S. AS WAGONS, TRAINS, ETC. APPROACH INDIAN VILLAGE.

BLAM

EXPLOSION EFFECT AS VEHICLES HIT VILLAGE. TEEPEES SCATTERED.

SFX. (BOWLING PINS)

EFFECT CLEARS SHOWING GULCH FREE OF TEEPEES BUT WITH TRACKS AND ROAD.

So, the Gophers were moved - lock, stock and tomahawk - to a reservation in the North...

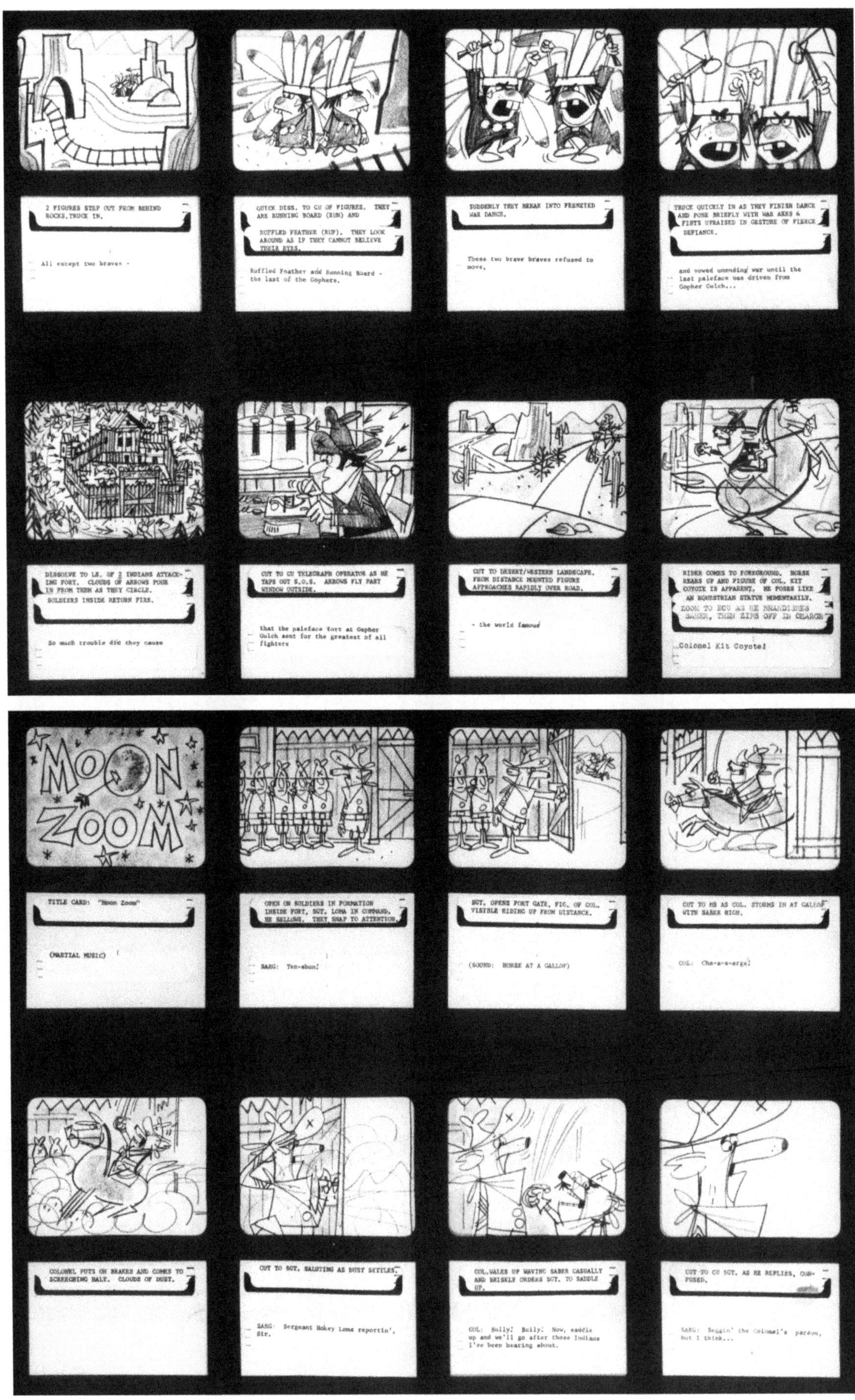
2 FIGURES STEP OUT FROM BEHIND ROCKS,TRUCK IN.
All except two braves -
QUICK DISS. TO CU OF FIGURES. THEY ARE RUNNING BOARD (RUN) AND
RUFFLED FEATHER (RUF). THEY LOOK AROUND AS IF THEY CANNOT BELIEVE THEIR EYES.
Ruffled Feather and Running Board - the last of the Gophers,
SUDDENLY THEY BREAK INTO FRENZIED WAR DANCE.
These two brave braves refused to move,
TRUCK QUICKLY IN AS THEY FINISH DANCE AND POSE BRIEFLY WITH WAR AXES & FISTS UPRAISED IN GESTURE OF FIERCE DEFIANCE.
and vowed unending war until the last paleface was driven from Gopher Gulch...
DISSOLVE TO LS. OF 2 INDIANS ATTACKING FORT. CLOUDS OF ARROWS POUR IN FROM THEM AS THEY CIRCLE.
SOLDIERS INSIDE RETURN FIRE.
So much trouble did they cause
CUT TO CU TELEGRAPH OPERATOR AS HE TAPS OUT S.O.S. ARROWS FLY PAST WINDOW OUTSIDE.
that the paleface fort at Gopher Gulch sent for the greatest of all fighters
CUT TO DESERT/WESTERN LANDSCAPE. FROM DISTANCE MOUNTED FIGURE APPROACHES RAPIDLY OVER ROAD.
- the world famous
RIDER COMES TO FOREGROUND. HORSE REARS UP AND FIGURE OF COL. KIT COYOTE IS APPARENT. HE POSES LIKE AN EQUESTRIAN STATUE MOMENTARILY.
ZOOM TO ECU AS HE BRANDISHES SABER, THEN ZIPS OFF IN CHARGE
...Colonel Kit Coyote!
MOON ZOOM
TITLE CARD: "Moon Zoom"
(MARTIAL MUSIC)
OPEN ON SOLDIERS IN FORMATION INSIDE FORT, SGT. LOMA IN COMMAND, HE BELLOWS. THEY SNAP TO ATTENTION.
SARG: Ten-shun!
SGT. OPENS FORT GATE, FIG. OF COL. VISIBLE RIDING UP FROM DISTANCE.
(SOUND: HORSE AT A GALLOP)
CUT TO MS AS COL. STORMS IN AT GALLOP WITH SABER HIGH.
COL: Cha-a-a-arge!
COLONEL PUTS ON BRAKES AND COMES TO SCREECHING HALT. CLOUDS OF DUST.
CUT TO SGT. SALUTING AS DUST SETTLES.
SARG: Sergeant Hokey Loma reportin', Sir.
COL. WALKS UP WAVING SABER CASUALLY AND BRISKLY ORDERS SGT. TO SADDLE UP.
COL: Bully! Bully! Now, saddle up and we'll go after those Indians I've been hearing about.
CUT TO CU SGT. AS HE REPLIES, CONFUSED.
SARG: Beggin' the Colonel's pardon, but I think...

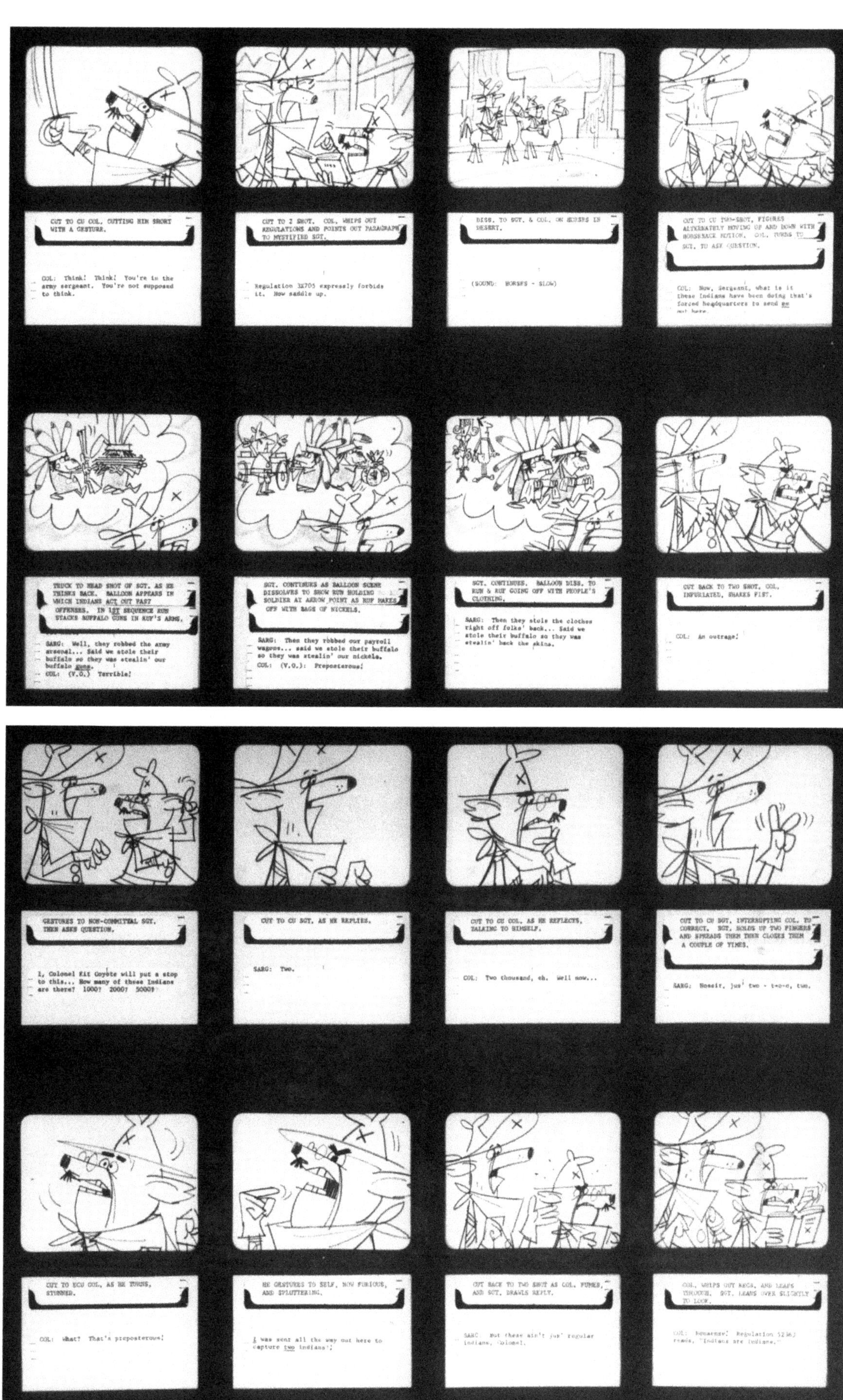
CUT TO CU COL. CUTTING HIM SHORT WITH A GESTURE.
COL: Think! Think! You're in the army sergeant. You're not supposed to think.
CUT TO 2 SHOT. COL. WHIPS OUT REGULATIONS AND POINTS OUT PASAGRAPH TO MYSTIFIED SGT.
Regulation 3X705 expressely forbids it. Now saddle up.
DISS. TO SGT. & COL. ON HORSES IN DESERT.
(SOUND: HORSES - SLOW)
CUT TO CU TWO-SHOT, FIGURES ALTERNATELY MOVING UP AND DOWN WITH HORSEBACK MOTION. COL. TURNS TO SGT. TO ASK QUESTION.
COL: Now, Sergeant, what is it these Indians have been doing that's forced headquarters to send me out here.
TRUCK TO HEAD SHOT OF SGT. AS HE THINKS BACK. BALLOON APPEARS IN WHICH INDIANS ACT OUT PAST OFFENSES. IN 1ST SEQUENCE RUN STACKS BUFFALO GUNS IN RUF'S ARMS.
SARG: Well, they robbed the army arsenal... Said we stole their buffalo so they was stealin' our buffalo guns.
COL: (V.O.) Terrible!
SGT. CONTINUES AS BALLOON SCENE DISSOLVES TO SHOW RUN HOLDING SOLDIER AT ARROW POINT AS RUF MAKES OFF WITH BAGS OF NICKELS.
SARG: Then they robbed our payroll wagons... said we stole their buffalo so they was stealin' our nickels.
COL: (V.O.): Preposterous!
SGT. CONTINUES. BALLOON DISS. TO RUN & RUF GOING OFF WITH PEOPLE'S CLOTHING.
SARG: Then they stole the clothes right off folks' back... Said we stole their buffalo so they was stealin' back the skins.
CUT BACK TO TWO SHOT. COL. INFURIATED, SHAKES FIST.
COL: An outrage!
GESTURES TO NON-COMMITAL SGT. THEN ASKS QUESTION.
I, Colonel Kit Coyote will put a stop to this... How many of these Indians are there? 1000? 2000? 5000?
CUT TO CU SGT. AS HE REPLIES.
SARG: Two.
CUT TO CU COL. AS HE REFLECTS, TALKING TO HIMSELF.
COL: Two thousand, eh. Well now...
CUT TO CU SGT. INTERRUPTING COL. TO CORRECT. SGT. HOLDS UP TWO FINGERS AND SPREADS THEM THEN CLOSES THEM A COUPLE OF TIMES.
SARG: Nossir, jus' two - t-o-o, two.
CUT TO ECU COL. AS HE TURNS, STUNNED.
COL: What? That's preposterous!
HE GESTURES TO SELF, NOW FURIOUS, AND SPLUTTERING.
I was sent all the way out here to capture two indians!
CUT BACK TO TWO SHOT AS COL. FUMES, AND SGT. DRAWLS REPLY.
SARG: But these ain't jus' regular indians, Colonel.
COL. WHIPS OUT REGS. AND LEAFS THROUGH. SGT. LEANS OVER SLIGHTLY TO LOOK.
COL: Nonsense! Regulation 52363 reads, "Indians are Indians."

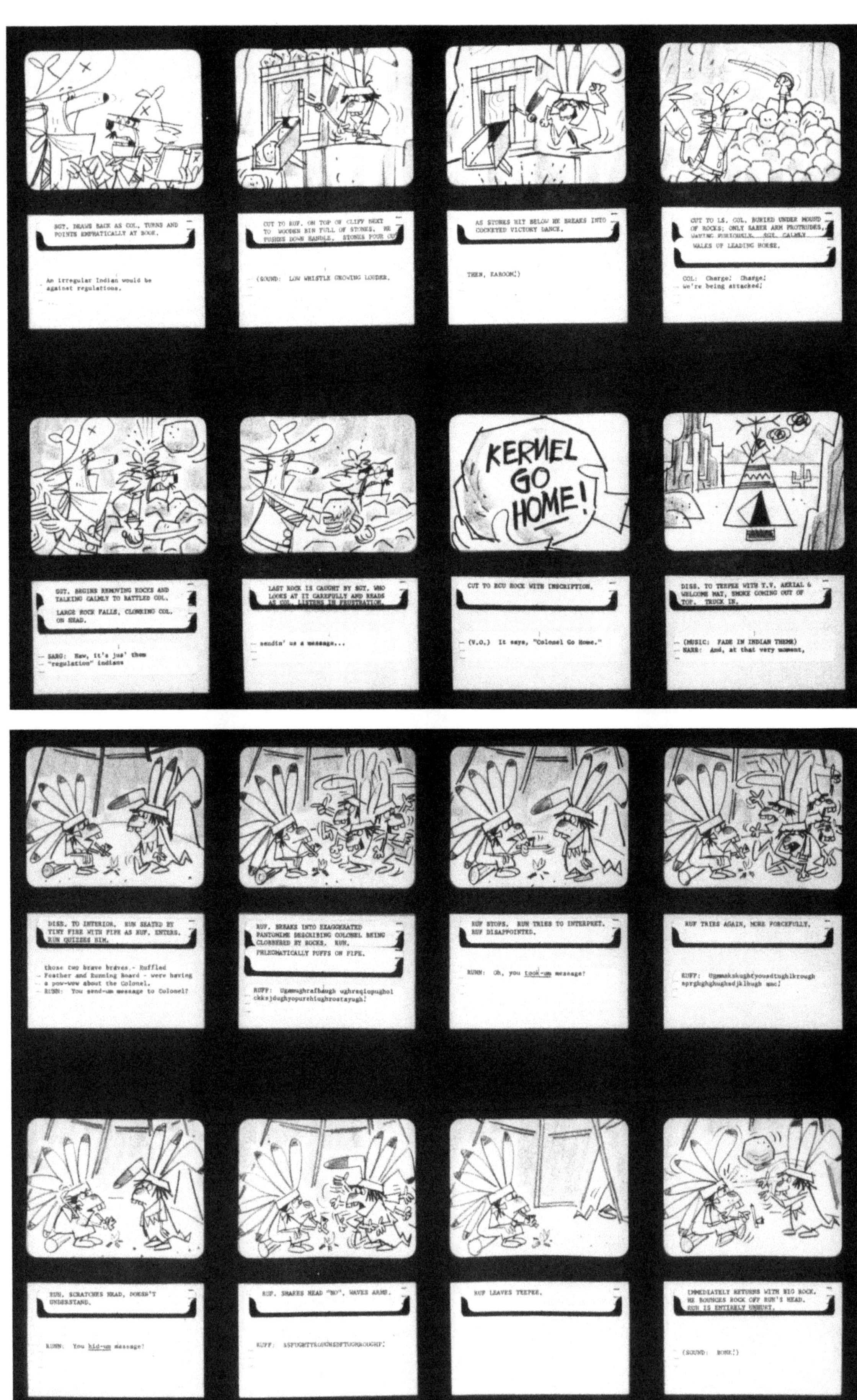
SGT. DRAWS BACK AS COL. TURNS AND POINTS EMPHATICALLY AT BOOK.
An irregular Indian would be against regulations.
CUT TO RUF. ON TOP OF CLIFF NEXT TO WOODEN BIN FULL OF STONES. HE PUSHES DOWN HANDLE. STONES POUR OUT
(SOUND: LOW WHISTLE GROWING LOUDER.
AS STONES HIT BELOW HE BREAKS INTO COCKEYED VICTORY DANCE.
THEN, KABOOM!)
CUT TO LS. COL. BURIED UNDER MOUND OF ROCKS; ONLY SABER ARM PROTRUDES, WAVING FURIOUSLY. SGT. CALMLY WALKS UP LEADING HORSE.
COL: Charge! Charge! We're being attacked!
SGT. BEGINS REMOVING ROCKS AND TALKING CALMLY TO BATTLED COL.
LARGE ROCK FALLS, CLONKING COL. ON HEAD.
SARG: Naw, it's jus' them "regulation" indians
LAST ROCK IS CAUGHT BY SGT. WHO LOOKS AT IT CAREFULLY AND READS AS COL. LISTENS IN FRUSTRATION.
sendin' us a message...
KERNEL GO HOME!
CUT TO ECU ROCK WITH INSCRIPTION.
(V.O.) It says, "Colonel Go Home."
DISS. TO TEEPEE WITH T.V. AERIAL & WELCOME MAT, SMOKE COMING OUT OF TOP. TRUCK IN.
(MUSIC: FADE IN INDIAN THEME)
NARR: And, at that very moment,
DISS. TO INTERIOR. RUN SEATED BY TINY FIRE WITH PIPE AS RUF. ENTERS. RUN QUIZZES HIM.
those two brave braves - Ruffled Feather and Running Board - were having a pow-wow about the Colonel.
RUNN: You send-um message to Colonel?
RUF. BREAKS INTO EXAGGERATED PANTOMIME DESCRIBING COLONEL BEING CLOBBERED BY ROCKS. RUN. PHLEGMATICALLY PUFFS ON PIPE.
RUFF: Ugamughrafbaugh ughraqiopughol ckksjdughyopurehiughrostayugh!
RUF STOPS. RUN TRIES TO INTERPRET. RUF DISAPPOINTED.
RUNN: Oh, you took-um message?
RUF TRIES AGAIN, MORE FORCEFULLY.
RUFF: Ugmmakshughtyousdtughlkrough sprghghghughsdjklbugh mmc!
RUN. SCRATCHES HEAD, DOESN'T UNDERSTAND.
RUNN: You hid-um message?
RUF. SHAKES HEAD "NO", WAVES ARMS.
RUF LEAVES TEEPEE.
IMMEDIATELY RETURNS WITH BIG ROCK. HE BOUNCES ROCK OFF RUN'S HEAD. RUN IS ENTIRELY UNHURT.
(SOUND: BONK!)

RUF'S ILLUSTRATION MAKES IT CLEAR TO RUN WHAT RUF HAS DONE. HE STANDS UP GIGGLING MERRILY AND HOLDING SIDE AS RUF NODS IN GAWKISH AFFIRMATIVE.
RUNN: Ohhh, you hit-um with message. Hee, hee, hee, hee. Whoopee Doopee!
RUN DELIGHTEDLY ASKS FOR MORE DETAILS.
...What him do?
RUF JUMPS UP, LANDS WITH A JAR FLAT ON BACK, FEET IN AIR.
RUF SITS UP, IMITATES MAN DETERMINEDLY RIDING HORSE. RUN BECOMES DISAPPOINTED AGAIN.
RUFF: Giftughtyroughfdesughlopd.
CUT TO CU AS RUN. PONDERS. RUF. LOOKS UP FROM HIS SEAT ON FLOOR.
RUNN: Him still coming? Pooey Phooey. Got-um be stopped.
RUF. POPS UP WAVING HAPPILY. RUN. TURNS TO HIM HOPEFULLY.
RUNN: You got-um plan?
RUF. REACHES OUT OF FRAME, WHIPS IN HAMMER, PANTOMIMES SLUGGING COL. OVER HEAD.
RUFF: Updagughpftyupughfrughop rouyghtyoutpougkytrugh..Crunch!
RUN. GESTURES "NO GOOD". RUF STOPS DISAPPOINTEDLY IN MIDST OF THIRD OR FOURTH BLOW.
RUNN: Ugh, no good. Hurt-um our hammer on his head.
RUF. DISCARDS HAMMER, DOES JOHN L. SULLIVAN ACT, ARMS FLAILING.
RUFF: Ugtaghyptygugh...Pow!... Pow! Rtyughpofhtyog...Pow! Ughfty.
RUN AGAIN GESTURES "NO." RUF WINDS DOWN IN MIDDLE OF PUNCHES.
RUNN: Ugh, no good. Hurt-um our fists on his face.
BOTH TURN AWAY AND PONDER.
RUF. HOPS UP VERY, VERY EXCITED. RUN TURNS, SURPRISED.
RUFF: (Very excited) Ughftryonpoert pordughtyoupfughtryerwcvbugh poutyoghtyrdfughrestughj...
CUT BACK TO LS. RUF GOES INTO INVOLVED, RAPID FLURRY OF ACTIONS AS RUN WATCHES HIM EXCITEDLY. HE IS IMITATING ROCKET LAUNCHING.
Bang! Zoom!
RUF. POPS UP IN SHORT ARC AND LANDS ON HEAD WITH HEAVY THUD. RUN IS OVERJOYED.
RUNN: Moon rocket!
RUN ENTHUSIASTICALLY SHAKES RUF'S HAND AND GESTURES TO SKY. RUF SHAKES HEAD WITH CRUSHED FEATHERS IN HAPPY AFFIRMATIVE.
You make-um Colonel man to moon! You-um genius!
DISS. TO RUN & RUF STUFFING POWDER KEGS INTO HOLLOW LOG MOUNTED ON TRIPOD ARRANGEMENT OF BIRCH BARK STABILIZERS.
(INDIAN MUSIC UP)

PULL BACK TO E.L.S. AS THEY STEP OVER TO CONTROL SHAFT STUCK IN MIDDLE OF NOTHING. RUN MOVES SHAFT. HUGE LOG ROCKET WITH TEEPEE ON TOP FOLDS UP ITS STABILIZERS AND BEGINS TO DESCEND INTO HOLE IN GROUND.
NARR: After having constructed the moon rocket,
ROCKET SINKS DOWN INTO GROUND LEAVING ONLY INNOCENT-LOOKING TEEPEE SHOWING.
the next problem for the brave braves was to get the Colonel into it.
DISS TO HUNN AND RUFF WALKING THROUGH BUSHY AREA LADEN WITH SIGNS AND DIGGING TOOLS
Immediately, they began work on the first step
RUFF STOPS, MARKS OUT A CIRCLE IN CLEARING AND BEGINS TO DIG
of an intricate plan designed to get the Colonel to the rocket.
STOP
DETOUR
GO AWAY
AS RUFF DIGS IN CLEARING, HUNN CONTINUES THROUGH TO OTHER SIDE OF BUSHES AND QUICKLY PUTS UP SIGNS
(SOUND: DIGGING AND HAMMERING)
DISS TO LS OF SPOT WHERE HUNN HAS PUT UP SIGNS AS SGT AND COL RIDE IN. COL REMARKS ON SIGNS
COL: Aha! A detour sign - an obvious Indian trick. Prepare to charge!
COL SUGGESTS THEY CHARGE. SGT HESITANT BUT COL'S HORSE IS ALREADY REARED UP AND READY.
SARG: Well now, Colonel, I'm not sure we oughta ...
COL: Enough! The army requires blind obedience...
CUT TO ECU COL AS HE BRANDISHES SABER AND PLUNGES ON.
Cha - a - a - arge!
ARMY GO HOME
CUT BACK TO LS AS SGT FOLLOWS COL INTO THICKET
(SOUND: HOOFBEATS)
LONG FALL AND THUD IS HEARD OFF-SCREEN. THUD CAUSES SCENE TO SHAKE.
(SOUND: CRASH!)
PAN RIGHT TO SHOW DEEP HOLE RUFF HAS DUG
CUT TO CU SGT GROPING IN DARKNESS AT BOTTOM OF HOLE
SARG: Well, I'm sure enough blind obedient now, Sir. Kaint see a thing!
PULL BACK TO SHOW COL POINTING OUT TUNNEL HE HAS DISCOVERED
COL: Never fear when you're with me, Sargeant. I've already found a handy tunnel.
CUT TO HUNN AND RUFF ON CLIFF AT END OF TUNNEL. HUNN PUTTING FINISHING TOUCHES ON DIGGING, RUFF STARING OUT AT SOMETHING BELOW.
NARR: Yes, the tunnel was handy, indeed - the other end of it only being finished at that very moment by Ruffled Feather and Running Board.
CUT TO ELS SHOWING HUNN JOINING RUFF AT EDGE OF HIGH CLIFF OVERLOOKING SOLITARY TEEPEE OF THE LOG ROCKET
CUT TO MS AS RUFF GOES THROUGH PANTOMIME INVOLVING TEEPEE AND TUNNEL. HUNN DOESN'T QUITE GET IT
RUFF: Hstuyughidpzvnughtredughugh

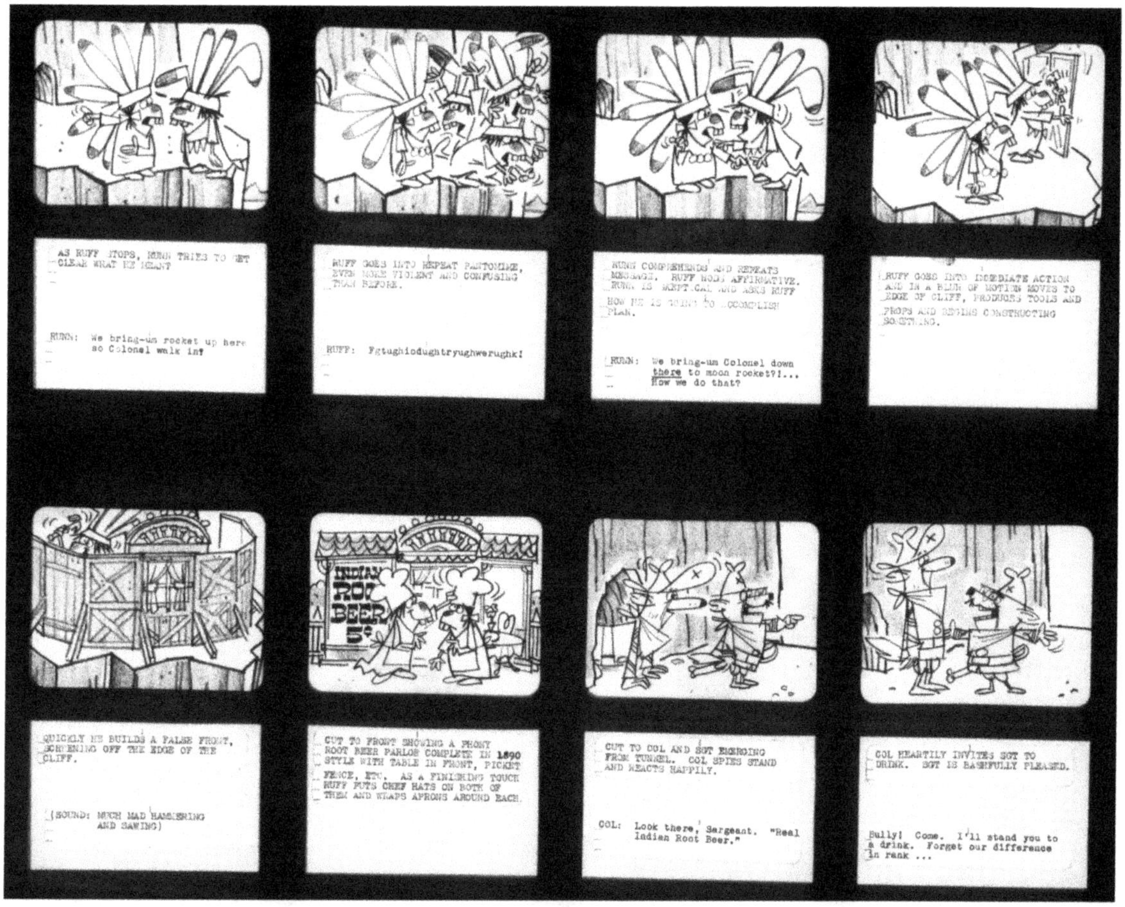

AS RUFF STOPS, RUNN TRIES TO GET CLEAR WHAT HE MEANT
RUNN: We bring-um rocket up here so Colonel walk in?
RUFF GOES INTO REPEAT PANTOMIME, EVEN MORE VIOLENT AND CONFUSING THAN BEFORE.
RUFF: Fgtughiodughtryughwerughk!
RUNN COMPREHENDS AND REPEATS MESSAGE. RUFF NODS AFFIRMATIVE. RUNN IS SKEPTICAL AND ASKS RUFF HOW HE IS GOING TO ACCOMPLISH PLAN.
RUNN: We bring-um Colonel down there to moon rocket?!... How we do that?
RUFF GOES INTO IMMEDIATE ACTION AND IN A BLUR OF MOTION MOVES TO EDGE OF CLIFF, PRODUCES TOOLS AND PROPS AND BEGINS CONSTRUCTING SOMETHING.
INDIAN ROOT BEER 5¢
QUICKLY HE BUILDS A FALSE FRONT, SCREENING OFF THE EDGE OF THE CLIFF.
(SOUND: MUCH MAD HAMMERING AND SAWING)
CUT TO FRONT SHOWING A PHONY ROOT BEER PARLOR COMPLETE IN 1890 STYLE WITH TABLE IN FRONT, PICKET FENCE, ETC. AS A FINISHING TOUCH RUFF PUTS CHEF HATS ON BOTH OF THEM AND WRAPS APRONS AROUND EACH.
CUT TO COL AND SGT EMERGING FROM TUNNEL. COL SPIES STAND AND REACTS HAPPILY.
COL: Look there, Sargeant. "Real Indian Root Beer."
COL HEARTILY INVITES SGT TO DRINK. SGT IS BASHFULLY PLEASED.
Bully! Come. I'll stand you to a drink. Forget our difference in rank ...

CUT TO STAND AS COL AND SGT WALK UP. COL ORDERS TWO ROOT BEERS.
...Two root beers my good man!
CUT TO ECU RUFF AS HE GOES INTO SUDDEN FLURRY OF GESTURES POINTING TO DOOR.
RUFF: Uytrughfkhyghjoptrughiou.
CUT TO SGT AND COL PUZZLED. COL LEANS OVER TO RUNN AND WHISPERS, ASKING WHAT RUFF MEANT.
COL: What'd he say?
RUNN GESTURES TO DOOR. COL AND SGT PLEASED.
RUNN: Him say back room reserved for Army.
CUT TO LS. AS COL AND SGT WALK IN THROUGH DOOR.
COL: Wonderful. Come along, Sargeant, we'll just...
TRUCK QUICKLY TO 2S RUFF AND RUNN POISED LISTENING, EARS CUPPED AS COL AND SGT PLUNGE OFF CLIFF.
(SOUND: POW! POW! SLIDE WHISTLE)
SCENE SHAKES GRATIFYINGLY.
(SOUND: THUD! THUD!)
RUNN AND RUFF SMILE SMUGLY AND SHAKE.
RUFF & RUNN: Hee, hee, hee, hee, hee!

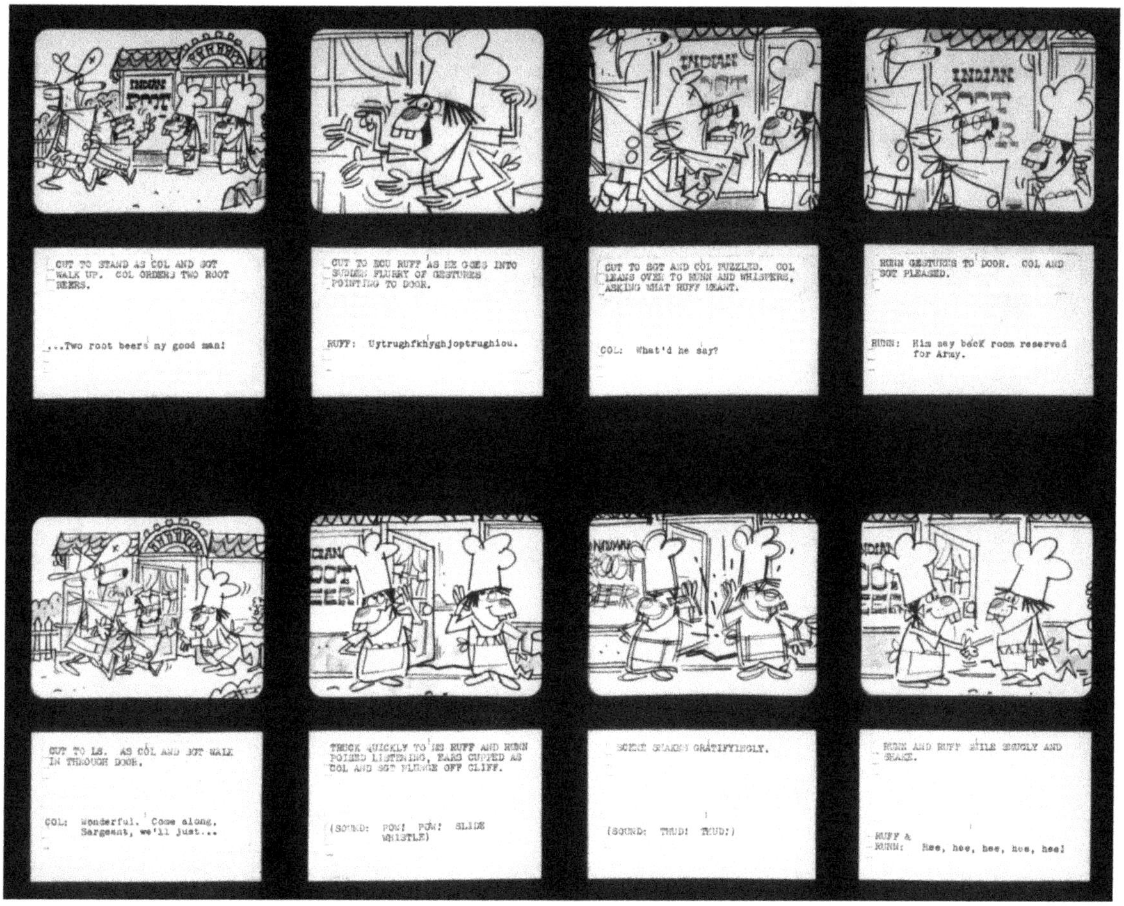

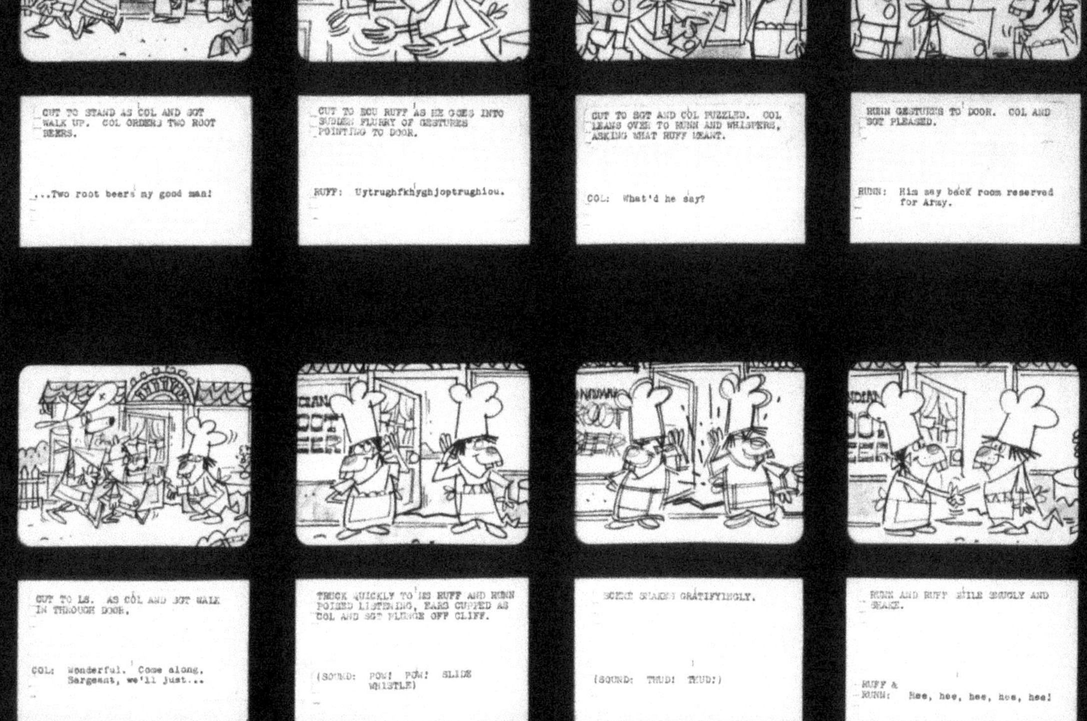

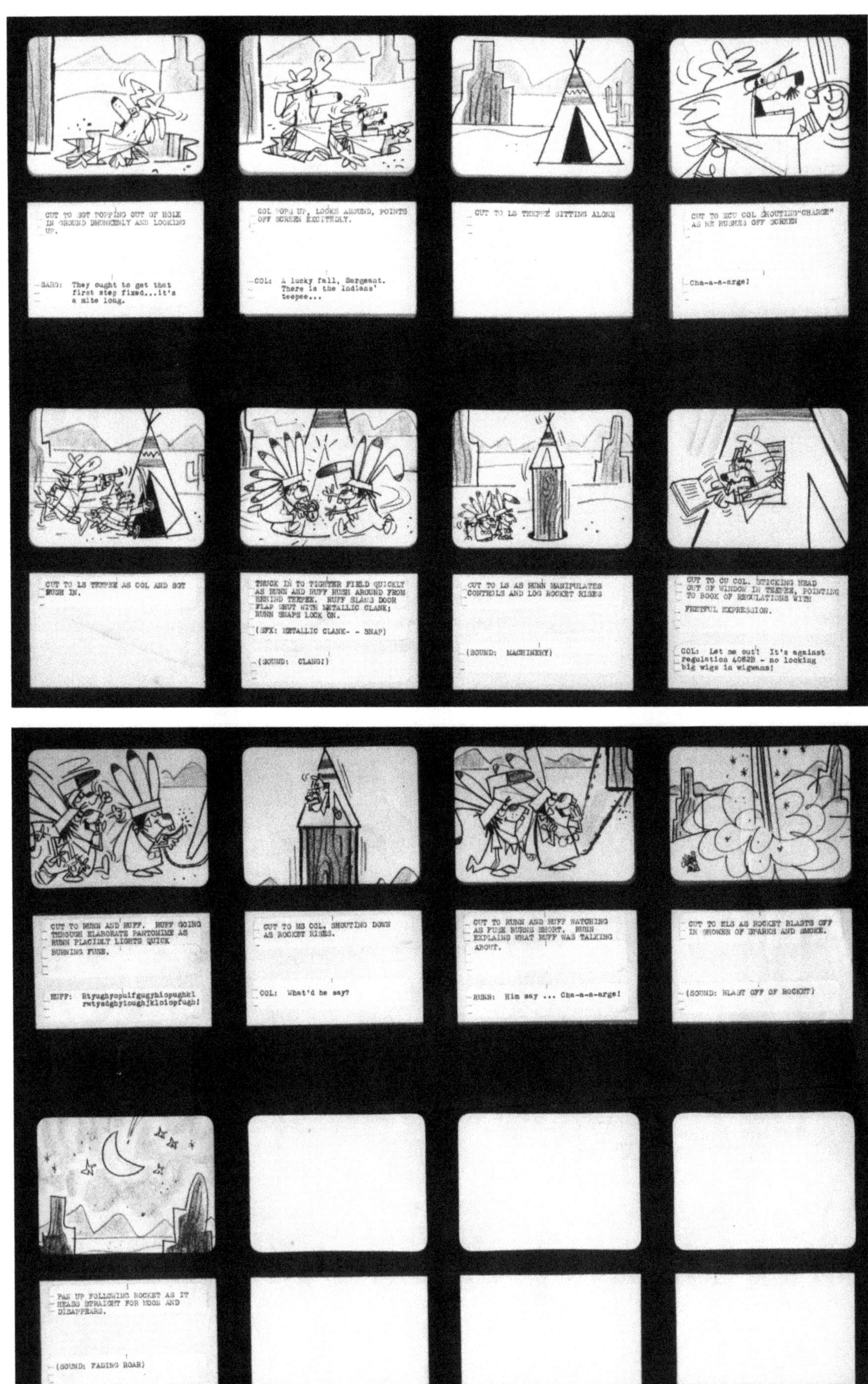
CUT TO SGT POPPING OUT OF HOLE IN GROUND DRUNKENLY AND LOOKING UP.
SARG: They ought to get that first step fixed...it's a mite long.
COL POPS UP, LOOKS AROUND, POINTS OFF SCREEN EXCITEDLY.
COL: A lucky fall, Sargeant. There is the Indians' teepee...
CUT TO LS TEEPEE SITTING ALONE
CUT TO ECU COL SHOUTING "CHARGE" AS HE RUSHES OFF SCREEN
Cha-a-a-arge!
CUT TO LS TEEPEE AS COL AND SGT RUSH IN.
TRUCK IN TO TIGHTER FIELD QUICKLY AS RUNN AND RUFF RUSH AROUND FROM BEHIND TEEPEE. RUFF SLAMS DOOR FLAP SHUT WITH METALLIC CLANK; RUNN SNAPS LOCK ON.
(SFX: METALLIC CLANK- - SNAP)
(SOUND: CLANG!)
CUT TO LS AS RUNN MANIPULATES CONTROLS AND LOG ROCKET RISES
(SOUND: MACHINERY)
CUT TO CU COL. STICKING HEAD OUT OF WINDOW IN TEEPEE, POINTING TO BOOK OF REGULATIONS WITH FRETFUL EXPRESSION.
COL: Let me out! It's against regulation 4082B - no locking big wigs in wigwams!
CUT TO RUNN AND RUFF. RUFF GOING THROUGH ELABORATE PANTOMIME AS RUNN PLACIDLY LIGHTS QUICK BURNING FUSE.
RUFF: Rtyughyopuifgugyhiopughkl rwtysdghyioughjkloiopfugh!
CUT TO MS COL. SHOUTING DOWN AS ROCKET RISES.
COL: What'd he say?
CUT TO RUNN AND RUFF WATCHING AS FUSE BURNS SHORT. RUNN EXPLAINS WHAT RUFF WAS TALKING ABOUT.
RUNN: Him say ... Cha-a-a-arge!
CUT TO ELS AS ROCKET BLASTS OFF IN SHOWER OF SPARKS AND SMOKE.
(SOUND: BLAST OFF OF ROCKET)
PAN UP FOLLOWING ROCKET AS IT HEADS STRAIGHT FOR MOON AND DISAPPEARS.
(SOUND: FADING ROAR)

IT'S A BIRD... IT'S A PLANE...

Dad and Chet were elated. They were looking forward to collecting money from a successful new business venture and were now taking a few extra minutes to celebrate during their regular lunch meeting at the 1812 House in Framingham, Massachusetts.

"We did it, buddy!", Dad said, as he toasted glasses with Chet. "I'm not sure, but I think this may prove to be the easiest money we've ever made. What are you going to do with your share?"

Chet thought for a moment.

"Put it in the bank," he answered with a smile.

"Good move," my father said, taking from his briefcase the cartoon script he and Chet were working on that week. "Okay... Now let's get to work."

In the 1960s, after they had successfully launched TTV, Dad and Chet decided that it would be wise to buy a plane, so they could be shuttled back and forth to their business meetings in New York City. And that is exactly what they did as well as hiring a retired Air Force pilot named Lynn. He was absolutely terrific.

Sometime during the past week, Dad and Chet had made an official bet with Lynn that he would not be able to coax my mother to take a ride in the plane. Why were they so sure my Mom would not go? I'll tell you. She was terrified of flying.

"Too dangerous!", my grandmother Nellie had told her. My grandmother had never flown, of course. She had been born in 1892, even before the Wright Brothers made their historic flight at Kitty Hawk, North Carolina. The closest she had ever come to getting on an airplane is watching one flying on a screen at the local movie theatre where she lived in Woodside, Queens.

By the time we moved to the Cape, my mother had developed such a fear of flying that she would usually have a panic attack if she got within 50 feet of an airport terminal. So, when Dad and Chet decided on a whim to make a bet with their pilot that he would not be able to get my mother to fly, they were certain that the money was already "in the bag". One thing was for certain, my father knew. Lynn would never, never be able to get my mother off the ground.

And so came the day when Lynn, as he had promised, invited my Mom out to the nearby Chatham airport to take a look at the plane that my father and Chet had recently purchased.

As Dad and Chet were having their lunch meeting at the 1812 House that early afternoon, my mother arrived at the airport looking absolutely stunning, as always: lovely dress, hair professionally coiffed, designer sunglasses and a touch of her trademark pink lipstick.

"Get in, Grace," Lynn suggested, "Take a look at the inside of the plane and we'll just taxi around the runway."

"Okay," said Mom, "As long as we stay on the runway. Promise?"

"I promise."

Lynn began to taxi on the runway, moving the plane in slow circles. After a few minutes, Lynn said casually: "Grace, as long as you're here, how about going up just for a minute? It's a beautiful day."

"Oh, no. You'll never get me up there, Lynn!", Mom laughed, shaking her head and putting her hands in front of her. But she had to admit, the weather was perfect.

As the little plane taxied around the runway for the sixth or seventh time, Lynn turned to my mother and said once again, "How about it, Grace? Want to go up?"

"I've been thinking about it Lynn, but, no." Mom sighed and Lynn decided to call it a day.

But then he got a surprise. Mom suddenly dug her nails into the seat and said, 'Lynn. I've changed my mind. Let's go up. If I don't do it now I never will, and I'll be the first person in my family to have flown!"

"Are you sure, Grace?", Lynn said.

"I'm sure!", Mom said, nodding. "Hurry before I change my mind!" She closed her eyes tightly and clutched the seat as Lynn started to pick up speed. Then, suddenly, the plane lifted into the clear blue sky.

Mom opened her eyes and gasped. The scene of the winding arm of Cape Cod, that she had seen so many times in photographs, simply took her breath away.

"My God!", Mom exclaimed, taking off her sunglasses, "It's absolutely gorgeous!"

Back at the restaurant, the manager suddenly tapped Dad on the shoulder. "Phone call for you, Mr. Biggers," he said. Dad and Chet looked at each other.

"It's your wife."

Dad got up and walked briskly to the front desk. He grabbed the phone.

"Watts?", he heard my mother say on the other line. She was ecstatic. "I'm going up a second time!"

As soon as school got out, Mom had my brother and I picked up and driven over to the Chatham airport where the two of us also took our first airplane ride. It was beautiful! And Lynn's expert piloting and thrilling narration made it all just perfect.

How much did my father end up losing on that bet? I don't know. And, to my knowledge, neither did my mother. According to Dad, he and Chet made a pact never to reveal the exact amount of money that they had to part with that day. Dad would only tell us that it was the closest he and Chet ever came to "losing their shirts".

No matter. From then on, whenever Lynn would fly over our beachfront home and wave the wing of the plane - Daddy would smile and wave back as if to say: "Job well done!" Because Lynn had done the impossible and paved the way for him and my mother to take all those fabulous vacations and NBC trips they were soon to make.

And on those particular days when my father and mother would be in the plane together flying over our house, Watts, Jr. and I could truly look up

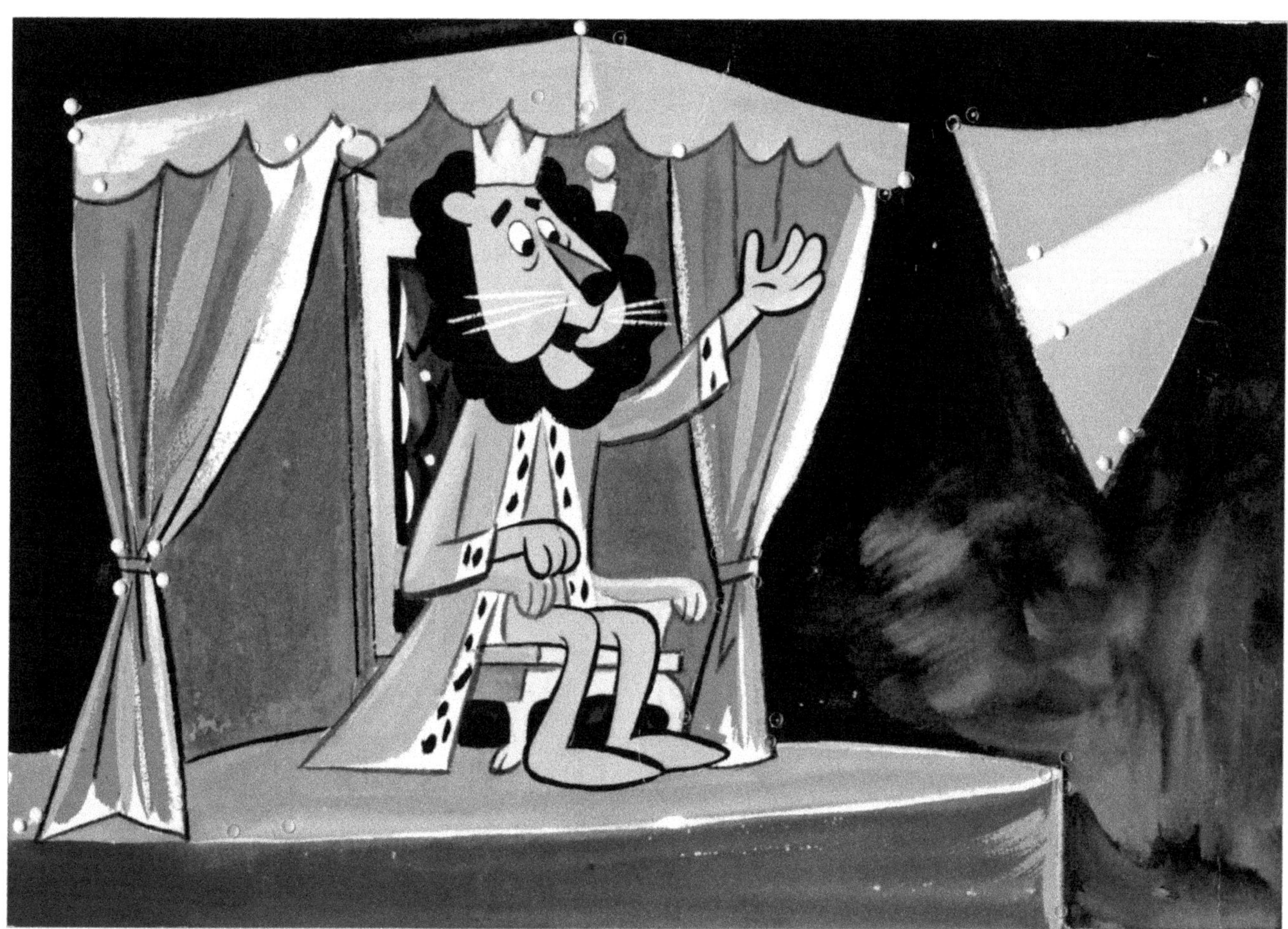

and shout, with a nod to Underdog: "Look, up in the sky. It's a bird …. It's a plane… It's Mom!"

IT'S TIME FOR THE BEAGLES!

Not many fans know that, in addition to being the co-writer of all the TTV cartoon scripts as well as the sole author of the music and lyrics for each show, Dad was also the voice of the announcer on *The Beagles*. Yep, that's right! When you see the man at the beginning of each episode shouting: "It's time for the Beagles!", it's my father's voice. If you listen closely, in fact, you can even hear Dad's slight Southern accent.

"I had no idea I'd be doing the final voice for that character," Dad once told me. "But I recorded the voice for a sample *Beagles* script and Tread liked it so much he asked me to do it permanently. Tread said that no one who auditioned could come close to the way I read it."

Dad also recorded several five-second "teasers" that are used in the show, too, such as: "Bet you don't know what's coming up next!"

I can never get over how wonderful Dad is in the role. Oh, well… I guess he was a natural-born actor!

One of my fondest childhood memories is sitting next to my father on the couch at home each time he finished writing a new *Beagles* song. As soon as one of these tunes was completed, Daddy would always make sure he'd play it for the family immediately. As my Mom, Watts, Jr. and I would sit down next to my Dad, we'd notice that he had pieces of paper all over the couch with music notes scribbled on them in black ink.

The tunes were always wonderful, but I always felt that "I Wanna Capture You" was one of my father's favorites - just from the way he swayed back and forth and tapped his foot on the floor whenever he'd perform that one. I could tell Daddy thought it was special. So did I! It was always my favorite, too!

And as for the *Beagles* theme song "Looking for the Beagles"? That stands out on its own because when the song was released, it was predicted to win one of the top 100 slots in the *Billboard* Charts on November 29, 1966. Wow, was my father proud of that! And, wow! Were we proud of my Dad!

FOR TWO BEAGLES WE CERTAINLY GET INTO A LOT OF DOG-GONE TROUBLE. IT'S ALL IN FUN.
THE BEAGLES
ALL NEW—ALL IN COLOR
12:30PM ON WCBS-TV 2

FIRE ALARM

One of the most wonderful memories I have as a child is the continual anticipation of what my father was going to invest in next. One of Dad's greatest qualities was his talent for being able to take an innovative idea and turn it into a reality. For example, although they are as plentiful now as grains of sand on the beach, when I was growing up, people who resided on Cape Cod didn't live in condos. In the 1960s, you either owned a house or rented an apartment. But Dad - and Chet Stover - helped change all that. One summer, Dad and Chet purchased a colony of beach cottages on Cape Cod Bay and decided to sell them all off individually. Something that was unheard of at the time. Many real estate agents warned them that they were certain to lose money. But in a very short time each and every one of the beach cottages were sold at a handsome profit. What did Dad and Chet do then? You guessed it. They immediately purchased a second cottage colony - this time on the opposite side of the Cape - and quickly sold those off, too! Another one of Dad and Chet's innovative ideas that turned to gold!

Then there was the time that Dad decided to buy an island. To this day, I don't even know where it was. All I remember is landing in our private plane with Mom and Dad in what seemed to be the middle of nowhere - with lots of green vegetation and trees but - as far as I could see - no homes, cars, or people. I'll never forget being met by a kind, older gentleman - perhaps the caretaker - who immediately bowed and presented me with a tiny porcelain cup and saucer etched with gold. "And this is for you," he said, proudly, with what sounded like a Dutch accent. He smiled from ear to ear, the two tufts of white hair on either side of his head blowing in the August breeze. "Thank you," I answered, curtsying in my pink summer frock. And with that we were off again in the plane... I later found out that Dad sold that island for much, much more than he bought it for. Another smart investment!

As you might guess, my father's talent for being able to spot new innovations in real estate went hand in hand with his love for any new innovation that came on the market, too. Especially anything for home use. Dad wanted the Biggers family, for example, to be one of the first in our neighborhood to get a fire alarm. Remember, this was the 1960s. There were no smoke alarms, then. Incredibly, flames had to be almost touching the round, metal disc on many fire alarms in those days - including ours - in order for the buzzer to sound. Thank goodness we never had a fire! But the day Daddy purchased that fire alarm is one I'll never forget. I distinctly remember my father lining us up - my mother, Watts, Jr. and I and - last but not least - our silver poodle, Petunia. In the next second, Dad had us all marching into the living room ."Okay, everyone," Dad said, "we're going to have our first fire drill."

"Right this minute, Dad?", Watts, Jr. asked.

"That's right," Daddy answered, quickly handing Petunia's leash to my mother. "Now, when you hear the alarm sound - don't panic - it's just a drill. But leave the house as quickly and quietly as you can. I'm going to time us."

Needless to say, the drill didn't go as planned. The next thing we knew, Dad climbed up a small stepladder, lit a match under the fire alarm, and then - as soon as the alarm sounded - everything went wrong. First, when Daddy blew the match out he didn't realize that the slight motion this caused would suddenly make the step ladder begin to sway. Dad started to slip down the step ladder but - by a miracle, he was able to stop his fall by landing with the palm of one hand and the fist of the other - (he still had the smoking match in it) - on the wall in front of him that the ladder was leaning against.

As he got his feet firmly on the ground - the alarm ringing with a deafening roar - Petunia started barking and running in a frenzy, so that - try as she might - Mom couldn't get the leash on her.

As for my brother and I, we realized that my Dad hadn't mentioned which of the five exits in that part of the house we were supposed to use. So - with the same instinct - he and I raced for the laundry room - at the very end of the house. As we scrambled ahead, Watts was attempting to put on his jacket - just like he might in a real emergency - and - in his haste to get to the exit - he got one arm caught firmly in its sleeve.

Meanwhile, my mother had succeeded in clipping the leash onto Petunia's collar and, huffing and puffing, the dog was practically dragging Mom behind her. Finally, when we all reached the exit - we started pulling on the doorknob only to find that it wouldn't budge. Yes, we had forgotten that the handy man was coming next week to fix a faulty lock on it.

"Hurry, Dad, open it!", Watts said, gesturing frantically with his free hand. Now, as my father started twisting and turning the doorknob, I covered my ears to try to block out some of the noise of the fire alarm. Somehow - my father yanked and yanked until the door finally opened. Almost in unison, we all piled out into the yard.

After a short pause, Mom patted Petunia reassuringly on the head and said to my father: "Well, Watts, how did we do?"

Dad looked at Mom incredulously, pointing to his watch as we all hurried back into the laundry room.

"Lousy," he answered. "That must have been the worst fire drill on record!"

He quickly walked back into the house to shut off the alarm with my brother following right behind him.

"Hey, Dad," Watts said, as they moved along, "Maybe we should have gone to see Mr. Whoopee first."

KICK START

During the years they worked together, Dad and Chet offered their expert services as consultants to many advertising firms and production companies. One day, they had just signed a lucrative agreement with a prestigious Manhattan firm and were walking down the hallway to the exit. As they got to the door, their client, a Vice President of the company, heartily shook hands with Dad and Chet. Then, briefcases in hand, they both started to walk out to the busy streets of Manhattan. But before they could even get two feet from the building, Daddy felt a light tap on his shoulder and turned again to see the VP waving him back.

"Oh, Buck," the man said excitedly. "Before you go, we wanted to show you and Chet something that just arrived. State of the art. We'd value your expert opinion on it."

Not sure of what to expect, Dad followed the man through the doorway again and into a side room and came face to face with - well - he didn't exactly know what it was. All he saw in front of him was a piece of equipment several feet in height. As he shot a sidelong glance at Chet - he quickly realized that he didn't know what it was, either.

Now, you have to remember that, in his long career in advertising Dad had directed many TV commercials and, like Chet, was familiar with virtually every current piece of post-production equipment used in the industry. Through the years, in fact, my father had directed several of his own productions. He even maintained a small editing suite at home. But at this moment both he and Chet were simply baffled by what they were looking at.

"Well, Buck," the VP continued, "What do you think?"

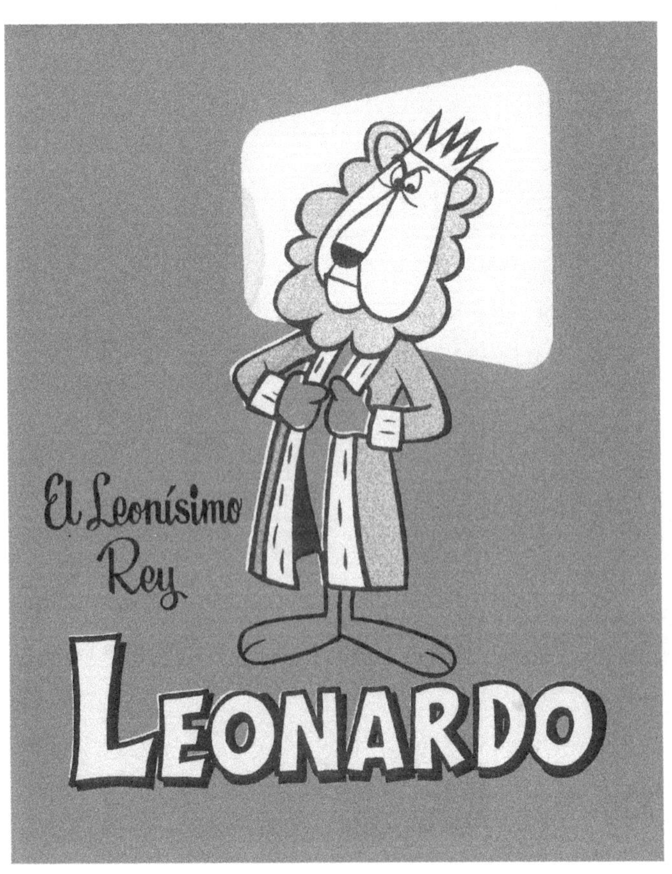

Suddenly, a frightening thought raced through Dad's mind. He realized that he had to be very careful about the answer he gave to their new client because he didn't want to jeopardize the contract he and Chet had just signed. Since Daddy didn't know what this monstrosity was in front of him, what in the world was he going to say? To make matters worse, several other members of the company had now entered the room and the expectant look on their faces told Dad that they, too, were waiting for his response.

Five seconds ticked by. All eyes were on my father. The room was so silent that you could hear a pin drop.

Slowly, Dad crept up to the machine and, stopping right in front of it, he carefully began to examine every button, dial and knob on the strange contraption. Finally, not knowing what else to do, Daddy took hold of the top of the machine with both hands, lifted one foot and gave the base of it a firm kick.

My father then turned to the group of men and, nodding his head in approval, announced: "Gentlemen, this piece of equipment is top of the line!"

Dad loved to tell people that, from then on, whenever he and Chet were about to walk into an office to meet with potential new clients, he would always try to jump start their energy levels by saying, "Okay - Chet - let's get in that meeting and kick some machines!"

THE HATFIELDS AND MCCOYS

Throughout the years, Total TeleVision had a number of cartoon shows that, for one reason or another, never materialized. There were a couple that I can think of, for example, that came very close to fruition and had already been completed as pilots. One of these was titled *Noah's Lark*. Why it didn't go on to win a weekly time slot is anyone's guess.

Other potential Total TeleVision series "bit the dust" when they were just beginning production, such as *The Colossal Show*, for which Dad wrote a fabulous circus-like theme song that had already been recorded in a studio. I still have a copy of the comic book showing the Roman characters on the cover and, somewhere in storage, the song, too.

Several other cartoon shows, like *The Three Muskrateers*, were far enough along in production that they had sample scripts and completed storyboards. Many of these are in my personal collection.

One of Chet and Dad's favorite programs that never got off the ground was a wonderful cartoon about a baseball team titled: *The Red White and Blue Sox*. Miraculously, a large, colorfully-painted storyboard that Chet Stover did still survives from this cartoon idea. It is a beautiful piece of artwork!

But one cartoon show that came very close to going into production before it, too, fell by the wayside was: *The Hatfields and McCoys*. Several scripts had already been written for this program and my brother and I had even gone into a studio and recorded two of the childrens' voices for one of the first episodes. That was a lot of fun.

But what I remember most about *The Hatfields and McCoys* is not only the foot-stomping, hand-clapping, authentic country music theme that my father wrote for the cartoon show, but the wonderful weekend my family spent recording the theme song at our beachfront home on Cape Cod.

It started out as a quiet, mid-summer weekend, but, when my father found out that not only my Aunt Edna and Uncle Rod were coming to visit, but my Uncle Harry and Aunt Kathleen and several other cousins as well, he decided to utilize the talents of the whole family to record a "rough" version of the *Hatfields and McCoys* theme song.

This was standard procedure for all TTV cartoon shows, including *Underdog* and *Tennessee Tuxedo*, even though the preliminary theme song version usually consisted of just my father singing and playing either the piano or the guitar. After completion, Dad would hand his "rough cut" over to

Tread Covington, who would use it as reference guide for the final version, which would later be recorded with singers and musicians in a professional studio.

Now, on this beautiful weekend on Cape Cod, Daddy got us all together in the living room, dragged out his reel-to-reel tape recorder and proceeded to pass out copies of the theme song he had written to everyone. Thus began one of the most memorable summer weekends my family ever spent together.

With my father directing the recording session and playing guitar, my mother strumming along on the bass fiddle, and the rest of the family singing and joining in with such authentic "hillbilly" instruments as the "jug" and the "washboard", *The Hatfields and McCoys* theme song sounded absolutely stupendous! The beginning of the lyrics to the song went like this:

"Oh, the Hatfields and McCoys
All them reckless girls and boys
They're sure havin' a lot of fun'n
While they feud.
Tommy Hatfield and his brother
Sure fooled poor ole' Bobby's mother
When they took off with the moonshine
That she brewed."

One of my Dad's ingenious touches was a natural beat he had in the song after the word "feud". During the short pause that followed this particular word, the audience was supposed to hear the sound of a rifle shot before the singers went into the next part of the lyrics. To make a realistic sound, each time we got ready to do a new "take" of the song, my Uncle Harry would blow up a small paper bag and then smash it with his hands the moment the pause came in so that it sounded exactly like a rifle shot.

All went well until later in the afternoon, when my Uncle started getting tired. That's when the gunshot sound between the words "feud" and "Tommy" started coming in later and later as Uncle Harry struggled to keep hitting the paper bags on time. On one take, the pause lasted for a full ten seconds! Oh, did we have fun that day! I don't think we ever laughed so much in our lives!

Finally, the song was completed, though, and - believe me - the result was fabulous! And, yes, somewhere in storage, the tape still exists.

For some reason that weekend brought our family even closer together than we were before. As the years went by, whenever family members would call each other and talk about the best times we had shared - someone would always say: "Hey - will you ever forget that weekend we recorded *The Hatfields and the McCoys?"*

"THE THREE MUSKRATEERS"

Series Storyline

This delightful new series is built around the wild and hilarious antics of three madcap muskrats - Maurie, Monk and Mervin. Against a background of Dixieland Jazz, the Three Muskrateers manage to maneuver themselves (or to be maneuvered by a wildcat lawyer name of "Squire Scat") into every conceivable type of situation... and a number of inconceivable ones as well.

The prime-mover for the Muskrateers appears to be money - or, really, the lack of money. Unable to hold any job for more than a few days or hours, the ~~Three~~ Muskrateers are forwer being tossed out of their boarding house for failure to pay rent or chased by a process server for failure to keep up certain installment payments or tossed into jail for failure to pay a fine or chased by a restaurateur for inability to pay their check.

Naturally, then, the Muskrateers are constantly searching for a quick way to make a lot of money; a new job with high pay; a new business with great growth potential; or a new subway grating where they can gum-fish for coins.

BUCK BIGGERS' HOLIDAY EXTRAVAGANZA

One Christmas, my parents decided to take us to Boston Common, to see the Christmas Lights. Boston Common has an interesting history: First it was a cow pasture, then it became a field where British soldiers mustered before the Revolutionary War and finally it became a public park. In the summer you can visit the colorful gardens there - oldest in the nation - and the famous Swan Boats. But in the winter the park becomes a glorious wonderland filled with the most beautifully lit trees you've ever seen!

The year we went to see the lights was very important for my father. It made such an impression on him that the day after we got home, he began decorating every tree in our front yard a different hue - just as he had seen in the Common - with different colored strings of electric lights. There were blue trees, yellow trees, red trees, green trees, orange trees, purple trees - the list went on and on. Then one day my father got an idea. Why not copy the Boston Common tradition completely by having Christmas music to accompany the display. But how? Unfortunately, there was virtually no way to pipe music from our house down to the trees on our property, which were a good fifty feet away. But my father - who had invented Mr. Whoopee, the man with all the answers - was not one to be put off so easily. After thinking the matter over for a day, he knew just what to do.

Dad bought a life-size Santa, painted on a six foot tall canvas, which he planted snugly in the ground. The next step was to surround Santa with several large wrapped gift boxes. Then, Dad got a small amplifier with a long, long cord, which he water-proofed so it wouldn't get wet in the snow. The last step was to hide the amplifier in one of the gift boxes at Santa's feet and then plug the other end of the cord into the hi-fi system in our living room, and - Voilà! - the result was spectacular.

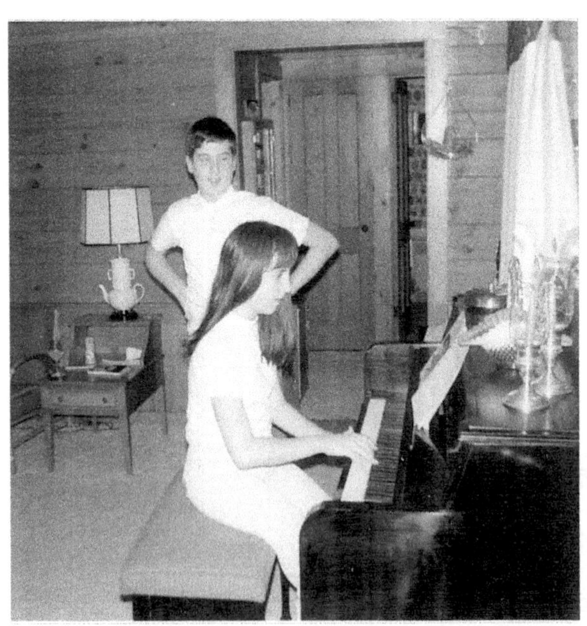

Victoria and Watts, Jr. All TTV theme songs were composed on this piano, including "Underdog" and "Go Go Gophers"!

For the entire holiday season, as soon as Daddy heard a car approaching, he would drop whatever script he was working on and quickly move to the window and peek out, a smile on his face. As Dad had expected, what happened next was always the same: Every time the car got to the edge of our property, it would always come to a full stop. Then, the driver would emerge from the vehicle and begin looking helplessly around - wondering where - on this deserted beach in the middle of the winter on Cape Cod - Christmas music could possibly be coming from.

As they would stand there at the side of the road, with snowflakes falling softly in the moonlight - and listen to the jubilant voices of the Ray Conniff Singers or the Mormon Tabernacle Choir, I'm sure that not one driver ever guessed that a small amplifier was hidden in a wrapped gift box just a few feet away!

THE EASTER SURPRISE

Holiday time was always special in our house. But there is one holiday - one very special Easter, that my brother and I could never forget. It all began when my parents told us that they had decided to take us all for a mini-vacation at the nearby Charter House Hotel on the Charles River in Boston. Make no mistake about it, Watts and I loved the Charter House. Every time we stayed there my parents always made sure we got a huge suite with a giant living room, and two separate bedrooms with a private bath - one bedroom and bath for my Mom and Dad and the other one for my brother and I.

The food was fantastic there. In those days, every hotel had both a fine dining restaurant and a coffee shop for family meals. Watts, Jr. and I loved the coffee shop with its circular booths. To make these trips more exciting, our private driver in Boston, Charlie, would take us on a narrated tour, always stopping at the famous Jack's Joke Shop and then The Museum of Science. One time he even arranged a private tour for us at the Old North Church.

But this vacation was going to be different. It would mean that we would not be spending Easter Sunday at home. And that meant no Easter Baskets and Easter egg hunts!

In the suite at the hotel in fact, the night before Easter, I was nestled in my father's arms, sobbing uncontrollably. "Daddy," I kept saying, tears rolling down my face, "Do you think the Easter Bunny will find us here?" Daddy hugged me closer.

"Victoria," he said, "I don't think so. But you'll have many, many more wonderful Easters to look forward to." That made me start crying even more.

Finally, with the pillow on my bed soaked in tears, I went to sleep.

The next morning, as I slowly opened my eyes, I thought I saw the sun streaming through the window in front of me. To my surprise, I was looking at gold tin foil lining a giant Easter Basket! I sat up in bed. There were Easter Baskets everywhere, filled to the brim with colorful plastic eggs and foil-wrapped Chocolate eggs. There were adorable stuffed bunny rabbits around me - each with a different face, and tiny pink and yellow baskets filled with jelly beans. Best of all, right next to the bed was a giant white sugar-spun egg with pink swirled icing and a small window to look though - with a delightful scene inside complete with a tiny church, green meadow, and little thatched-roof houses.

The morning was capped off with a wonderful Easter egg hunt for my brother and I right in our hotel suite. But that's not the ending to the story. When we arrived home the next day my brother and I stopped short the second we walked into the living room. For there, on the coffee table, were two more huge Easter Baskets filled with wrapped gifts - more goodies from the Bunny for my brother and I!

And here lies a mystery: How did the baskets get there? In order to reach the garage outside, you had to pass by the coffee table in the living room and, believe me, when the four of us were walking out to the car together to leave for Boston, that coffee table was empty. No one had a key to our home and my parents were careful never to let anyone into the house when we were not there. Even close friends. So.... Who put the Easter baskets on the table? Every few years, my brother and I would ask my father the same

question. But all we ever got for an answer was a shrug and a little smile as Daddy continued writing in his notebook. Which leads me to the conclusion that I've known all along: Yes, Victoria, there is an Easter Bunny!

DADDY AND THE PEACOCK

In the 1970s my father made a decision to relocate the Biggers family to New York City. There, we got a beautiful, spacious three bedroom apartment on 79th Street on the upper East side. A fabulous location. For a couple of years, Daddy was back at DFS on Madison Avenue, but he quickly moved over to NBC and became Vice President of Advertising and Promotion for both the East and West coasts. Wow! What a switch from writing cartoon shows!

For me, this proved to be one of the most spectacular times in my life. Being able to watch comic greats like Steve Martin in private rehearsals, getting front-row VIP seats at *Saturday Night Live* telecasts and having the honor of meeting many of the world's most famous stars in my father's office were experiences like no other. One of my biggest thrills of all, however, took place one evening at an NBC party. I had been speaking with Bill Murray (who was as funny off-stage as he was on), when I suddenly turned to see Mick Jagger and David Bowie standing in front of me. "Well, here's a well-dressed young lady!" Mick said in that unforgettable British accent. A beautiful smile lit up his face as he reached out his arms and took my hands in his. In the background, slow romantic music began to play as he gently laid my head on his shoulder, wrapped his strong arms around me and held me tightly against his chest. And then - like magic - Mick Jagger was whirling me around and around the room. What a terrific dancer! What a gentleman! And wow! What an evening!

Daddy went into the work full speed ahead. And, as with all of his previous undertakings, he and his talented staff helped usher in several new trends in the television industry, including the five-second promo. But, by far, the most important of Dad's accomplishments when he took over the advertising department was re-introducing something to NBC that many people - including both TV viewers and network personnel - lamented as being long gone. Yes - believe it or not - Dad and his wonderful advertising department were responsible for bringing back the NBC Peacock!

Let me explain: Before my father arrived at NBC, the network had made a decision to scrap the Peacock because they felt that the famed icon was too connected with the past and they wanted something new for the 70s. So, they came up with a blue and red logo that looked something like two triangles fitted together. That didn't thrill Dad. He thought, quite frankly, that the design did nothing to promote the network. That it simply wasn't exciting enough. That's when Daddy and other network executives began talking about bringing back the peacock.

"Why not invent an entirely new Peacock?", Dad said to himself, "Something that could combine the best elements of the old familiar Peacock with a whole new design - one that would give the bird a distinctly modern look."

And that's exactly what happened. After research confirmed that audiences were anxious for the peacock's return, Daddy and his fabulous team at 30 Rockefeller Plaza went to work and quickly came up with a fantastic streamlined logo paired with a brand new slogan: "NBC - Proud as a Peacock!" Their original peacock design still graces the NBC network today!

FRED SILVERMAN

I met Fred Silverman at several NBC parties and he was wonderful - full of energy and always so complimentary about Dad's talents. What a presence! Fred was amazing to listen to because he was constantly coming up with tremendous new ideas for shows. With his long track record in the television industry, believe me, he knew exactly what viewers wanted to watch. My father loved working with him.

One evening, Dad told me that Fred had an interesting, out-of-the-ordinary way of describing to his NBC employees exactly what was on his mind at any given moment. Almost like a secret language.

"Really?", I said, "What do you mean?"

"Well", Daddy answered, matter-of-factly, "Sometimes Fred talks in vegetables."

"Talks in vegetables?", I repeated, staring at my father in disbelief. I didn't have a clue what he was referring to.

Then, two nights later, the gold-plated, 1920s French phone that Dad had given me one Christmas rang in my room - the ringer was so loud you could hear it in the next apartment! When I picked it up Fred Silverman was on the line. This was nothing unusual. Fred sometimes called my father several times a night. But, naturally, any family member who picked up the phone always made sure Dad got the call right away.

Jumping up from my easy chair, I ran down the long hallway and into the living room where my father was busily watching - you guessed it - the NBC network. That was part of his job. Dad always made sure he stayed glued to the television set from the minute he got home from work until he went to bed. He even ate his dinner, in fact, right in front of the TV.

"Daddy, Fred's on the phone!", I whispered.

In a flash, Daddy removed his glasses and quickly walked toward the phone in the kitchen.

Back in my own room, I picked up the receiver again and immediately heard the "click" that told me that Daddy was on the line. Then, very quietly, I slowly started to hang up the phone.

"Buck," I heard Fred say, just as I was about to put the receiver back on the hook, "What's all that spinach on the TV screen?"

Fred Silverman, R.I.P.

THE ROOM

When I was a child, Thanksgiving always brought us to my Aunt and Uncle's magnificent home in the town of Hicksville, Long Island. It was an easy, half-day drive, even in the 1960s, when parts of Interstate 95 hadn't been completed yet. On most occasions, however, the Biggers family would wind up spending the night enroute, just because my parents loved hotels. (Our yearly visits to my grandfather in Marietta, Georgia, always turned into an "extended vacation" for this reason. We would end up spending the night in virtually every state we drove through on the way, including New York, Pennsylvania, Maryland, Virginia, North Carolina and South Carolina.)

It wasn't only my parents' love of hotels, of course, but my father's poor sense of direction that made these holiday trips even longer. For example, even though we had visited my Aunt and Uncle every Thanksgiving since leaving New York in 1961, my father would always make several wrong turns before we got to our overnight accommodations. The fact that he had driven the same route each year made no difference. As soon as we would cross over the familiar waters of the Cape Cod Canal, he would suddenly become disoriented. Oh, if only the GPS had been invented in those days!

To make matters worse, during the entire trip our dog, Petunia, would continue to watch my father's right foot. Whenever he suddenly put his foot on the brake, Petunia would begin to pant and throw herself onto my mother's lap in sheer terror. The animal's huffing and puffing would get even louder, it seemed, whenever Mom would yell: "Left! Left! I told you to turn left!"

"Sorry, Grace," Dad would say, shaking his head, "I missed the exit again!" Inevitably, by the time we circled back to the expressway for the third or fourth time, we would see the sun just beginning to set. That was always my mother's cue to take the Howard Johnson's hotel guide out of the glove compartment and begin thumbing through the pages.

Believe it or not, the Howard Johnson's franchise had started out in the 1930s with one single restaurant located on - coincidentally - Cape Cod, Massachusetts. By the 1960s, however, it had turned into one of the largest family-friendly hotel chains in the United States. Not only did Howard Johnson's restaurants - with their colorful orange-tiled roofs - have 28 flavors of ice cream - but - as a bonus - each and every one of their motels had its own special charm. I remember one accommodation on the way to Georgia had an enormous swimming pool shaped like a whale - and another one in South Carolina had an enchanting Cinderella theme - complete with a carriage to ride in that looked like a giant pumpkin.

By far our favorite Howard Johnson's, though, was in the New England town of Darien, Connecticut. In addition to the regular Howard Johnson's coffee shop and ice-cream parlor, it had a lovely first-class restaurant with fine china and linen tablecloths. Here, we not only tried "Steak Diane" for the first time but ended up buying a Lava Lamp that we saw in the eatery gift shop. Yes, we were the first people on our block to have one of those, too!

The following Thanksgiving, The restaurant's maître d' made quite an impression on my parents the night he suggested we try yet another new dish - "fondue". How did that vacation end? As you might expect: For the next few months we would sit at our dinner table at home placing small cubes of beef on long, slender forks so we could dip them in sizzling oil to cook in the beautiful red fondue pot my father had purchased. Just as the maître d' had taught us to do at Howard Johnson's. What fun!

That's why my brother and I were so disappointed when - on one of our overnight trips on the way home one Thanksgiving - we found that the Howard Johnson's in Darien was sold out. We had no choice but to stay at a smaller, "Mom and Pop" hotel nearby. A disappointment at the time, yes. But - as luck would have it - this would turn out to be one of the most memorable overnights the Biggers children ever had. Here's what happened: As soon as we arrived at our motel, Dad opened the door and quickly ushered my brother and I inside. Beyond the entrance was a sitting room with two comfortable-looking bedrooms on either side of it. Throughout was cozy knotty pine wood paneling, similar to what we had at home.

"I want to talk to you both," Daddy said. "Sit over here on the couch." My brother and I looked at each other. What could my father possibly have to talk to us about now? We sat down.

In the furthest bedroom, my Mom was busy unpacking one of the suitcases and feeding Petunia as my Dad started to speak.

"I know you're both disappointed because we couldn't get our room at the Howard Johnson's," Dad said, "but I have a little surprise for you."

Watts and I glanced at each other again. "I chose this particular motel for a very special reason." I moved closer to listen.

"Somewhere in this motel room - but I won't tell you where - is a secret panel that opens into a hidden room."

"A hidden room!", Watts and I exclaimed at the same time.

"That's right," Dad nodded.

"But how can we find it?", Watts wanted to know.

"When you put pressure on the correct part of the wall," Dad said, pushing his hands out in front of him for emphasis, "the panel will immediately slide open."

"Well ,where on the wall do we start pushing?", I asked, wrinkling my nose.

Dad raised his eyebrows and smiled as he began moving away from the couch. "You'll have to find that out for yourselves," he said. "Now if you need me, I'll be in the other room, working on my script."

With that, my brother and I leaped off the couch and began pressing on the knotty pine walls. Just before we had pulled into the motel the four of us had stopped for an early dinner at a nearby restaurant. Now, as we worked our way around the motel room, pushing and pressing on every part of the walls, we started getting sleepy. On and on we went, getting closer, we were sure, every minute to locating the mysterious "hidden room".

"I think I see a button on the wall!", Watts suddenly yelled.

"You're just imagining it," I said. "I don't see anything!"

Finally, as another hour wore on, Watts and I got so tired that we decided to sit down on the beds to rest a minute. The next thing we knew - it was daylight! We both woke up to find ourselves tucked in under warm blankets. As you might guess, despite our pleas the next morning, my father never would tell Watts and I where that "secret panel" was. "But while you were looking", he smiled, "I was able to finish the whole script I was working on."

There's a footnote to this story: Some time after this trip my father read to my brother and I an *Underdog* script that our Darien, Connecticut adventure had given him an idea for. In the show, the TV audience could distinctly hear - but not see - a group of monsters that Simon Bar Sinister has collected in a mysterious hidden room. As my father read the script out loud to Watts and I - making the terrifying sounds of all the "creatures" himself - we thought about that memorable night when we had so much fun searching for "the hidden room" at our motel.

Thanks for the memories, Dad!

UNDERDOG LIVES ON

The fact that *Underdog*, by far the most famous of all the TTV cartoon shows, has continued to be so popular through the decades since its television premiere in 1964, is something my dad was very, very proud of. Who would have thought, for example, that Disney would end up producing a live action version of *Underdog* in 2007? It was so wonderful to be able to stand next to my father on the red carpet during the premiere of that movie and then watch Dad's reaction when his entire *Underdog* theme song played as the film began. Daddy was so happy that Disney had made the decision to use it in the movie. Watching him smile, I remembered the day I had asked him how he came up with the words and music for the famous song.

"It was remarkable," he told me, "I only knew that I wanted the piece to begin with the type of minor chords that were in the original *King Kong* movie. Then, just as I sat down at the piano - the entire *Underdog* theme song - words and music - suddenly popped into my head!"

Now, more than half a century since Underdog first leaped into the sky, the amount of merchandise that continues to appear on the market related to the loveable cartoon character seems to keep growing. There are Underdog lunch boxes, mugs, plush toys, etc., and on a more personal note, as the years go by, I'm always reminded of Underdog's continuing popularity whenever I happen to run into him in delightful yet unexpected ways.

Not long ago, for example, I was walking along the harbor front in Newport, Rhode Island, when I suddenly came upon a private yacht in the water carrying a group of people singing the *Underdog* song! And more recently I was astounded when - during a visit to the library in a quaint, New England town - I suddenly found myself face to face with - who else? - Underdog! Next to a giant poster of the famous caped canine was a sign that read: "There's no need to fear - the *Underdog* DVD's are Here!"

More importantly, not only has Underdog left an indelible mark on popular culture, but the courageous ideals he stood for continue to manifest themselves in diverse and powerful ways. Whether it's a young boxer defeating a world champion, an unsung hero vanquishing an ominous criminal, or a tenacious individual down on his or her luck who comes back winning against all odds - Underdog endures.

April 9, 1964

Traed -

Just a quick note about Underdog episodes "Fearo The Ferocious." In these episodes there are two characters which come in quite a bit - at least in the first three parts. Here's a quick briefing on them:

Captain Coward - He looks and talks like Charlie Weaver in Navy XXXXXX Uniform - glasses on end of nose, hair stringing out from under cap, etc.

MATE - The First Mate is much more of a typical sailor, with something of the "blimey" added to hå voice.

That's it.

Best -

Letter from Daddy to Tread.

CREDITS AND CONTACTS

THE BEAGLES

In Color Saturdays, Premiere: September 10, 1966, 12:30-1:00 PM, CNYT

FORMAT:	Musical comedy in animated cartoons
CAST:	THE BEAGLES: Stringer and Tubby Scotty, their manager Various individual episode characters
PRODUCTION:	Total Television Productions, Inc. A CBS Television Network Program

CLIENTS:	AGENCIES:
Remco Industries Cape May Street Harrison, N.J.	The Gumbinner-North Co., Inc. 655 Madison Avenue New York, New York YOUR CONTACT: Gale Gilchrist
Deluxe Reading, Inc. 107 Trumbull Street Elizabeth, N.J.	Dancer-Fitzgerald-Sample, Inc. 347 Madison Avenue New York, New York YOUR CONTACT: Beverly Black
General Mills, Inc. 9200 Wayzata Blvd. Minneapolis, Minn.	Dancer-Fitzgerald-Sample, Inc. 347 Madison Ave. New York, New York YOUR CONTACT: Madelaine Betch, Jerry Golod

FORM 174M REV. 5-58 AMB.

DANCER - FITZGERALD - SAMPLE
INCORPORATED

CONFERENCE REPORT

No. 9-64

CLIENT General Mills, Inc. PRODUCT Cereals DATE 1/30/64

DATE OF MEETING 1/30/64 PLACE OF MEETING DFS

PERSONS PRESENT
For GMI: Messrs. C.W. Plattes, R.S.Carlson, R.F.Bodeau
For DFS: Messrs. G.E. Johnson, C.Hotchkiss, W. Doughten, A.M.Bruehl
For PAT: Mr. P. Piech
For GAMMA: Messrs. H. Siegle, S. Faillace
TOTAL TV: Messrs. W. Biggers, C. Stover, J. Harris, T. Covington

UNDERDOG

It was agreed to authorize production of 52 4-1/2 minute episodes of Underdog rather than the original schedule of 26 Underdog episodes and 26 Go-Go-Gopher, subject to network approval.

It was agreed that this change which will enable the strong Underdog episode to get double exposure in each half hour, will strengthen the show's impact.

In addition, it was agreed to authorize production of 8 4-1/2 minute Go-Go-Gopher episodes under the same terms and conditions except that if no further product is produced after a period of time, rights for Go-Go-Gopher will eventually revert to the producers. It was felt that this additional production would serve two purposes: It enables us to launch and establish a new character which can give us flexibility in future production; and it strengthens our position with the network in terms of negotiating underwriting commitments.

SCRIPTS Underdog script numbers four through nine were approved as submitted.

AMB/bhs

Tuesday May 19, 64

Dear Tread -

Attached is:

:10 Promo for Tennessee. Have typed and copy sent for board.

:10 Promo for Underdog. Same.

XXX Revised script for Three Muskrateers. With the Mexico bit going on, we have time to have secretary retype this decently with some carons (or process). As soon as completed, rush copy to me but at least two copies to Chet who will, per my long memo, cover with Gordon. For the moment, nothing need be done about revising board or track.

My throat really flattened me and put me behind, but I'm struggling now to catch up. Hope to get merchandising memo in mail by tomorrow.

Please send me copy of all Go-Go lyrics sent to you as well as recorded music. This will help us in doing the second Go-Go :30 opening.

More later....

Best -

Another letter from Daddy to Tread.

UNDERDOG :10 PROMO

LS UNDERDOG IN AIR ROCKETING XXX IN AND OUT OF BLDGS.

JET, (SOUND:/MUSIC AND CRIES OF HELP FROM POLLY)

HE LANDS ON SIDEWALK BESIDE SIMON WHO HAS POLLY TIED TO TELEPHONE POLE. UNDERDOG SLUGS SIMON STRAIGHT UP IN THE AIR AND UNTIES POLLY WITH ONE FLIP OF THE WRIST.

UNDER: There's no need to fear - Underdog is here!

(SOUND: POW..... FLIP)

NARR: (OVER ABOVE SOUNDS) Yes, Underdog is here - Every Saturday morning on this station!

SIMON COMES DOWN AND FLOORS UNDER AND POL.

(SOUND: PLOP!)

(FADE)

Underdog - NBC-TV
Element Schedule
1964-65 Broadcast Year
Eff Saturday 10/3/64 10-10:30 AM

Show #	Airdate	Underdog #	Go Go Gopher #	Hunter #	
1	10/3/64	8- 9	1	126	
2	10/10	10-11	2	14 (2)	
3	10/17	1- 2	3	7 (2)	
4	10/24	4- 5	4	23 (2)	
5	10/31	6- 7	5	102 (2)	
6	11/7	12-13	6	103 (2)	
7	11/14	14-15	7	104 (2)	
8	11/21	16-17	8	123 (2)	
9	11/28	18-19	9	106 (2)	
10	12/5	20-21	10	16 (2)	
11	12/12	22-23	11	109 (2)	
12	12/19	24-25	12	110 (2)	
13	12/26 (Repeat)	8- 9 (1)	13	112 (2)	
14	1/2/65 (Repeat)	10-11 (1)	1 (1)	113 (2)	
15	1/9	26-27	2 (1)	114 (2)	
16	1/16	28-29	3 (1)	115 (2)	
17	1/23	30-31	4 (1)	117 (2)	
18	1/30	32- 3	5 (1)	118 (2)	
19	2/6	33-34	6 (1)	119 (2)	
20	2/13	35-36	7 (1)	120 (2)	
21	2/20	37-38	8 (1)	121 (2)	
22	2/27	39-40	9 (1)	122 (2)	
23	3/6	41-42	10 (1)	124 (2)	
24	3/13	43-44	11 (1)	125 (2)	
25	3/20	45-46	12 (1)	5 (2)	
26	3/27	47-48	13 (1)	101 (2)	
27	4/3	49-50		2 (3)	46 (2)
28	4/10	51-52		10 (3)	1 (3)
29	4/17	1- 2 (1)		19 (3)	31 (1)
30	4/24	4- 5 (1)		15 (2)	33 (2)
31	5/1	6- 7 (1)		27 (2)	4 (3)
32	5/8	12-13 (1)		28 (2)	6 (2)
33	5/15	14-15 (1)		30 (2)	11 (2)
34	5/22	16-17 (1)		32 (2)	13 (2)
35	5/29	18-19 (1)		105 (2)	17 (2)
36	6/5	20-21 (1)		107 (2)	18 (2)
37	6/12	22-23 (1)		108 (2)	24 (2)
38	6/19	24-25 (1)		111 (2)	25 (2)
39	6/26	26-27 (1)		116 (2)	37 (2)
40	7/3	28-29 (1)	1 (2)	3 (2)	
41	7/10	30-31 (1)	2 (2)	9 (3)	
42	7/17	32- 3 (1)	3 (2)	20 (3)	
43	7/24	33-34 (1)	4 (2)	29 (2)	
44	7/31	35-36 (1)	5 (2)	34 (2)	
45	8/7	37-38 (1)	6 (2)	35 (2)	
46	8/14	39-40 (1)	7 (2)	38 (2)	
47	8/21	41-42 (1)	8 (2)	39 (2)	
48	8/28	43-44 (1)	9 (2)	40 (2)	
49	9/4	45-46 (1)	10 (2)	41 (2)	
50	9/11	47-48 (1)	11 (2)	42 (2)	
51	9/18	49-50 (1)	12 (2)	44 (2)	
52	9/25	51-52 (1)	13 (2)	45 (2)	

() indicates number of previous network runs.

Network Film requirements: 1-35mm color print
2-16mm black & white prints

Notes: Shows #1-26; 40-52 contain 2 Underdogs; 1 Go Go Gopher and 1 Hunter element

Shows #27-39 contain 2 Underdogs and 2 Hunter elements

8/20/64

A Total TeleVision production

"Go Go Gophers"

Episode #1: "Moon Zoom" - 6:00

LONG SHOT OF GREAT PLAINS AND MOUNTAINS.	NARR: (OVER INDIAN DRUMS) Many moons ago, somewhere west of Horace Greely, lay the Gulch
DOLLY IN TO HUGE INDIAN TEPEE VILLAGE.	of the Gopher Indians. Unfortunately, Gopher Gulch stood right in the path of paleface progress.
TRAIN ROARS RIGHT THROUGH TEPEES KNOCKING THEM ASUNDER... REST OF TEEPEES VANISH, LEAVING TWO TINY FIGURES ON THE VAST LANDSCAPE.	(SOUND: THUNDER OF TRAIN) So, the Gophers were moved - lock, stock and tomahawk - to a reservation in the North ... All except two braves -
MOVE IN TIGHT ON THE TWO FIGURES IN FULL WAR HEAD-PIECES.	Ruffled Feather and Running Board - the last of the
TWO BRAVES JUMP ON HORSES AND RIDE OFF SCREEN.	Gophers. These two brave braves refused to move.
CUT TO STOCKADE - TYPE FORT, LONGSHOT OF TWO INDIANS CIRCLING FORT AT GREAT SPEED, RAINING ARROWS OVER WALL.	So much trouble did they cause that the paleface fort at Gopher Gulch sent for the
CUT TO COLONEL RIDING LIKE MAD, BRANDISHING SWORD.	greatest of all fighters - the world famous Colonel Kit Coyote!

(DISSOLVE)

Hoppity Hooper - ABC-TV
1964-65 Broadcast Year
Element Schedule
Eff. Saturday 9/12/64 12:30-1:00 PM

Show #	Airdate	Hoppity #	Fairytale #	Peabody #
1	9/12/64	1- 2	89 (1)	83 (3)
2	9/19	3- 4	88 (1)	89 (2)
3	9/26	5- 6	81 (2)	88 (4)
4	10/3	7- 8	80 (2)	74 (2)
5	10/10	9-10	79 (3)	75 (4)
6	10/17	11-12	76 (3)	77 (2)
7	10/24	13-14	78 (2)	90 (2)
8	10/31	15-16	21 (4)	85 (2)
9	11/7	17-18	20 (2)	84 (2)
10	11/14	19-20	77 (3)	78 (3)
11	11/21	21-22	75 (2)	73 (1)
12	11/28	23-24	74 (2)	72 (1)
13	12/5	25-26	68 (3)	71 (1)
14	12/12	27-28	19 (3)	70 (2)
15	12/19	29-30	66 (3)	69 (3)
16	12/26	31-32	64 (3)	67 (1)
17	1/2/65 Repeat	1- 2 (1)	63 (3)	66 (1)
18	1/9 Repeat	3- 4 (1)	62 (3)	64 (1)
19	1/16	33-34	61 (3)	62 (2)
20	1/23	35-36	55 (2)	61 (3)
21	1/30	37-38	54 (2)	60 (2)
22	2/6	39-40	53 (2)	59 (1)
23	2/13	41-42	52 (2)	58 (2)
24	2/20	43-44	51 (3)	57 (2)
25	2/27	45-46	50 (2)	56 (2)
26	3/6	47-48	49 (2)	55 (2)
27	3/13	49-50	48 (2)	28 (3)
28	3/20	51-52	16 (2)	29 (2)
29	3/27	5- 6 (1)	46 (2)	30 (2)
30	4/3	7- 8 (1)	45 (2)	81 (3)
31	4/10	9-10 (1)	43 (3)	31 (2)
32	4/17	11-12 (1)	42 (2)	32 (2)
33	4/24	13-14 (1)	41 (4)	33 (4)
34	5/1	15-16 (1)	40 (2)	34 (2)
35	5/8	17-18 (1)	39 (3)	35 (2)
36	5/15	19-20 (1)	38 (6)	36 (4)
37	5/22	21-22 (1)	37 (2)	37 (2)
38	5/29	23-24 (1)	36 (2)	38 (1)
39	6/5	25-26 (1)	35 (2)	39 (2)
40	6/12	27-28 (1)	34 (3)	40 (2)
41	6/19	29-30 (1)	33 (1)	54 (2)
42	6/26	31-32 (1)	32 (1)	53 (3)
43	7/3	33-34 (1)	31 (4)	52 (2)
44	7/10	35-36 (1)	30 (4)	51 (2)
45	7/17	37-38 (1)	29 (4)	50 (2)
46	7/24	39-40 (1)	28 (4)	27 (4)
47	7/31	41-42 (1)	27 (2)	26 (2)
48	8/7	43-44 (1)	26 (2)	25 (4)
49	8/14	45-46 (1)	25 (2)	23 (4)
50	8/21	47-48 (1)	24 (3)	22 (2)
51	8/28	49-50 (1)	23 (2)	21 (4)
52	9/4	51-52 (1)	22 (5)	20 (4)

( ) indicate combined number of previous ABC & NBC runs.

Network Film requirements: 2-16 mm color prints
3-16 mm black & white prints

Note: No duplication of Fairytale or Peabody episodes.

8/20/64

LIAISON FILMS, INC.
630 NINTH AVENUE
NEW YORK 36, N. Y.
PHONE: JUDSON 6-1651

KING & ODIE 15 MINUTE FORMAT

:05	OPENING TITLES
:10	BILLBOARD
:15	MUSICAL OPENING
:45	COMMERCIAL #1
4:30	KING & ODIE # ________
:60	COMMERCIAL #2
1:30	TWINKLES # ________
:15	COMMERCIAL #3
4:15	HUNTER # ________
:60	COMMERCIAL #4
:15	MUSICAL CLOSING
:10	CLOSING BILLBOARD (GPBB-6)
:10	CREDITS
14:20	

APRIL, 1964

GENERAL MILLS, INC.
King and Odie Market List

Market	Station	Time Period
CHICAGO	WBKB	8:45-9:00 AM
ATLANTA	WAGA	7:45-8:00AM
Albany/Schenectady/Troy	W-TEN	7:45-8:00AM
Albuquerque	KOB-TV	7:45-8:00AM
Amarillo	KGNC-TV	8:45-9:00AM
Bakersfield	KERO-TV	8:45-9:00AM
Baltimore	WMAR-TV	7:45-8:00AM
Boston	WNAC-TV	8:15-8:30AM
Cedar Rapids	KCRG-TV	12:30-12:45PM
Charleston, W. Va.	WHTN-TV	10:15-10:30AM
Cincinnati	WCPO-TV	9:30-10:30AM
Cleveland	WEWS	12:15-12:30PM
Columbus	WTVN-TV	8:45-9:00AM
Dallas	WFAA-TV	8:15-8:30AM
Dayton	WHIO	8:45-9:00AM
Denver	KBTV	8:00-8:15AM
Des Moines	KRNT-TV	7:30-7:45AM
Detroit	WJBK-TV	7:45-8:00AM
Fargo	KXJB-TV	7:45-8:00AM
Flint/Saginaw	WJRT-TV	10:45-11:00AM
Fort Wayne	WKJG-TV	9:15-9:30AM
Green Bay	WFRV-TV	12:15-12:30PM
Indianapolis	WLW-I	9:45-10:00AM
Joplin	KODE-TV	7:45-8:00AM
Kansas City	KCMO-TV	7:45-8:00AM
Los Angeles	KHJ-TV	9:00-9:15AM
Lubbock	KLBK-TV	7:45-8:00AM
Miami	WLBW-TV	9:45-10:00AM
Milwaukee	WITI-TV	8:15-8:30AM
Minneapolis	WTCN-TV	12:45-1:00PM
New Haven	WNHC-TV	7:55-8:10AM
New York	~~WABC-TV~~ WNEW TV 4/30	7:45-8:00AM
Oklahoma City	KOCO-TV	9:15-9:30AM
Omaha	KETV	9:00-9:15AM
Peoria	WEEK-TV	12:30-12:45PM
Phoenix	KTVK-TV	8:45-9:00AM
Pittsburgh	WTAE	8:30-8:45AM
Portland, Me.	WMTW-TV	9:00-9:15AM
Portland, Ore.	KPTV	8:15-8:30AM
Providence	WPRO-TV	7:30-7:45AM
Rochester, N.Y.	WOKR	9:45-10:00AM
Rockford	WTVO	12:45-1:00PM
Sacramento	KXTV	7:45-8:00AM
St. Louis	KTVI	9:15-9:30AM
Salt Lake City	KCPX-TV	8:15-8:30AM
San Francisco	KPIX	7:45-8:00AM
Seattle	KIRO-TV	8:15-8:30AM
Sioux City	KTIV	12:30-12:45AM
South Bend	WNDU-TV	9:30-9:45AM
Spokane	KREM-TV	8:45-9:00AM
Springfield, Mass.	WHYN-TV	9:45-10:00AM
Toledo	WTOL-TV	9:30-9:45AM
Tulsa	KTUL-TV	8:15-8:30AM
Washington, D.C.	WTOP-TV	7:45-8:00AM
Wheeling/Steubenville	WSTV-TV	7:45-8:00AM
SALINAS/SAN JOSE	KNTV	9:45-10:00AM

"UNDERDOG"

A New Television Cartoon Series

Created and Produced by

Total TeleVision productions

TENNESSEE TUXEDO - CBS-TV
SHOW FORMAT
EFFECTIVE 9/26/64

CODE	TIMING	CUME TIMING	ELEMENT
1	:30		Action cuts - Preview today's show
2	:10		Show opening billboard
3	:05		Commercial billboard
4	1:00	1:45	Commercial #1
5	:30		Opening to show & Tennessee episode
6	4:30		Tennessee Tuxedo - first half
7	1:00	7:45	Commercial #2
8	4:30		Tennessee Tuxedo - second half
9	1:00	13:15	Commercial #3
10	:10		Closing first half show billboard
11	:05		Commercial billboard
12	:05		"Stay Tuned" card
13	:10		Second half show opening billboard
14	:05		Commercial billboard
15	:30		Opening to second half show
16	1:00	15:20	Commercial #4
17	:25		Riddle
18	4:30		Tooter episode
19	1:00	21:15	Commercial #5
20	:25		Riddle
21	4:30		King & Odie episode
22	1:00	27:10	Commercial #6
23	:10		Lead-in to action to come
24	:30		Action cuts - Preview (next week's show)
25	:10		Show closing billboard
26	:05		Commercial billboard
27	:20	28:25	Credits
	28:25 approximate timing		

Revision I
11/5/64

TOOTER TURTLE

Episodes Unused From Original 26 Title Summaries:

13. Lossie (Doggone Dope)
18. T-Turtle (Counterfiet Feat)
23. Bee Sweet (Buzz, Buzz, Buzz)

Additional 13 Episodes:

30. The Master Builder (Rivet Riot)
31. Taxi-Turtle (My Flag Is Gone)
32. Canned Camera (Peek-A-Boob)
33. Man In The Gray Flannel Soot (Mad Avenue)
34. Slowshoe Mountie (Snow Snook) Here
35. Duck Haunter (Decoy Drip)
36. Bull Flighter (O'Lay Down)
37. News Nuisance (Sub-Scribe) Here
38. Foreign Fleegion (Sand Stupe)
39. Waggin' Train (California Bust) Here
40. Anchors A-woe (Nautical Nut)
41. Vaudevillain (Song And Dunce Man)
42. Rod And Reeling (Field And Scream)
43. Man In the Blue Denim Suit (Hay! Hay!)

Vet, Ambulance Driver, architect, Artist, Chef, Barber, Arthur Murray, Dentist

97 TTV Characters according to Joe Harris (I got 98):

1. King Leonardo
2. Odie Colognie
3. Biggy Rat
4. Professor Messer
5. Mr. Mad
6. Duke
7. Earl
8. King Leonardo's Mama
9. Carlota Colognie
10. Lynetta Lion
11. Sewonya Button
12. The Duchess
13. Death Valley O'Days
14. General Custard
15. The Black Baron
16. Tooter Turtle
17. Mr. Wizard the Lizard
18. Lois Loon
19. The Hunter
20. The Fox
21. Officer Flim Flanagan
22. Horrors Hunter
23. Tennessee Tuxedo
24. Chumley
25. Phineas J. Whoopee
26. Stanley Livingstone
27. Baldy Eagle
28. Flunky
29. Yakkety Yak
30. Sergeant Badge
31. Mr. Hothead
32. Jerboa Jump
33. Tiger Tornado
34. Platypus
35. Rocky Monanoff
36. Samantha
37. Pretzel
38. Mayor of Megapolis
39. Slippery Hood
40. Gopher Brother
41. Gopher Brother
42. Beaver Brother
43. Beaver Brother
44. Big Bill Bear
45. Mr. Stonecutter
46. Plumber
47. Commander McBragg
48. Colonel Kit Coyote
49. Sergeant Okey Homa
50. Ruffled Feathers
51. Running Board
52. General Nuisance
53. Corporal Crimp
54. Underdog
55. Shoeshine Boy
56. Sweet Polly Purebred
57. Simon Bar Sinister
58. Cad Lackey
59. Riff Raff
60. Mooch
61. Giant Monster with Red Sweater
62. King Klobber
63. Goggol
64. Irving and Ralph, the two-headed dragon
65. O.J. Skweez
66. King Cumulus
67. Mange the Mole King
68. Bubblehead Emperor
69. Overcat
70. Captain Marblehead
71. Princess Glissando
72. Bubblehead Empress
73. Tap Tap the Chiseler
74. Wicked Witch of Pickeyoon
75. Aunt Flora
76. Lady who says, "It's a frog!"
77. Just in Case the Witch Doctor
78. Klondike Kat
79. Major Minor

80. Savoir Fare
81. Malemutt
82. Scotty
83. Tubby
84. Stringer
85. Professor X
86. C.B. Shlemiel
87. Gene Hattree
88. Rabbit Foot
89. Tortilla Fats
90. Cauliflower Cabby
91. The Champion
92. Pinky Knees
93. Boston Bully
94. Shifty
95. Sing-a-Long Father
96. Sing-a-Long Mother
97. Sing-a-Long Son
98. Sing-a-Long Daughter

BIBLIOGRAPHY

Arnold, Mark, *Created and Produced by Total TeleVision productions*, BearManor Media, 2009

Biggers, Buck, and Chet Stover, *How Underdog Was Born*, BearManor Media, 2005

Scott, Keith, *The Moose That Roared*, St. Martin's Press, 2000

Van Citters, Darrell, *The Art of Jay Ward Productions*, Oxberry Press, 2013

INDEX

ABC - 168, 242
ACME pegs - 17
Adams, Don - 170, 192, 201
Advertising Age - 28
Aesop and Son - 26, 59, 69
Akron, Ohio - 156-157
Ali, Muhammad - 192
Allen, Woody - 59, 166
Almond Joy - 12
Alvin and the Chipmunks - 42
Amazon - 30
American Airlines - 12
American Bandstand - 204-205
American International Development (AID) - 23-24
Andrina, Frank - 2, 170
Animato - 1
Animation International - 24, 29
Arambula, Roman - 5-6, 18, 21, 170
Argentina - 14, 18
Arngrim, Alison - 177
Arnold, Mark - 1, 3, 5, 8-9, 11-29
Art of Jay Ward Productions, The - 11, 14
Atlanta, Georgia - 185, 189
Aunt Edna - 223
Aunt Kathleen - 223
Aunt Lizzie - 201-202
Avondale Estates, Georgia - 185

Bakshi, Ralph - 89
Baldwin, Gerard - 14, 25
Ball, Lucille - 174, 184
Barefoot Executive, The - 174
'Be My Valentine" - 121-123
Beagles, The - 1, 23, 28, 60, 68, 168-169, 186, 198, 217-219, 236
BearManor Media - 1
Beatles, The - 168, 201
Beck, Jackson - 42, 171, 192
Becker, Sandy - 171-172
Beinler, Hans - 19
Berle, Milton - 190
Betch, Madelaine -236
Betty Crocker - 43
Betty Crocker Cookbook - 189
"Big Drip, The" - 196
Biggers, Grace (Mom) - 187-188, 202, 204, 216-218, 220-221, 224, 227, 231-232
Biggers Jr., Watts (brother) - 215-217, 220-221, 223. 226-228, 232-233
Biggers, Lloyd - 185
Biggers, Victoria - 1, 185-202, 204-206, 215-218, 220-224, 226-234
Biggers, Watts "Buck" (Dad) - 1, 3, 22, 80, 172, 182, 185-202, 204-206, 215-218, 220-224, 226-234, 237
Biggy Rat - 41, 46, 192, 195
Billboard - 218
Black, Beverly - 236
Blackthorne Publishing - 90, 93
Bluto - 170
Bodargus, Ellie - 173
Bodeau, R. F. - 28, 237
Bohlman, Sean - 25
Bolke, Bradley - 58, 173, 193-194
Bonwit Teller - 187
Boomerang Media - 2
Borden - 156
Boston, Massachusetts - 227
Boston Common, Massachusetts - 226
Bowie, David - 228
British Academy - 15
Britt, Ponsonby - 1
Broadway Danny Rose - 59, 166

Bruehl, A. M. - 237
"Bubble-Heads, The" - 82, 86
Bugs Bunny - 79
Bullwinkle Moose - 1, 11, 13, 16, 21, 24, 26-27, 41, 44, 54, 59, 78, 118, 156, 163-165
Bullwinkle Show, The - 24, 26
Bullwinkle's - 80
Bullwinkle's Corner - 60, 168
Burbank, California - 5
Burgos, Daniel - 5

Cad Lackey - 4, 7, 80-81, 87, 90, 99, 116-117, 120, 122-123, 125, 127, 129-130, 162, 166
Callanese - 20
Cancun, Mexico - 15
Canton, Angel - 5
Canton, Cesar - 5
Cape Cod, Massachusetts - 194, 197, 199, 215-216, 220, 223-224, 226, 231
Captain Coward - 88, 235
Captain Marblehead - 101-102
Carlin, Cynthia - 13
Carlin, Roger - 13
Carlson, George - 13, 18, 237
Carmen, Mexico - 15
Cartoon Carnival - 42
Cartoon Color - 16
Cartoon Lagoon Studios - 49, 59
Cartoon Cut-Ups - 49
Casper Show, The - 30
Casper, the Friendly Ghost - 79, 177
Cauliflower Cabby - 60, 78
CBS - 34, 37, 50-51, 64, 66, 68, 168, 219, 236, 246
Charles River - 227
Charlie - 227
Charlton Comics - 114, 120
Charter House Hotel - 227
Chatham Airport - 216
Cheerios - 28, 39, 41-42
"Chew Gum Charlie" - 82
Chief Running Board - 53, 82, 88, 138-141, 147-149, 153, 197, 207-214, 241
Chip and Dale - 26
Christmas - 226
Chuck Gammage Animation - 49, 59
Chumley Walrus - 4, 43, 53, 55, 57-58, 192-194, 196
Cinderella - 231
Clarabelle Cow - 6
Clark, Dick - 204-205
Classic Media - 2, 27
Clay, Cassius - 192
Cloyd - 13, 26
Coca-Cola - 154
Cocoa Puffs - 28, 41
Collegeville Costumes - 79
Colonel Kit Coyote - 53, 57, 88, 136-137, 139-145, 148-153, 197, 207-210, 212-214, 241
Colossal Show, The - 89, 223
Columbia Pictures - 31, 38, 49
Columbia Records - 187
Columbia Screen Gems - 31
Commander McBragg - 23, 50, 58-60, 66-78, 168
Conniff, Ray - 226
Cooper Union School of Engineering - 12
Coppola, Francis Ford - 30
County Cork, Ireland - 202
Covington, Tread - 1, 8-9, 22-23, 193, 217, 224, 237-238
Cox, Wally - 86, 88, 166, 173-174
Cream of Wheat - 185
Created and Produced by Total TeleVision productions - 1, 11, 21, 30, 49, 59
Culhane, Jimmy "Shamus" - 11, 13-14
Culver City, California - 16

Dallas, Texas - 5
Dancer Fitzgerald Sample (DFS) - 22, 26, 60, 83, 187-189, 195, 228, 236-237
Dancer, Mix - 188-189
Darien, Connecticut - 231-233
de la Torre, Sergio - 5
Defoe, Daniel - 197
Delmar, Kenny - 30, 42, 174-175, 193
Delmar Jr., Ken - 193

Delmonico steaks -194
DeLuxe Reading Corporation - 83
DePatie-Freleng - 25
DFS Program Exchange - 60
Dino the Dinosaur - 156
Donald Duck - 156, 165
Doughton, W. - 237
Dr. Seuss - 25
Dracula - 30
DreamWorks Animation - 2
DreamWorks Classics, LLC - 2, 49
Dudley Do-Right - 26, 41, 53
Dudley Do-Right Emporium - 27
Duncan, Herb - 175
Dunsford, David R. - 31, 49, 59
Durango, Mexico - 18
DVD - 31, 49, 57, 168, 196, 233

Easter - 227-228
Eisman, Hy - 4
Elsie the Cow - 156
Emergency +4 - 89
Emery University - 185
English - 15, 26
"Eye On the Ball" - 88

Faillace, Sal - 3, 14, 26, 175, 237
Faith, Percy - 187, 198
Farmer Brown - 86
Farrow, Mia - 166
FBI, The - 11-12
Fearo the Ferocious - 88, 235
Felix the Cat - 86, 167
Fillmore Bear - 45
Flair pens - 196
Flynn, Joe - 174
FM2 - 14-15
Fox and the Crow, The - 31, 38
Fox, Charles - 175
Fox, The - 43, 46, 82, 229
Fractured Fairy Tales - 26, 242
Framingham, Massachusetts - 215
Frankenstein - 202
Fred Calvert Productions - 89
Fred Flintstone - 3
Fresno, California - 40
Friends - 59
Frosty-O's - 55
Frosty-O's Bear - 41
Fulton the Camel - 41, 46-48

Gamma Productions - 5, 11-12, 18-22, 24, 26, 28-30, 89
Garfield - 180
Gene Hattree - 60, 78
General Mills - 11-13, 22, 24-27, 29, 31, 41-42, 46-49, 55, 57, 83, 189-191, 195, 236-237, 244
Georgia - 186
Georgia Serenaders, The - 185
Gidney - 13, 26
Gilbert, Herschel Burke - 175
Gilchrist, Gale - 236
Gillette - 12
Glen Burnie, Maryland - 167
Go Go Gophers - 10, 50, 53, 57, 59-60, 65-66, 72-78, 85, 88, 136-153, 186, 195, 237, 205-214, 238, 240-241
Gold Key Comics - 57, 89
Golod, Jerry - 236
Gomer Pyle - 193
Gonzara, Rodolfo - 5
Goodyear Tire & Rubber Company - 84, 154-157, 165, 167
Goofy - 6
Google - 23
Gottfredson, Norm - 175
Gourley, Bud - 19-21, 24-26
GPS - 231
"Grand Canyon Caper" - 82
Grandmother Nelly - 215
"Great Gold Robbery, The" - 88

Grinch, The - 180
Guadalajara, México - 15
Guarnier, Lu - 176
Guerrero, Julio - 5
Gumbinner-North Company, The - 236
Gumby Show, The - 30

Hanmer, Ronald - 176
Hanna-Barbera - 3, 5, 26, 30-31
Happy Dragon, The - 156, 163
Harris, Joe - 1, 3-4, 7, 9-10, 22-23, 29, 155, 164, 167-169, 176, 202, 237, 248
Harrison, George - 168
Harrison, New Jersey - 236
Hartsdale, New York - 197
Hatcher, Norman "Hatch" - 185
Hatfields and McCoys, The - 223-224
Henson, Tex - 5, 26
Heritage Auctions - 89
Hicksville, Long Island, New York - 231
Higgins ink - 17
Hippopotamus - 46
Hogan's Alley - 1
Hollywood, California - 26-27
Hoppity Hooper - 11, 27, 41, 44, 54
Hoppity Hooper - 23-24, 27, 242
Horrors Hunter - 81
Hotchkiss, C. - 237
Hotel Roosevelt - 18
How Underdog Was Born - 1
Howard Johnson's - 231-232
Huffine, Charlotte - 176
Hunter, The - 31, 36-39, 42, 44, 46, 50, 59, 82, 85, 88, 193, 197. 228, 240, 243
Hurtz, Bill - 25
Hyperion Productions - 5

I Am the Greatest: The Adventures of Muhammad Ali - 89
"I Wanna Capture You" - 218
"Introducing Mr. Mad" - 30
Irving, George S. - 49, 176-177
Ishi, Chris - 14
Italy - 18
Itchy Brother - 42, 46, 195, 221

Jack's Joke Shop - 227
Jackson Heights, New York - 187
Jagger, Mick - 228
Japan - 13, 24
Jaws - 79
Jay Ward Productions - 1, 13-14, 21, 23-27, 29, 50, 59-60, 168
Jenkins, Frank - 156
Johnson, Frank - 114, 120
Johnson, Gordon - 21-22, 190-192, 237-238
Jordan, Will - 192

Kaboom - 22
Kai, Sammy - 26
Karloff, Boris - 202
Ka-Vee Grape Drink - 56
Kelvin - 17, 25
Kemp Balloons - 167
Key, Leonard - 13, 21
Key, Ted - 13
Kickstarter - 168
Kilgore, Al - 10
Kimbal, Charlie - 19
King and Odie, The - 31-34, 50, 243, 246
King and Odie Show, The - 30-31, 243
King Kong - 233
King Leonardo - 41-42, 46, 85, 192, 197, 217, 222
King Leonardo and his Short Subjects - 1, 24, 30-31, 35-36, 38-40, 89, 186, 195, 197
Kitty Hawk, North Carolina - 215
Klein, Izzy - 22
Klondike Kat - 23, 60, 68, 72-78, 168, 186
KMJ-TV - 40
Koala Bear - 41, 47
Kodak - 17, 20
Korean War - 11

Labor Day - 197
Lassie - 86
Lennon, John - 168
Leow's Theatre - 186
Liaison Films - 243
Li'l Abner - 31
Lincoln, Abraham - 12
Linus the Lionhearted - 156, 163
Lion - 45, 47
Lipton Cup-a-Soup - 190
Long and Short of It, The - 185
"Looking for the Beagles" - 218
Lopez, Ernesto - 20
Los Angeles, California - 5, 16, 24
Lucky Charms - 12, 28, 54
Ludwick, William "Bill" - 156
Lynn - 215-216

MacMillan, Norma - 177
Macy's Thanksgiving Day Parade - 59, 83-84, 154-167
Magilla Gorilla - 193
Magnet Men, The - 96, 117-118
Man of La Mancha, The - 22
Manhattan, New York - 187-188, 222
Manriquez, Carlos - 19, 22, 26, 178
"Marbleheads, The" - 101-106, 112-113
Marietta, Georgia - 231
Marine Corp - 11
Marshal, Mort - 178
Martin, Steve - 228
Maryland - 231
Martinez, Jesus "Chuy" - 18, 20-21, 23
Marvel Productions - 5
Maurie Muskrat - 225
McCann, Chuck - 178
McCartney, Paul - 168
"Medicine Men" - 81
Melvin, Allan - 193
Melvin Muskrat - 225
Menfield, Joe - 28
Mercer, Jack - 171
Mervin Muskrat - 225
Mexico - 14-15, 17-26, 29
Mexico City, Mexico - 5, 11, 14, 16, 18, 24-25
Miami, Florida - 185
Mickey Mouse - 5-6, 18, 163
Milano, Frank - 179
Miller, Mitch - 187
Minneapolis, Minnesota - 24, 191, 236
Minnie Mouse - 6
Mishkin, Lee - 179
Monk Muskrat - 225
Montell, Joe - 22, 26
Mooch - 91-92
"Moon Zoom" - 208, 241
Mooney, Gerry - 10
Moose That Roared, The - 21
Moosylvania - 78
Morgan, Frank - 192
Mormon Tabernacle Choir - 226
Mounds - 12
Mr. Know-it-All - 60, 168
Mr. Mad - 30, 42
Mr. Magoo Show, The - 30
Mr. Novak - 86
Mr. Peabody - 41, 43, 45
Mr. Peepers - 173
Mr. Wizard the Lizard - 46, 195, 230
Mrs. Baldy - 49
Murphy, Marty - 179
Murray, Bill - 228
Museum of Science, The - 227

Nantucket Sound, Massachusetts - 194
NBC - 31-33, 35, 37-38, 59-60, 62, 65, 67, 82-86, 88. 154-157, 162, 166, 189, 192, 216. 228-230, 240
NBCUniversal - 2
Nell Fenwick - 53
New Orleans, Louisiana - 185
Newport, Rhode Island - 233
New York City, New York - 12, 22, 26, 29, 49, 59, 89, 157, 167, 185-187, 191, 193, 201, 215, 228, 231, 236, 243

New York Public Library - 186
New Yorker, The - 59, 164
Nicholson, Sam - 180
Nixon, Richard M. - 23
Noah's Lark - 223
North Carolina - 15. 231
North Georgia Military College - 185

O.J. Squeeze - 88
Odie Cologne - 41, 46, 195
Of Moose and Men - 26
Old Doddering Nincompoop, The (fake comic book) - 58
Olivares, Eduardo - 5
Oxberry pegs - 17
Oxford camera - 25

Paige Albert, Ashley - 49
Paramount Pictures - 29
Peabody's Improbable History - 242
Pennsylvania - 231
Peter Paul Candy - 12
Petunia - 220-221, 231
Phillips, Chris - 49
Phillips, Van - 179
Phineas J. Whoopee - 53, 57, 192, 221, 226
"Phoney Booths, The" - 114
Piech, Peter - 11, 13-14, 20, 24-25, 80, 85-86
Plattes, Cyril "Cy" - 11, 22, 24-25, 28, 237
Plattes, Heather - 24
Platypus - 47
Playa del Carmen - 15
"Ponda That Moose" - 49
Popeye the Sailor - 156, 165
"Power Play" - 130
Producer's Associates of Television (PAT) - 13, 24, 26-27
Professor Moby Von Ahab - 82
Pruitt, Robb - 49
Purbeck, Nancy - 172

Questel, Mae - 171
Quick Draw McGraw - 30

Ray Conniff Singers - 226
Ray, Gerry - 28-29, 179
RCA - 17
Red White and Blue Sox, The - 223
Rehfeld, Kurt - 180
Remco Industries - 236
Revolutionary War - 226
Reyes, Terraro - 20
Reynosa, Mexico - 20
Riff Raff - 27, 78, 88, 91-92, 108-110
Rockmart, Georgia - 156-157, 165
Rocky and his Friends - 24, 30-31
Rocky Show, The - 30
Rocky, the Flying Squirrel - 1, 13, 21, 24, 26, 41, 43-44, 85
Roman, Dun - 180
Roman, Phil - 180
Roosevelt Hotel - 185
Rose, Norman - 30, 180
"Rubber Duck, The" - 133-135
Ruff and Reddy - 30-31
Ruffled Feather - 53, 82, 88, 137-141, 146-149, 151, 153, 197, 207-214, 241

Sally Sergeant - 89
Sandoval, Carlos - 20, 22, 26
Sanford the Parrot - 41, 46-48
Santa Claus - 226
Saturday Night Live - 228
Schleh, Bob - 18-19, 21, 25-26
Schoolhouse Rock - 3
Scotty - 169, 218, 236
Sesame Street - 24
Sgt. Okey Homa - 57, 136-137, 139-140, 144-145, 152-153, 197, 207-210, 212-214
Sharples, Winston - 30, 180
Sherman - 41, 43-44
Shoeshine Boy - 78, 91-93, 97, 105-106, 117, 121
Shout Factory - 30, 49
Siegel, Drew - 15
Siegel, Eileen - 15, 22
Siegel, Harvey - 3, 5-6, 11-29, 181, 237

Siegel, Laurie - 15
Siegel, Scott - 15
Silverman, Fred - 229-231
Simon Bar Sinister - 4, 7, 27, 78, 80-81, 83-85, 87, 90, 98-100, 114-117, 120, 122-123, 125, 127-130, 162, 166, 192, 233, 239
"Simon Says, 'No Thanksgiving'" - 59, 83
Sinclair Oil - 156
Sing-a-Long Family, The - 60, 69, 73, 77, 168-169
Singer, George - 14, 18, 26, 181
Scotch tape - 25
Smith, Bob - 59, 154-167
Smith, Sid - 156
Smith Special Productions / Balloonworks - 154
Smokey Bear - 163
Snidely Whiplash - 53
Snoopy - 163
South Carolina - 231
Spanish - 15, 18, 20, 26
Squire Scat - 225
St. Joan of Arc Church - 187
St. Thomas Episcopal - 12
Starr, Ringo - 168
Stern, Ben - 181, 193-194
Stern, Howard - 181, 193
Stewie - 154
Storch, Larry - 171, 181-182, 192-193
Stover, Chet - 1, 22, 182, 194-196, 201, 215-216, 220, 222-223, 237-238
Stringer - 169, 218-219, 236
Sullivan, Ed - 192
Supercar - 42
Superman - 167, `184
SWAT - 12
Sweet Polly Purebred - 4, 7, 27, 78, 80-84, 88, 93, 98, 106, 115, 117, 120, 122-123, 132, 166
Swift, Allen - 42, 182, 192

Tecamachalco - 19-20
Tennessee Tuxedo - 3-4, 15, 21, 41, 44, 49-53, 55-58, 60, 69-77, 85, 170, 192, 196, 198, 238, 246
Tennessee Tuxedo and Chumley - 49, 52. 58-59
Tennessee Tuxedo and his Friends (fake comic book) - 57
Tennessee Tuxedo and his Tales - 1, 24, 27-28, 30, 34, 37, 49-52, 57, 66, 89, 186, 192-196, 223, 246
Tennessee Tuxedo Riddle - 50, 246
"Termite Trainers" - 81
Terrazas, Ernie - 14, 19, 26, 183
Terrytoons - 29, 89
Thanksgiving - 59, 83, 88, 157, 162, 167, 231-232
"That is Horse" - 49
"The Big Shrink" - 79
Three Muskrateers, The - 223, 225, 238
Tiger - 41
Tiger Tornado - 192-193
Timberg, Sammy - 29, 183
"Tin Man Alley" - 116-118
Tojo Studios - 13
Tom & Jerry - 180
Tomlinson, Ernest - 183
Tommy Hatfield - 224
Tompkins - 29
Tooter Turtle - 23. 31, 34-36, 41, 45-46, 50, 76, 186, 195, 230, 246-247
Tootsie Roll - 206
Toronto, Ontario - 49, 59
Torres, Jaime - 5, 20-21, 26
Total TeleVision productions (TTV) - 1-3, 9-11, 15, 23-31, 49-50, 59, 84, 155, 168, 170, 189, 192-193, 206, 215, 217, 223, 233, 236, 241, 245, 248
Travis, Bob - 22
Trix - 49
Trix Rabbit - 12, 23-24, 28, 41
"Trojan Totem, The" - 82
Tubby - 169, 218-219, 236
Tucker, Sophie - 185
TV Cooking Capers - 43
TV Guide - 31, 49, 59, 164
TV Magazine - 164
TV Spots - 29
Twinkles - 31, 38, 41, 46-48, 54, 243
"Two for the Turkey Trot" - 81

Uncle Harry - 223-224

Uncle Rod - 223

Underdog - 4, 7, 10-11, 13, 15, 17, 21, 23, 27, 29, 57, 59-65, 70-88, 90-92, 94-100. 108-111, 114-115, 117-120, 122-132, 134-135, 154-166, 171, 184, 202-203, 217, 233-234, 238-240

Underdog (2007 movie) - 78, 233-234

Underdog Fan Club Card - 80

Underdog Show, The - 1, 19, 24, 26, 28, 30-31, 36, 49, 59-65, 67-69, 82-89, 155, 166, 169, 186, 195, 201, 223, 233, 237, 240, 245

Underdog: The Adventure Continues - 59, 78

Underdog 3-D - 90

Underdog Theme Song 45, The - 162

United States of America (USA) - 5,14-15, 18, 20, 23-24, 26, 29

University of Guadalajara - 15

Upson, Stuart - 183

US Navy - 15

Valdez, Gustavo - 18, 20, 23

Valenzuela, Alberto - 19

Val-Mar - 18-19, 21, 23, 26

Van Citters, Darrell - 11, 14-15,17-19, 21, 23

Viacom International - 89

Virginia - 231

Von Bernewitz, Fred - 183

Walt Disney Productions - 5, 11, 18, 19, 26, 174, 233

Ward, Jay - 1, 13-15, 21, 23-27, 31

Ward, Tiffany - 26

Warner Bros. - 5

Washam, Ben - 184

Weaver, Charlie - 235

Weidman, David - 184

"Whistler's Father" - 107-111

Wikipedia - 12, 89

Wilbur the Monkey - 41, 46-48

Winsor-Newton Brushes - 19

Woodside, Queens, New York - 215

Wright, Frank Lloyd - 185

Yakkety Yak - 49, 199

Young, Victor - 184

YouTube - 49, 59

Zamora, Rudy - 184

Zebra - 46, 48

Drawings from the unsold *The Otters* and *Marjorie* presentations by Joe Harris. Little more is known about these pilots than these drawings.

ABOUT THE AUTHORS

Mark Arnold was born in San Jose, and grew up in Saratoga, California. He is a comic book and animation historian, and has had many articles published in various publications. He has also written books on TTV (Underdog, Tennessee Tuxedo), Cracked *Magazine, The Beatles, Disney, DFE (Pink Panther), Dennis the Menace, The Chipmunks and The Monkees. He is currently working on a book about* Mad *magazine. He has also produced and recorded DVD commentaries for Shout! Factory and Kino Lorber. He currently resides in Springfield, Oregon.*

Victoria Biggers began her career as a casting director for film and television in New York and Boston. Her syndicated TV variety column ran in over 200 newspapers nationwide, including the Cleveland Plaindealer, *the* St. Louis Post-Dispatch, *the* San Antonio Light, *the* Honolulu Advertiser *and the* New Orleans Times-Picayune. *She is an award-winning documentary producer and lives on Cape Cod, Massachusetts.*